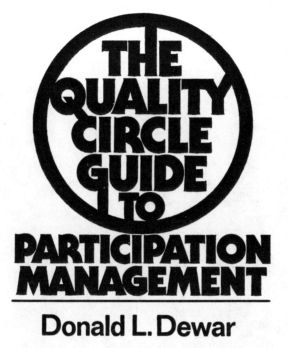

THE QUALITY CIRCLE GUIDE TO PARTICIPATION MANAGEMENT

Donald L. Dewar

PRENTICE-HALL, INC., Englewood Cliffs, N.J. 07632

The Quality Circle Guide to
Participation Management
by Donald L. Dewar
Copyright © 1980 Under UCC
by Quality Circle Institute

Printed in the United States of America

Prentice-Hall International, Inc., London
Prentice-Hall of Australia, Pty. Ltd., Sydney
Prentice-Hall of Canada, Ltd., Toronto
Prentice-Hall of India Private Ltd., New Delhi
Prentice-Hall of Japan, Inc., Tokyo
Prentice-Hall of Southeast Asia Pte. Ltd., Singapore
Whitehall Books Limited, Wellington, New Zealand

10 9 8 7 6 5 4 3 2 1

Library of Congress Cataloging in Publication Data

Dewar, Donald L.
   The quality circle to participation management.

   1. Quality circles. I. Title. II. Title:
Participation management.
HD66.D48 1982   658.4'036   81-15724
ISBN 0-13-744987-9
ISBN 0-13-744979-8 {PBK.}

ACKNOWLEDGEMENT

A very special thanks to my wife Elizabeth for her patience and support over what seemed to be an eternity.

PREFACE

Worker participation activities, under the stimulus of keen competition and a consumer demand for "quality" products and services, are assuming an increasingly important role in every kind of organization.

Quality Circles, one of the rising stars in the area of worker participation, is such an activity. Although relatively new in the Western World, it has grown to phenomenal proportions in Japan since its shakey beginning in 1962. There it is credited with having contributed greatly to that nation's ascendency to economic and industrial strength.

"What is this magic?" people are asking in vast numbers. The bandwagon is rolling and everyone seems to want on--now! Therein lies a potentially serious dilemma. The Western World, already known for its impatience, and with a past littered with the wreckages of other "programs" that fell by the wayside, is desperately in need of direction.

This has led to the need for a Quality Circle guidebook, which brings together in one place and in a form convenient for reference, all of the knowledge which has been developed in this field.

TABLE OF CONTENTS

CONTENTS OF THE LEADER MANUAL AND MEMBER MANUAL
PORTION OF THIS BOOK

SUGGESTED FORMS

WHAT AND WHY

There was a period of time during the 1970's when the question was, "Can Quality Circles succeed in the Western World?" This is no longer an issue. Quality Circles are having widespread success in a number of nations. This book describes many basic features about this exciting concept and how it has progressed since leaving the country of its birth--Japan. Its rapid growth lends hope that a new era has begun in the way we manage our organizations whereby the people who do the hands-on work will be brought into the mainstream and properly recognized as a potentially more powerful and valuable resource.

Quality Circles is one name of this phenomenon which is rapidly becoming a genuine movement throughout the industrialized world. The movement is known by a number of different names, such as "Quality Circles," "QC Circles," "Teams," and many others. This concept is concerned with an organization's most valuable (and most expensive) resource--one that is virtually untapped--its work force.

Quality Circles can be a most powerful ally in solving problems and effecting significant

1

efficiencies in an organization's operations. Dramatic gains will result by putting these people on the team.

WHAT IS IT?

A quick answer is, "A Quality Circle is a way of capturing the creative and innovative power that lies within the work force."

A more formal definition is: A group of workers from the same area who usually meet for an hour each week to discuss their problems, investigate causes, recommend solutions, and take corrective actions when authority is in their purview.

OBJECTIVES

To effect improvements in:

* Quality
* Productivity
* Motivation

Quality

"Quality" is a thought that resides in every executive's mind. Participative management is the vehicle that puts it in the mind of every employee in an organization. Without attention to quality, sooner of later any organization will fail.

Productivity

Clients and customers want quality services and products. Management alone cannot carry the burden of responding to these basic tenets of organizational survival. The intelligence and creative capacity of employees must be tapped to stem the complacency toward poor quality and its inherent high cost.

Motivation

Every organization using Quality Circles reports improvement in employee morale; and the change can be observed in many ways. Commonly, an organization will recognize that improvements in employee morale are indicated by reduced absenteeism and lower employee turnover. The author's experience indicates that workers readily accept involvement in Quality Circles and that the activity is a powerful motivating force. It also indicates that an informed and properly trained work force can often solve problems faster than anyone else because they are closest to them.

WHY?

"Workers don't care anymore! They have lost their desire to work." "Absenteeism and worker turnover are soaring!" "The workers' 'I don't care' attitude is resulting in poor workmanship, deteriorating morale, and a serious decline in productivity." "Our ability to compete is eroding constantly; and we don't know how long we can survive!" These remarks are being heard with increasing frequency; but there is now a way to turn this frightening trend around.

Despite all the apparent indications to the contrary, employees still have a latent and keen desire to belong to the organizations for which they work, to help to make them successful, and to be able to be proud among their peers that "their" organizations are ahead of all of their competitors.

This is a provable fact and should never be doubted. Every organization, with management that firmly believes this, is well on its way to results never dreamed possible.

It is absolutely essential to remain aware that a tremendous productive potential exists in every office and shop; and there are practical ways for both workers and their organizations to benefit from it. These people want to be part of the team; and they <u>will be</u> in the presence of a people-building philosophy.

The key is participative management, and this approach should be encouraged from top to bottom of every organization. Responsibility for the quality of work should be returned to the worker; and he or she should be able to influence how the job can best be done. The worker's ideas and resourcefulness can often make the difference between success or failure of the best engineering concepts. The worker <u>can</u> make a good idea better --he or she is closest to the work itself. Success is assured when participation is encouraged, because it results in a strong commitment to attainment.

Belief in this most powerful and important resource is essential; and there is no risk of failure in having faith in workers' loyalty and integrity when they can participate in management in an optimum manner.

Employees who are treated as important resources, and who are truly part of the team will make "their" organizations formidable competitors in any field.

This is not just an idea or a dream, it's a reality that's spreading across the industrial, business, and governmental scene at an accelerating pace.

HISTORY

A study of the history of Quality Circles begins in Japan. In 1961 a series of exploratory meetings were sponsored by the Union of Japanese Scientists and Engineers (JUSE). Their objective was to develop a way that would allow the people doing hands-on work the opportunity to contribute to the benefit of the company. Thus, Japan was the testing ground for this exciting and innovative technique; which, after sweeping the nation of its birth, has continued to spread throughout the entire world.

QUALITY CIRCLES IN JAPAN

Quality Control Before 1940

For decades the Japanese were viewed as producers of junk merchandise. Today, Japanese exports are sought after because of their reputation for high standards of design and quality. What factor influenced this astounding reversal? How did they attain it, and at what cost? Dr. Joseph M. Juran, an internationally recognized American author, lecturer, and consultant on Quality Control, predicted in 1966 that "Japan is engaged in an all-out effort to seize world

leadership in quality by 1980." He further predicted they would succeed, "Because no other
nation is moving toward that goal at the same
rate." It is doubtful that many agreed with him
at the time. Now, Japan's quality reputation is
enviable and highly regarded around the world,
and, there are millions who feel that the Japanese
actually did achieve world leadership in quality
by 1980!

This transition was due in part to General
Douglas MacArthur, who served as commander of the
U.S. occupation forces in Japan following World
War II. He determined to get the Japanese back on
their financial feet as quickly as possible.
He was acutely aware that Japan's lack of natural
resources would require international trading
arrangements. He knew that Japan's reputation for
shoddy workmanship would limit the acceptance of
their merchandise. Japanese leaders in government
and industry indicated a willingness to help.
With that, MacArthur obtained the services of
various Americans to assist the Japanese in
raising the quality levels of their products.
Among them was Dr. Edward W. Deming. Dr. Deming
introduced statistical quality control (SQC) to
them; and the Japanese proved to be excellent and
highly receptive students.

Their receptivity was dramatically enhanced
after Dr. Deming made the prediction that if Japan
were to embrace the principles of statistical
quality control, the nations of the world would be
imposing import quotas and limitations against
Japanese goods within five years because they
would be so much in demand. That statement
excited the Japanese and helped to double their
commitment toward obtaining quality control.
Deming's impact on the development of a quality
control science in Japan has been enormous. In
1951 the Union of Japanese Scientists and Engi-

neers (JUSE) created the annual corporate and individual Deming awards. These prestigious honors are highly sought after in Japan.

Dr. Deming has just recently been "discovered" in the United States as an expert--not only in quality control, but in the allied field of productivity. A one-and-a-half-hour documentary on productivity was broadcast nationally during June, 1980.

The JUSE organization brought Dr. Joseph M. Juran to Japan in 1954 to lecture on the subject, "Management of Quality Control." He was favorably received by management personnel who found his approach more readily acceptable than statistical quality control. Juran's approach to quality laid the framework that helped to round out Japan's subsequent success.

Incentives were offered by the Japanese government to further increase the level of quality of Japanese products. The use of the "JIS" symbol on exported products was considered a symbol of prestige. It could appear only on products meeting the very highest quality standards. The Minister of International Trade and Industry gave additional awards and incentives. In 1960 the government declared November as "National Quality Month"; and it has become commonplace to see quality posters and "Q" (Quality) banners. Quality-oriented seminars and conferences occur everywhere in Japan during November.

In 1956 the government-sponsored educational radio broadcasted a weekly series on the subject of quality. It was repeated annually until 1962. During 1960 the government-sponsored educational television network beamed a series of video programs on the subject of quality.

HISTORY OF QC CIRCLES

QC Circles in Japan were conceived in 1961. During that year the Japanese magazine, Quality Control, sponsored a symposium from which two concepts developed: (1) A quality control magazine directed to shop foremen was necessary. Existing publications tended to be "over the foreman's head." (2) Rarely were foremen included in conferences on the subject of quality control outside of the company. The editorial board of Quality Control took the lead by promoting the inclusion of foremen in the annual quality control conference held during November,1961. Foremen were invited to take part on the panel.

The editors went one step further by sponsoring a new magazine called, The Foremen and QC. Its first issue appeared during July, 1962, as a quarterly. Since then it has become a monthly publication. It was priced attractively to enable supervisors and workers to buy it with their own money, if necessary.

Not only did a new magazine enter the scene, but it was decided that now was the time to launch a new and exciting concept which was given the name "QC Circles." A QC Circle would be lead by a supervisor. Member companies of the JUSE organization were solicited with the hope they would be willing to experiment with this new QC Circle concept. There was considerable interest but also an enormous amount of skepticism. Three circles were registered with JUSE during May of 1962, and by the end of the year there were twenty.

QC CIRCLE MOVEMENT BEGINS TO GROW

The growth of QC Circles in Japan can be attributed to the promotional activities of the Union of Japanese Scientists and Engineers. JUSE is a non-profit organization, much like any other professional organization. One of the boosters of QC Circles within the JUSE organization was Dr. Kaoru Ishikawa, who was an engineering professor at the University of Tokyo. He has served JUSE in many important leadership roles including their national governing board which functions in a leadership role for the Japanese QC Circle activities. Dr. Ishikawa has been instrumental in building training courses and materials for the JUSE organization.

JUSE is widely recognized in Japan and is divided into several geographical regions, each headed by a leading executive from a company in that area.

Much of the credit for the phenomenal success of Quality Circles in Japan is directly attributable to the leadership provided by JUSE. Since 1962 the activity has spread spectacularly until today it is estimated that 10 million Japanese are involved as members of QC Circles.

HISTORY OF QUALITY CIRCLES

IN THE WESTERN WORLD

Dr. Juran's article, "The QC Circle Phenomenon," alerted the Western World in 1967 about Japan's QC Circle activities.

In 1968 further word of QC Circles was carried from Japan by a visiting team of QC Circle leaders. This team, sponsored by JUSE, was put together to provide the participants the opportunity to learn more about quality control and industrial practices outside of Japan. Typically, each team member prepared a paper to present to American audiences. This excursion by a Japanese group of QC Circle leaders has continued as an annual activity and now extends into Europe as well as the U.S.

The American Society for Quality Control
(ASQC) promoted the Quality Circle concept through
its numerous articles and its many speakers
on that subject at its national, regional, and
chapter conferences.

"IT WON'T WORK HERE, THE JAPANESE ARE DIFFERENT"

If Quality Circles were so successful in
Japan, why did it take so long for them to reach
the Western World? Two reasons seemed to dominate. First, the belief that the Japanese were
different. The author, on going to Japan in
1973, with the express purpose of studying Quality
Circles, was disturbed by the hundreds of individuals who voiced this opinion. Few could
identify why the Japanese were different; but
those who tried would usually talk about the
permanent employment feature of the Japanese
firms. Also, the Japanese had traditionally
been considered imitators rather than innovators.
Perhaps they were so firmly cast in that role that
it was difficult to realize that they had taken a
leadership position.

Permanent employment is a feature of many
Japanese businesses. Certainly, permanent employment has been important to the success of Quality
Circles in Japan. However, it has been a changing
concept. At one time, prior to World War II,
it was for salaried employees only. When labor
unions became prominent after the war the concept
of permanent employment spread to all levels in
the organization. However, companies have, in
addition to their permanent employees, temporary
employees who may constitute around 20% of a total
work force. These temporary employees are subject
to layoffs caused by downturns in the business.
These temporary employees are often workers who
have retired and have been rehired. Also included
are women. In Japan, retirement usually occurs at
age 55; however, many employees remain on the job

as temporary workers at considerably less than
their former remuneration.

There are many Japanese executives who
predict that ultimately permanent employment will
not survive in Japan.   Despite Japanese manage-
ments' desire to retain all employees on the
payroll, they will allow the red ink to flow only
so long. The recession of 1974 tested the ability
of the Japanese to weather this kind of storm.
There was a considerable reluctance to release
employees at that time. The recession would not
last forever and soon these people would be needed
again. To let them go meant they would surely be
absorbed by other companies. This would result
in great difficulty in rebuilding a capable and
productive work force. Initially, this dilemma
was handled by the company finding other firms
that would take their workers on a temporary
basis. When this approach failed, some companies
released these employees.

The twice-a-year bonus that almost all
Japanese workers receive is mentioned almost as
much as permanent employment. Historically, it
was based on whether or not a company was making
money. Over the years, it has evolved into a
twice-a-year institution; and it no longer relates
to company profits. Companies tend to pay the
bonus regardless of profitability. Often, a
company with financial problems will borrow the
money needed to enable it to pay the semi-annual
bonus. In some companies the author visited in
1973, he was told that the amount of the bonus was
often negotiated for the employees by the labor
union that represented them. While at one company, the author asked, "Isn't it the same as
the company withholding a little bit of each
paycheck and then giving it back to the employee
every six months?" The Japanese agreed that the
analogy was essentially correct, but laughed when
it was suggested that some Japanese might prefer

to get larger regular paychecks and not bother with the bonus system, especially if the overall amount was the same one way or the other. They said, "It is inconceivable that we would ever do away with the six-month bonus. It has become an institution in Japan. Our system of credit depends on it. Bonuses are 'spent' before they are even received."

STUDY TRIP TO JAPAN

In November, 1973, the author was one of six Lockheed employees who journeyed to Japan to study QC Circles. This group visited the Circles at a number of Japanese companies; and enthusiasm built as members of the team became more and more convinced that the concept would work in the Western World. The author remained in Japan for sometime, studying the QC Circle idea in depth.

Later, on several occasions, when teams of Japanese QC Circle leaders visited in the U.S., the author heard them questioned; and they responded with answers that were exactly the same as applied in the United States. The Lockheed people were so convinced that the Japanese model was correct that they did little to change it.

EARLY U.S. EXPERIMENTS

Quality Circles were started at Lockheed in November, 1974. The success at Lockheed drew the attention of many companies elsewhere in the U.S. and in Europe. However, little occurred until 1977 when five companies in the U.S. actually started Circles; and from there the activity has grown steadily. In 1980 the number of companies using Quality Circles in the U.S. was conservatively estimated at 230.

<u>Growth of Quality Circles Elsewhere In The Western World.</u> Quality Circles is now literally

in every continent of the world. Its spread in
the Western World, although slow initially, is
accelerating, and is now experiencing dramatic
growth.

THE INTERNATIONAL ASSOCIATION
OF QUALITY CIRCLES (IAQC)

The enormous success of Quality Circles in
Japan is due to the brilliance of the leadership
of the Union of Japanese Scientists and Engineers.
However, their influence was not directed to
Western World countries. An international organization was needed to provide guidance to those who
wanted to initiate Quality Circle activities.
There were attempts to have existing organizations
accept this role, but the timing was off and none
were willing to make the commitment.

The International Association of Quality
Circles (IAQC) was formed in late 1977, with the
author as its first president. Headquarters are
in the United States, located in Midwest City,
Oklahoma, U.S.A.

The IAQC serves as a repository and clearing
house for Quality Circle information.

What Are The Objectives Of The IAQC?

* To serve the educational needs of its members

* To promote the recognition and spread of
  the Quality Circle concept

* To act as a central international clearing
  house for Quality Circle information

How Does IAQC Carry Out Its Objectives?

Issuance of a Publication. The official
magazine of the IAQC provides a wide variety of

articles and pictures in an effort to respond more
fully to the needs of its members. It includes:

* Technical articles written by qualified
  individuals

* Up-to-date current events on Quality Circles

* Reports of government legislation effecting
  worker participation

* New techniques used successfully by others

* Articles by Circle members

* Special features of interest to management
  personnel, facilitators, leaders, and
  members

Encouraging the Development of Local
Chapters. The first IAQC chapter was started by
Bernie Perry, Facilitator, U.S. Naval Ordnance
Station, Louisville, Kentucky, U.S.A. The
charter, granted in February, 1980, was announced
at the Second Annual Conference and was featured
in the 1st Quarter IAQC magazine. The second
chapter of the IAQC, following closely on the
heels of the first, was organized in the Cleveland
area by Price Gibson, Facilitator, for the Brush
Wellman Company. These initial acts of leadership
provided a spur that triggered a rapid series of
chapter formations.

Sponsoring Conferences. In February 1979,
in San Francisco, with barely over 100 members,
IAQC gambled on its first annual conference. The
big unknown was, "Will anyone come?" The fact
that 150 attended was amazing; because rarely does
an organization attract more than its total
membership to a convention.

Regional conferences represent current
planning in the IAQC so that more members can be

served.   Likewise, leaders and members are more
likely to be able to attend when travel requirements are minimized.

Chapter Conferences are encouraged by the
IAQC to carry the benefits of the regional conference to its ultimate height--including attendance and involvement, low cost, and ready accessi-
bility.

IAQC CODE OF ETHICS

I recognize that every person, no matter
where in the organization, desires to do
quality work and be a respected and contributing citizen.

I will aid in the advancement of human
welfare by helping to make peoples' lives
more meaningful through enabling them to
obtain maximum satisfaction from their
work.

I will insure that credit for the work of
others is given to those to whom it is
due.

I will not compete unfairly with others. I
will assume responsibility for my own mis-
takes and refrain from shifting blame to
others.

I will always keep an open mind and look for
merit in the ideas of others.

I will maintain a reputation for good moral
character, good citizenship, and honesty.

I will strive to keep informed of all the
latest developments in the area of employee
participation and will work toward implementing such advancements as appropriate
to improve working conditions.

I will aid in the professional development
and advancement of my colleagues, and those
in my employ or under my supervision.

I will earnestly endeavor to aid the work of
the Association and to extend public knowledge of its purposes and activities.

RESULTS

What attracts people to Quality Circles? What helps them to sell the concept to others in their organizations? What is it that holds management's continuing support as it operates? What is it that keeps the Circle members enthusiastic?

The answer is RESULTS--positive results that pay off in terms of improved quality, reduced costs, increased safety, and better attitudes.

The following are typical examples--only a few of the many that could be related.

Problem: A clerical group was "overly organized." Information on one specific account might be contained in several different specialized files. Considerable labor was expended when cross-checking was necessary. Over 200,000 accounts were being maintained.

Solution: All the separate files were combined by account so that everything pertaining to one of them would be found in one folder.

Results: Clerical costs were reduced over 40%. Accounts were balanced without increased difficulty.

- o -

Problem: Customer statements were mailed each month. One final task before enclosing them in envelopes was to date each statement by hand. Time requirement was 3 hours.

Solution: Type the data on a master printing plate. All statements were run through the printing press in 10 minutes.

Result: A monotonous manual job reduced from 3 hours to 10 minutes.

- o -

Problem: A group of janitors voiced frustration at how their work assignments were made. Assignments were highly specialized. Complaints about undone work were common. It was difficult to pinpoint blame.

Solution: The janitorial Circle members reorganized their assignments so that one man had total responsibility for everything in one part of a building.

Results: Complaints fell to almost zero. Janitors said their jobs were more interesting. In their own "territories" they were "bosses." Reduction of 30% (reassigned) of the janitors was effected—as a direct result of their recommendations.

- o -

Problem: A purchasing department Circle was concerned about material overshipments to its company.

Solution: All vendors were notified by letter that henceforth, excess supplies would either become the property of the company (without payment), or be returned at vendor expense plus handling costs.

Results: First year savings of $636,000. Overshipments are continuing to be tracked; and an on-going decline has been noted.

- o -

Problem: Plastic bags used as packaging material for computer tapes are being torn.

Solution: Analysis showed that the bags were being torn when the reels were placed on the conveyor. The Circle tested several types of conveyor belts. One did not tear the bags. The belt was purchased and installed.

Result: Savings of $45,000.

- o -

Problem: A machine shop was experiencing quality problems due to prematurely worn and broken taps.

Solution: Data was carefully collected in a number of categories that could have contributed to the problem. The coolant flow and fixturing proved to be the key factors. The optimum settings were identified.

Result: Tap life increased from an average of
           1,600 holes per tap to more than 3,000.

                          - o -

Problem: How to redesign jobs and work flow in an
           insurance company to improve quality,
           productivity, and attitudes.

Solution: Two examples are reported here.   Both
           involved job redesign.

           1.   Automatic bank checking unit

           2.   Word-processing center

Results: 1.   The automatic bank checking unit
                reduced staffing by 17% despite
                a 16% increase in workload.

           2.   The word-processing center has
                experienced an almost 20% drop
                in errors.

                          - o -

Problem: Excessive rework despite an intensive
           campaign by management to minimize
           it. Level was approximately 21%.

Solution: A variety of improvements were recom-
           mended and many implemented.

Result: Rework dropped to below 8%.

                          - o -

Problem: Drafting errors were causing excessive
           scrap and rework of newly designed
           tooling. The average number of defects
           existing at the tool manufacturing
           stage was 1.20 per drawing.

Solution: A detailed checklist was prepared to be used by all draftsmen. Feedback systems were also incorporated.

Results: The number of defects decreased to .16 per drawing. Further, when a draftsman's error rate dropped below .20 per drawing, his work was checked thereafter on a sampling basis only. This resulted in a 70% saving of the time of the checker.

- o -

Problem: To reduce the time to get new procedures implemented.

Solution: All steps in the process were organized into a Pareto chart and the top cate-gories were analyzed.

Result: Time requirements were reduced to 32.8% of what they were.

- o -

Problem: Excessive time requirements and inade-quate control of errors in a manufactur-ing change-order department.

Solution: An analysis resulted in the development of a mask to reduce the probability of errors. After a thorough testing to remove the "bugs," the idea was approved and implemented.

Result: Time requirements were reduced by 19% primarily due to the avoidance of errors.

- o -

Problem: Clerical employees prepare and route
          job packages through other departments.
          Each person receiving a package examines
          it and takes specific and appropriate
          action. Very difficult to track the
          location of the job package during
          its movement. Often, excessive delays
          occur due to a package awaiting atten-
          tion on someone's desk.

Solution: The Circle utilized a variety of
          techniques: brainstorming, data
          collecting, Pareto analysis, and
          cause-and-effect problem solving
          to analyze it. A routing slip was
          designed to accompany each package. The
          routing slip controlled who would need
          to see the job package and each would
          initial it.

Results: The error rate fell by 50% with no
          more lost or misrouted job packages.
          First-year savings were $62,400.

                        - o -

Problem: Warehouse inventory counts. Counting
          done on unscheduled basis throughout
          the day. Error rate was unacceptable.

Solution: Elimination of constant interruptions
          by not "opening for business" for
          the first 45 minutes.

Results: Error rate has declined steadily.
          As each new target is achieved, the
          Circle establishes higher goals. It
          is currently targeting to reduce the
          error rate to 5%.

                        - o -

Problem: One product line was experiencing costs that prevented competitive pricing in the market place.

Solution: Circle members (including the inspector) worked out a procedure to inspect their own work, thus eliminating the need for a full-time inspector!

Result: Not only were production schedules maintained, but no degradation in product quality occurred.

- o -

Problem: Excessive product costs.

Solution: Three Circles established goals to reduce product costs by 20% over a 6-month period.

Results: Assembly hours per unit reduced by 39%. Total savings: $154,000.

- o -

Problem: Excessive rejection rate of 9.9% for high-frequency overtone crystals.

Solution: Analysis of accepted and rejected crystals disclosed differences in the angles of cuts made in the crystals. A series of tests followed using a variety of angles of cuts. Detailed records were maintained to record all variations. A recommended angle of cut was made and thoroughly tested.

Result: Rejections decreased to approximately 1%.

- o -

Problem: Fuel costs for the boilers in a paper
           mill were excessive. This had been
           verified by a comparison with other
           mills.

Solution: Several approaches were pursued:

           1. Coal samples were tested for their
               caloric content. They disclosed
               the alarming fact that coal being
               delivered was inferior to the
               grade being purchased.

           2. Excessive amounts of unburned
               carbon were present in the ash. The
               Circle maintained detailed records
               as it tested for the optimum grate
               height, which it recommended be
               lowered by about 20%.

Result: Paper production costs decreased 15%.

                        - o -

Problem: Excessive labor costs in an electronic
           assembly area. A goal was agreed on
           to reduce these costs by 20%.

Solution: Various Quality Circle techniques,
           including process cause-and-effect
           problem analysis, were utilized to
           identify a number of contributing
           causes. Corrective action was initiated
           on as many as possible.

Result: Costs were reduced 46%. At no time
           was concern expressed about a reduction
           in the work force. Employees just
           wanted to get the job done with a
           minimum number of obstacles.

                        - o -

Problem: An electronics Circle wanted to improve its yield rate of 72%.

Solution: The Circle set a yield-rate goal of 75%. Data were collected and the results prioritized using Pareto charts. Cause-and-effect analysis identified the prime causes. Corrective action was initiated by the Circles.

Result: First-year savings: $125,000.

- o -

Problem: Excessive defects encountered in fabricating and joining five separate plastic parts.

Solution: Technique developed whereby the five separate parts could be reduced to two larger parts and then joined.

Result: Estimated savings over the life of the contract: $160,000.

- o -

Problem: Constant delays being experienced due to tools being out for calibration.

Solution: The Circle coordinated with quality control in developing a schedule that established nonconflicting times for the calibration sequences. This included doing much of the calibration on a different shift.

Result: Annual savings of $86,000.

- o -

Problem: A Circle of working mothers wanted to reduce the work day to 7-1/2 hours.

Management was unable to comply because of production quotas.

Solution: The Circle instituted improvements that permitted them to hold daily production quotas in 7-1/2 hours.

Result: Productivity improvement of over 6% with no reduction in the level of quality.

- o -

QUALITY PERFORMANCE (YIELD RATE)

The following examples are indications of what can be done to effect improvements in the yield rate (Percentage of completed units with no errors).

	Start (%)	1-Year Later (%)
Camera units	64	98.3
Business forms	88	100.0
Plastic parts assemblies	82	91.0
Cosmetics	56	93.0

OPINION SURVEYS

Organizations with Quality Circle activities are encouraged to solicit information regarding the opinions of those involved in a direct way, such as Circle leaders and members.

The results of one such survey are shown on the following pages. It was taken toward the end of the first year of Quality Circles in a rather large company.

Circle leaders and members responded anonymously to a series of questions.

(Results are shown in percentages)

	Leader	Member
HOUR-LONG MEETINGS ARE -		
Too long	0	0
Too short	17	12
Just right	83	86
No opinion/Other	0	2
ONCE-A-WEEK MEETINGS ARE -		
Too frequent	17	2
Not frequent enough	0	6
Just right	83	82
No opinion/Other	0	10
BEST SIZE OF CIRCLE IS -		
3 to 5 members	0	0
5 to 10 "	100	53
10 to 15 "	0	25
15 or more members	0	10
No opinion/Other	0	12
FOR CIRCLES TO MAKE MANAGEMENT PRESENTATIONS IS -		
A good idea	100	96
A bad idea	0	0
No opinion/Other	0	4
TAKING PART IN QUALITY CIRCLES -		
Makes job more enjoyable	83	71
Makes no change	17	27
Makes job less enjoyable	0	2
HAVE SPENT OWN TIME ON CIRCLE ACTIVITIES		
Yes	100	44
No	0	52
No indication	0	4

QUALITY OF WORK IN MY AREA –

Has improved	67	73
Has not changed	33	19
Has worsened	0	0
No opinion/Other	0	8

RELATIONSHIP WITH OTHERS IN MY UNIT HAS –

Improved	83	65
Remained unchanged	17	33
Worsened	0	0
No opinion/Other	0	2

PRODUCTIVITY IN MY UNIT HAS –

Improved	100	69
Remained unchanged	0	27
Worsened	0	0
No opinion/Other	0	4

RELATIONSHIP WITH WORKERS IN OTHER UNITS HAS –

Improved	50	33
Remained unchanged	50	65
Worsened	0	0
No opinion/Other	0	2

I THINK MANAGEMENT IN MY AREA –

Is glad we have Circles	66	65
Doesn't care	17	14
Is sorry we have Circles	17	4
No opinion/Other	0	17

QUALITY CIRCLES SHOULD BE –

Continued and spread	100	92
Discontinued	0	2
No opinion/Other	0	6

IN LEADING MEETINGS, THE LEADER HAS BEEN –

Doing a good job	0	81
Doing a fair job	67	17
Doing a poor job	0	0
No opinion/Other	33	2

REGARDING CIRCLE MEMBERSHIP,
EMPLOYEES SHOULD BE –

Free to join or not	100	94
Requested to join	0	4
No opinion/Other	0	2

TIME SPENT ON CIRCLE ACTIVITIES
IS JUSTIFIED BY THE IMPROVE-
MENTS MADE IN MY AREA –

Yes	100	90
No	0	4
No opinion/Other	0	6

HAVING THE FACILITATOR AT
MEETINGS –

Helped	100	94
Had little effect	0	2
Interfered	0	0
No opinion/Other	0	4

TRAINING RECIEVED IN THE
FIRST 8 WEEKS WAS –

Very helpful	67	74
Somewhat helpful	33	10
A waste of time	0	0
No opinion/Other	0	16

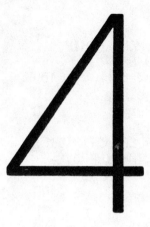

QUALITY CIRCLE OPERATION

AN OVER-VIEW

The following diagram illustrates the various processes that take place in the operation of Quality Circles.

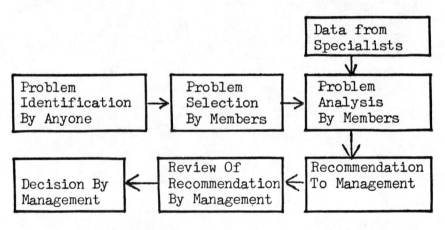

PROBLEM IDENTIFICATION

Organizing The Circle

The leader begins to organize a Circle as soon as his or her training course is completed;

and, normally, the first meeting takes place within one or two weeks.

If the leaders' first Circles can't be started in operation within two weeks of the completion of the training course, it is usually advisable for the facilitator to meet with the leaders, prior to the actual starting of their Circles, and review the techniques they learned.

Start Training

The training of Circle members is done by the leader and begins at the first meeting; and the basic subjects are usually covered in about 8 weeks. Training is best assimilated by the members when it is combined with the actual solving of problems in their work areas. The identification of the problems the Circle could consider working on normally occurs during the second half of the third meeting.

Identifying Problems

The problems usually identified by Circle members are the uninteresting, mundane ones that are not particularly exciting to anyone else. These are the problems either that no one else is aware of; or, if they do know they exist, they are either too busy to give them attention, or are simply not interested enough to care. Someone ought to be concerned about these "little" impediments to progress; and there is probably no one more qualified to identify, analyze, and solve them than the people who put up with them every day. They are truly the experts!

Circle members should not put any attention on identifying the big inter-organizational problems that management is undoubtedly both fully aware of and has been attempting to solve-- perhaps for years.

Problems (often referred to as projects or themes) are suggested mostly by Circle members. However, the Circle should encourage ideas from as many others as possible. Typically, the management personnel, staff personnel and even non-members are candidates for suggesting additional problems on which the Circle could consider working.

How Problems Are Identified

There is a variety of techniques used, but the most effective seems to be through the brain-storming approach. Some leaders have met on a one-to-one basis with each Circle member to solicit ideas. Facilitators sometimes do the same. However, research done by Bernard Perry of the U.S. Naval Ordnance Depot in Louisville, Kentucky, demonstrates that brainstorming is the most effective way, both in terms of cost and time.

PROBLEM SELECTION

Who Selects The Problem?

The list of problems developed in the previous step is carefully reviewed by the Circle members and prioritized. The number one problem they wish to adopt as their Circle project is selected by the leaders and the members.

Possible Reaction From Management

There have been instances where management reacts unfavorably to the idea that Circle members select their own problems. "If I'm the boss around here, I'll tell them who is going to work on what!" This concern about management authority being eroded is unnecessary. In fact, if the manager does dictate what the Circle will work on, the usual reaction by Circle members is, "Just as we thought. Another management con game. This isn't any different than it ever was."

Reasons Why Members Should Select The Problem

The members of the Circles are the experts in the areas where they work. Problems are, or at least should be, selected from that area of expertise. It must be remembered that the Circle members know more about the job they are doing than anyone else; and that includes the managers and staff people. Management insists that certain quality standards, cost limitations, and prescribed schedule commitments be adhered to. The members know better than anyone else what impediments or obstructions are making it difficult for them to do these things. About the best guidance they can receive at the time they are selecting a problem is toward keeping it within their own work areas--where they are the experts.

PROBLEM ANALYSIS

Who Does It?

Now the Circle has selected a problem it wishes to work on. Who actually does the analysis? The answer is, of course, the Circle. The reason is just as obvious as the reason stated for having the Circle members select the problems they wish to work on. They are the experts in the areas where they work.

How Do They Do It?

At this point it might be very tempting to simply turn their problem over to the "experts." This is precisely what many of the older Circle members want to do! They probably have years of experience in an environment where the boss or staff people were the problem solvers. That was standard practice then; so is anything

really any different now? Realizing that the
Circle members themselves will be taking the
extra step and getting involved in the analysis is
often a new learning experience. But from the
standpoint of the organization, it is the proven
most cost effective way to do it. There is more
than one reason for its positive effect on holding
costs down. Member involvement in something that
will change the way they do their work is important to assure acceptance of the change. It's no
longer something imposed upon them from above
or from some other part of the organization.

Leaders Should Avoid Solving Problems By Themselves

The author has seen leaders who have taken
problems suggested by the Circles and developed
solutions for them on their own. They report to
the next meeting, "Well, I solved that problem.
We can now move on to the next one." Unfortunately, this occurs more often than it should.
The members do not get the satisfaction of being
involved in the actual problem analysis process.
They may even resent the fact that the leader has
solved the problem in a manner with which they may
not totally agree. Their involvement would possibly have resulted in a more efficient and cost
effective solution. Perhaps the biggest negative
aspect of this approach is the fact that the
leader is preventing a people-building opportunity
from occurring. A further detrimental effect can
be the fact that the leader may soon start voicing
the complaint, "I already had enough to do before
Circles started, but now I'm busier than ever.
I can't keep up this pace."

Developing An Action Plan

As a first step in getting into the analysis
of a problem, the Circle will develop an action
plan or a schedule whereby its project is planned
with a schedule of objectives that are broken

into milestones and responsibilities assigned to various members of the Circle. Circles using schedules to accomplish their objectives are the ones that produce the most dramatic results. Circle progress is not a haphazard occurrence. It results from an organized approach.

Assistance From Staff Specialists

Sometimes, when people are being introduced to Quality Circles, they see that Circles are encouraged to call in outside specialists to give them an occasional helping hand. They often view this as one of the weaknesses of the concept.

Everyone who seeks to attain objectives is likely to need the assistance of someone with specialized knowledge at times. "Now we know why Circles are so successful. They simply call in the experts and get their problems solved that way!" In actual fact, it is not a weakness, but one of the strengths of the concept. The act of calling in an expert to help when one is confronted by a problem that requires assistance is a sign of good management. Executives and higher level management do it all the time. So should the Circles; and they are urged to do so. It is vital that individuals brought in to give this momentary assistance do not try to take over the problems. It is preferable that only the assistance asked for be given; and then the experts step aside and let the Circles continue as before.

RECOMMENDED SOLUTIONS

The process of communicating the recommendations to the manager is one of the most exciting phases of Quality Circle operation.

Why Not Written Communications?

Most people have had unpleasant experiences depending on written communication. Often, the

person with good ideas does a relatively poor job
of communicating them to others. An example of
this occurred at a large airplane manufacturing
company. A mechanic in the wing panel section
developed a complex tool at home in his basement
workshop, using his own lathe to build it. He
wrote it up on a suggestion form using a total of
four lines to describe it. It was completely
misunderstood. In fact, it was perceived to be so
obviously without merit, it was rejected without
further investigation. Later an accidental
encounter with a member of the industrial engineering staff brought the tool out of the bottom
of a tool box where it was kept. The mechanic
said, "I knew it was good; but if they thought it
was useless, then why should the company get
the benefit of it?" When put to use, it saved
nearly a half-million dollars a year in the wing
panel section alone.

Oral Communications

The management presentation is conducted as
a stand-up function whereby the members take part
and use charts and graphs that they have prepared
themselves. It is common that preparations for
the management presentation take place on employees' own time at break, lunch, and after
work. Nobody asks them to do this. They do it
because it's important to them to do the best
possible job. It is a powerful and exciting way
to communicate what they have done. It is also a
fantastic method of giving recognition to the
Circles. The author knows of many Circle programs
where there is no form of recognition or reward of
any sort other than the management presentation.

Incidentally, the mechanic who failed miser-
ably to communicate his half-million-dollar idea
via the written form, would have done quite well
in a management presentation. He was capable of
communicating verbally and demonstration of the

use of the tool he developed would have been a firm and immediate convincer.

SOLUTION REVIEW BY MANAGEMENT

Normal Channels

Quality Circles operate through the normal management channels. The presentation is made to the individual to whom the supervisor (normally the Circle leader) reports. It is not made to the steering committee, or to somebody on the high executive level. The normal channels are followed precisely. That is not to say that higher-level management may not be present at a management presentation. In fact, it is likely that higher-level management people will often be present; but they are there as observers, not as decision makers.

Length Of Review

The review may take place over a period of several weeks; but that is uncommon. If the manager feels that it needs some verification studies done, he will either commission some staff person to do these or refer the recommendation back to the Circle for further work.

DECISION BY MANAGEMENT

There is nothing automatic about implementing a Quality Circle solution. The decision whether or not to do it has to come first. The manager of the organization decides if it is the proper thing to do.

When Is The Decision Made?

The decision to accept a Quality Circle recommendation is frequently made during the meeting in which it is presented. This is

because the manager usually knows what the Circle
has been working on, and what its recommendation
is going to be, long before the presentation takes
place. This is reasonable, because the supervisor
who is normally the Circle leader should be
keeping his superior informed as to what is going
on in his work area concerning normal work functions. Quality Circles is simply one of several
normal work tasks. Leaders should communicate on
Circle activities as well as other aspects of the
job. Thus, the manager is usually in a position
to make a decision at the time the presentation
occurs.

Implementing The Idea

Implementation of the accepted idea can be an
entirely different problem for the manager. It is
one thing to say that an idea will be implemented.
It might be more difficult to make it happen.

Does Cost Often Prohibit Implementation Of An Idea?

It is unusual for Circle members to advocate
recommendations that would result in large outlays
of cash for implementation. Circle members are
capable money managers. They do a rather good
job of distributing limited funds to a wide
variety of necessities and other factors in their
personal lives. They are just as concerned with
making wise decisions on the job. There are
many illustrations which show that when various
alternatives to implement a recommendation have
been made by the Circle, the members will ultimately select that which is a low-cost and
cost-effective solution.

The Manager May Refuse To Approve Of A Circle's Recommendation

Organizations report that from 85 to 100% of
Circle suggestions are approved by the manager.

When a manager must decline to accept a recommendation, he or she can prevent an adverse effect on
the Circle's enthusiasm by thoroughly explaining
why he or she had to do so.   Sometimes a refusal
is not final.   An alternative solution may be
feasible.   Mostly, if refused, it is because of
cost considerations.   It might also have something
to do with inter-organizational effects that the
proposed solution could have.   As stated elsewhere, it is important for Circles to concentrate
on finding problems to work on that lie totally
within their own areas of expertise.   The objective is to have them apply their effort where the
chance for success is best.   They need successes,
particularly in their early months of existence.
However, the facilitator should not expect to
experience serious problems because a recommendation is rejected, particularly if the manager
takes the time to provide logical reasons why the
refusal is necessary.

MOTIVATION AND QUALITY CIRCLES

Being motivated is clearly a case of being attracted--not <u>pushed</u> toward goals.

No study of Quality Circles would be complete without attention being given to the changes in attitude that so often result from involvement with the activity.

Improved employee attitudes can lead to a greater willingness to work toward goals set by the organization--especially where personal goals are also being achieved in the process.

No facilitator's training is complete without a study of human motivation--of what it is that "turns people on."

The facilitator is expectd to know. He or she should be familiar with basic theories and should know who those behavioral scientists are that have influenced so many millions.

The Motivation Cycle

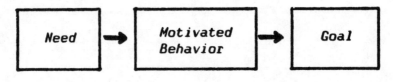

The Motivation Cycle is triggered by a need. If that need is strong enough, the goal one forms is likely to enable its achievement. For example, one is hungry. Food is the obvious need. The goal could take a variety of forms. It might be as simple as going to a nearby restaurant; or, perhaps, to buy food at a grocery store. The effort displayed to achieve that goal is termed "motivated behavior." On one hand, it might require little more than a 1-minute stroll to the restaurant; but on the other hand, it might require a 1-hour walk. In either case it is motivated behavior.

Once filled, a need no longer motivates. To illustrate: after eating a full meal it is extremely doubtful that one would be motivated to want food, even if no effort were required to obtain it. Again, a filled need does not motivate.

THE BEHAVIORAL SCIENTISTS

No study of motivation would be complete without reference to some of the theories of the behavioral scientists. For the purposes of this discussion, three have been selected: Abraham Maslow, Frederick Herzberg, and Douglas McGregor.

MASLOW

Maslow contended that an individual could have an almost endless number of needs. However, he has grouped all of these needs into five major categories as depicted below:

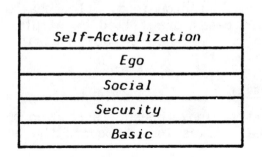

| Self-Actualization |
| Ego |
| Social |
| Security |
| Basic |

The order is important and moves from the bottom (Basic) to the top (Self-Actualization). The most crucial grouping is the basic needs-- those necessary to sustain life itself such as: air, food, clothing, and shelter. Although most important, they are the easiest to fill. After basic needs are taken care of, one turns attention to satisfying security needs. As one continues up through the other major groupings, the difficulty in filling the needs increases. One's ego needs and self-actualization needs are enormous. Until one need group is satisfied, a person's behavior is not motivated by the next higher-level need. For example, if one's basic needs are not taken care of, one is not likely to be worried about his or her security needs.

An Example

Basic

Suppose a man is shipwrecked. He grasps a large plank and hangs on. Bobbing about in the ocean, he finally washes up on a remote and apparently deserted island. His needs? Survival, first and foremost! His goals will be to locate food, water, and shelter--just to sustain life itself. The effort he expends in doing this can be termed motivated behavior. Once the essential needs are filled, they will cease to motivate. At this point, could one expect this unwilling Robinson Crusoe to stretch out and relax in the sun on the beach? After all, his basic needs have been met. No, he still has myriads of other needs in the other four groupings. (In today's society, one's basic needs are filled by simply getting a job. The pay is used to buy what is needed to sustain life.)

Security

His attention, though, is focused on security needs. He affixes logs to guard the entrance to his cave. Fences are erected to protect his food and water supply. Spears, bows, and arrows are fashioned from wood and stone. In the process of doing all this, a great amount of movement (motivated behavior) is exhibited. This motivated behavior will begin to diminish as he feels he has met his security needs. (In today's society we meet our security needs with locked doors, guns, police protection, pension plans, job security, and insurance.)

Social Needs

Fortunately, he still has a mass of other needs. He now knows that a group of natives occupy the island. They seem peaceful, even willing to be friendly. He no longer has hope of rescue. He concedes that these natives may be the only humans he will know. He wants to belong and he is gratified that they accept him. A general affection develops between them. Included completely, he finally realizes his social needs are filled.

(In today's society he would want to be accepted as "one of the guys" at work, or, to be a member of some sports or social club.)

Ego

Eventually it is not enough to be simply "one of the group." He wants to be "somebody special." When he introduces the crossbow he is heralded as a hero. This adulation swells his ego. He discovers that his needs in this category tend to be enormous. He maintains his special status in the group by a continuous outpouring of technical advances gleaned from his prior experience. (In today's society our ego needs are met by job advances, titles, personal publicity, adulation, recognition. Everyone has ego needs— some more than others. People in the spotlight

such as show business personalities and politi-
cians, are generally considered to have larger
esteem needs. In many, ego needs carry negative
connotations; but history is repleat with examples
of business, political, educational, and military
leaders driven by enormous ego appetites, who have
provided better lives for countless others far
less fortunate than themselves.)

Self-Actualization

The shipwrecked victim is doing well. The
island society, despite its simplicity, is meeting
his needs quite effectively. His lower needs:
basic, security, social, and ego are being satisfied. Mentally and physically, he is comfortable and happy. Gradually his innermost thoughts
begin to revolve around what he had at one time
hoped to do with his life. From childhood he
had dreamed of becoming a teacher. Suddenly he
realizes that he needn't wait. The island people
are eager for his knowledge. He becomes their
seer--the learned one who is to dedicate his
life to developing them and their culture. It
becomes the fulfillment of his dreams. He is
doing exactly what he wants to do. His life is
exciting and fulfilled. (In today's society,
although not necessarily so, we tend to picture
artists, writers, teachers, statesmen, mission-
aries, and doctors as the lucky ones who lead
fulfilled lives doing exactly what they want to
do.) The limits of needs at this level are
infinite--they are unlikely ever to be filled.
Further, the self-generator that keeps it happening helps create an on-going and seemingly limitless source of motivation.

At Which Level Is Any Individual At Any One Time?

This is not an easy question to answer. More
likely, it is at what percentage involvement in
each level? At any given time, one particular

need will dominate one's behavior. For example, one individual may be primarily at the social level, but can also have needs at both the security and ego levels. Additionally, one may, on occasion, shift abruptly from one to the other. To illustrate: a man operating largely at the self-actualization level is told his company has just gone bankrupt and that this is his final day! At what level would he operate? Perhaps he will plunge to a sudden concern for the basic needs. "How will I buy food? How do I make payments on the house?"

Needs in Business and Industry

It is important to realize that employees cannot bring only their basic needs to work and leave their other needs at home. They will attempt to satisfy all of them at work or through work.

HERZBERG

Herzberg divided the factors that motivate employees into two major groups:

| Hygiene Factors |
| Motivational Factors |

The first group contains the hygiene factors, so-called because they operate in a manner similar to public health or hygiene, whereby people are not made healthy but are prevented from being unhealthy. While hygiene factors do not make employees happy or satisfied, they do prevent them from being unhappy and dissatisfied. The other

major group contains factors that provide positive
motivation and are called "motivators."

When one looks at the following side-by-side
comparison, Herzberg and Maslow appear to have
been saying somewhat the same thing.

SELF-ACTUALIZATION Need to do the work we want	MOTIVATIONAL FACTORS 　The work itself 　Challenging work 　Meaningful work
EGO Need to feel respected and important	Recognition 　Responsibility

SOCIAL Need for love--to be part of a group	HYGIENE FACTORS 　Friendly co-workers 　Good working 　　conditions
SECURITY Need to feel safe	Insurance 　Pensions 　Job security
BASIC Need to stay alone	Good pay

Today, most employers provide for the lower
level needs--those Herzberg identified as the
hygiene factors. And, if these needs are met,
they do not function as motivators.

To suggest that hygiene factors motivate
makes about as much sense as a man hoping that
providing his wife with a home and new clothes

will motivate her to be a better wife. Such
incentives are very temporary.

How the Circle Motivates

Many of today's jobs in the office and the
factory are enormously dull, routine, and boring.
That is, they may be essentially devoid of the
characteristics that motivate. How can the Circle
make any real difference?

First, a review of Herzberg's motivators
is in order: interesting and challenging work,
opportunity to perform meaningful work, recognition, and responsibility.

Participation in Circle activities definitely
provides these vital motivators. Members assume
responsibility to identify and analyze problems
in their work areas. This opportunity to do
interesting and meaningful work provides a new and
exciting challenge. The management presentation
is a dramatic form of recognition for the Circle
members.

"Wait just a moment," is a possible re-
joinder, "the Circle meeting lasts for only an
hour." True, but the employees must return to
doing their regular jobs for the other 39 hours--
often the same boring, unrewarding routine that
existed before. But there is a difference.
Circle members talk about Circle activities during
breaks and lunch times. They continue to think
about their projects. So, rather than one very
separate and isolated hour each week, it becomes
one very special hour (the Circle meeting) that
thoroughly permeates the other 39 hours.

MCGREGOR

Theory X and Theory Y are assumptions that
Douglas McGregor used to describe management
styles.

Theory X Assumptions

Theory X is identified as management's conventional perception of employees' attitudes They include:

* The average person dislikes work and will avoid it if possible.

* Because of this dislike of work, people must be coerced, controlled, directed, or threatened with punishment to get them to put forth adequate effort toward the achievement of organizational objectives.

* On the average, people prefer to be directed, don't want responsibility, have little ambition, and desire security above all.

The carrot and the stick approach is often used to illustrate this kind of method of handling employees. It carries the connotation that employees will respond to either the carrot or the stick, or some combination thereof.

It also implies that the employee has to be manipulated.

McGregor says that the Theory X style is the traditionally accepted way to get a motivated employee to increase productivity.

When a person behaves toward work in the manner that Theory X assumes, McGregor sees the organization to blame, not the employee; because people are basically not lazy, uncooperative, or uncreative. McGregor sees the negative behavior of Theory X as one fundamentally created by management through its excessive degree of control.

Theory Y Assumptions

Theory Y is a set of assumptions about people that are quite different from those of most traditional management philosophies. They include:

* Physical and mental effort in work are as natural as rest and play.

* External control and the threat of punishment are not the only means of getting people to strive toward the organization's objectives. They will exercise self-control and self-direction toward achieving objectives if they are committed.

* Commitment to objectives is a function of the rewards associated with their achievements (esteem and self-actualization, for example).

* The average person learns, under the proper conditions, not only to accept but to seek responsibility.

* Most people are capable of a relatively high degree of imagination, ingenuity, and creativity in solving organizational problems.

* Under the conditions of contemporary industrial life, the average person's intellectual potential is being only partially utilized.

Self-Fulfilling Prophecy

The manager employing a Theory X management style knows he is right. He has Theory X assumptions concerning his employees attitudes; and, of

course, they respond in a manner which proves
him right! Truly, a self-fulfilling prophecy! It
is as though an employee were saying, "If that is
your unfaltering opinion of me, why should I
waste my time trying to change your views?"

If, on the other hand, the manager has Theory
Y assumptions about his employees, there is every
likelihood they will respond by proving him right.
Again, a self-fulfilling prophecy!

Congruency of Goals

Matching the needs and goals of the individual to those of the organization is necessary to
maximize employee commitment. An example is the
sales manager who tries to attune the goals of an
individual sales person to those of the organization. The organization's goals might be simply to
increase sales by 10%. An individual sales person
may have difficulty in relating to such a goal.
He or she has personal goals--those he or she
understands and to which he or she is committed.
A major goal might be to build a swimming pool in
the backyard.

How does one arrive at a congruency of goals
when it is unclear what the employer's goals are?
The sales manager should be direct and ask. The
ensuing discussion will likely result in a heightened realization that increased sales on the part
of the sales person will not only make the pool a
reality sooner, but the organization will inch
closer to its goals as well. Other areas of
congruency may also emerge. For example, an
appeal to the employee's pride in working for a
vigorous growing company might add additional
elements of congruency.

The manager will do better by henceforth
talking in terms of the employee's goals rather
than the organization's. McGregor says that

employees will exercise self-direction and become better involved in working toward organizational objectives only to the degree they are committed to those objectives. If commitment is minimal, only a minimal amount of self-direction will result, and external control will be needed. If commitment is great, conventional controls are superfluous, and possibly self-defeating. The determining variable is the employee's perception of the situation, regardless of the objective reality.

Interpreting the Motivational Cycle

Near the beginning of this chapter, the motivational cycle was described. It is triggered by a need. A goal is formulated to fill the need.

The process of meeting the goal was described as the effort exerted that could be termed motivated behavior.

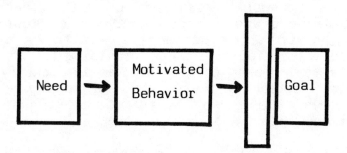

What happens if the barrier prevents attainment of the goal? Certainly a degree of frustration results. If this frustration lasts long enough, the employee will begin to exhibit one or several types of behavior:

* Anger
* Apathy
* Compromise

Anger and apathy are self-explanatory. Compromise behavior is where the employee may decide to leave the company; transfer to another department; start up a part-time business with the hope of leaving the business someday; thrust himself into some activity not necessarily an organization's goal, such as union activities.

In any case, the resulting behavior may not necessarily be supportive of the organization's goals. More likely, it is be contrary to its interests.

How can the Circle help in this area? Circle activities provide a way for employees to meet their personal goals and still be fulfilling organization goals.

There is no way that an organization can provide job advancement to all the employees deserving of it. This may be possible only in rare instances, where an organization is undergoing tremendous expansion; but it is not an on-going process. Some other method must be provided to allow personal goals to be met. Circle activities do this by providing the opportunity for members to get involved in identifying problems affecting their jobs and to engage in analyzing these difficulties and presenting solutions.

It may be the only opportunity to make a real difference.

JOB ENRICHMENT

The question often is asked, "Can one build into a job the factors that Herzberg calls 'motivators'?" These motivators, of course, are: responsibility, recognition, meaningful work, challenging work, and the work itself.

The "Taylorization" (Frederick W. Taylor was the father of scientific management) of our work areas--highly specialized, fragmented tasks that are both incredibly simple and almost totally devoid of challenge--leads to economies in the cost of production. But, the application of scientific management principles has not been without consequences. The major negative factor has been an enormous under-utilization of our most costly and valuable resource: our people.

What Is Job Enrichment?

Job enrichment involves deliberately building into the job content the motivating factors that permit people to build their own internal generators. The accompanying diagram helps to explain why it is often referred to as vertical job loading.

JOB ENRICHMENT

(Vertical Job Loading)

* Regular job duties are the same except that the overall depth is greater

* Some "managerial" responsibilities have been delegated to employees

* Involves participation and decision-making responsibility

* Entire process contains several satisfiers to stimulate and motivate

How Job Enrichment Works

...Employee continues doing his basic job

...Employee is delegated some management level function

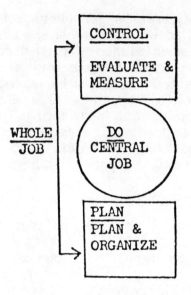

...Provides for degree of participation in job design

...Allows for some choice between alternatives

...Includes employee involvement in design of feedback system to permit employee degree of control

Job Enrichment—-An Illustration

An examination of what people do in their spare time can aid in understanding job enrichment.

A golfer typically experiences the following:

...Freedom to set his own goals. He chooses to spend his time golfing. He makes a choice and thereby has ownership in the goals. Thus, there is more commitment to attaining them.

...<u>Personal responsibility for attaining goals</u>. When he goes to the golf course he knows he has personal responsibility and involvement in attaining the goals that were set. He will carry his clubs, clean his club heads, and personally swing at the ball. He also has some freedom in choosing the methods for attaining these goals: "Will I use my number 4 wood or my number 3 iron?"

...<u>Challenging goals</u>. The game contains many built-in obstacles that remove any assurance of easy access to a good score. One must pit his or her skills and ingenuity against the harsh realities of the course. It provides stimulation and challenge. One can feel proud of a game well played.

...<u>Prompt feedback</u>. People want to know how they are doing during, not after, the game. The golfer understands the fairness of the scoring system. He knows that it applies the same to whoever plays that course. Best of all, the feedback is prompt and continuous.

...<u>Recognition</u>. Reward and recognition must be related to the degree of achievement. A mediocre score would provide much less personal reward than a good one. This relationship, while apparent on the golf course, is much less obvious on the job, where personality and political considerations are encountered.

...<u>Support and encouragement</u>. Teammates provide encouragement. Support can be obtained <u>if</u> desired; for example: golf lessons. On the job, the supervisor has the task as coach and counselor, assisting as requested. He does not assume the

role of a judge who decides what is needed
by the employee and when it will be
administered.

Job Enrichment And Quality Circles

Do games contain a magic that can turn
employees on? Maybe so; and maybe there are
lessons that businesses can learn from them.

Perhaps the work environment stifles employee
motivation and productivity. Incorporating some
of the features contained in golfing (or any other
game) may unleash a whole new vitality.

The redesign of jobs is often limited by
machine and other factors. The Quality Circle may
not be able to alter the entire job; but the
effect of involving one hour each week with
Herzberg's motivators can dramatically influence
and permeate the other thirty-nine. As stated
previously, Circle members do discuss Circle
activities during breaks and the lunch period; and
minds are activated, excited, and challenged so
that members think about it while working on their
regular jobs.

GROUP DYNAMICS

Group dynamics is a highly complex subject that deals with the interaction between people. Relationships in the Quality Circle sense will be explored here with suggestions on ways to maximize the effectiveness of Circle activities.

In the U.S., more money is now being spent by business, industry, and government on leadership and management training and development than is spent in running all of the schools, colleges, and universities in the nation.

PEOPLE BUILDING

People building is the art of making people better than they already are. It is done by helping them to acquire knowledge and skills; and, just as important, to improve their attitudes-- making them feel·better about themselves.

People-Building Techniques

The following are a few of the more obvious ways in which a Circle leader may bring about these people-building changes:

*Circle assignments for members such as:

- Collecting data
- Taking minutes of Circle meetings
- Writing Circle news items for company or community newspapers
- Leading brainstorming sessions
- Writing down ideas at brainstorming sessions
- Posting charts

*Management presentation participation such as:

- Preparing agenda
- Setting up meeting room
- Preparing presentation charts
- Making presentations
- Assisting by hanging charts on the wall as speakers finish with them

*Training:

- Assisting leaders by performing portions of training instruction
- Assisting members who need special help during training
- Appointing and training one or more assistant Circle leaders

Give People Status

People want to feel appreciated and important.

To illustrate: automobiles, homes, and clothes are examples of status symbols that people often employ to tell the world, "I'm important."

There are a number of status symbols that can make members feel important. It costs little or nothing, but carries with it a big payoff. Simply treating members in a courteous way is giving them status.

Remembering names, birthdays, hobbies, and other interests are ways of giving status.

Status should be built into Circle activities. Status creates the motivation that carries benefits for Circle members, the Circle, and the organization as a whole.

Members should be kept informed. Everyone wants to "Be in on things"; and they should hear about them from the leader.

Pygmalion Effect (Self-Fulfilling Prophecy)

Most supervisors and/or Circle leaders have had people-building experience long before they attained their present positions.

This is true if they have children. People want their youngsters to be not only as good as they themselves are, but much better! They put a lot of effort and attention in the drive to assure that this occurs. Education, trips, hobbies, special lessons, etc., all play a role. There is no question, "Is this the right thing to do?" Or, "Will it have a payback?" They simply know it will! They believe! The youngsters pick up this positive conviction, this confidence in them, and perform positively. Truly, this is a self-fulfilling prophecy.

It need not be any different in Circle activities. The leader who works with the Circle members by giving them the best and expecting the best, who helps them set challenging goals and objectives, will get the best results. "Expect a lot and you get a lot!"

It can work just as dramatically in reverse. A low expectation can also be a self-fulfilling prophecy. "You think I'm a loser? Okay, you're probably right."   "Why try?" is the conclusion often reached.

Studies have shown that attitudes and behavior throughout a person's life are strongly influenced by parental expectations. Also significant is the effect of the first supervisor's expectations when he or she first enters the business world. Likewise, the first supervisor in each new organization worked for exerts a powerful influence on subsequent performance.

The phenomenal influence of the Circle leader's expectations on another's behavior is no exception. It is truly an awesome responsibility!

The leader must remember that all Circle members have abilities that are waiting to be discovered. Encouragement, compliments, and assurances of their worth will stimulate them to reach for new heights!

Some psychologists have stated that nearly 90% of the actions we take are prompted by our wish to be important. The point is--all persons have an innate desire to take positive action toward this end.

That's how each person tends to feel about himself.   But the manner in which people treat each other often communicates a different kind of message. "You will never make anything of your-self." "You're dead wrong." "You don't have a chance in the world to do what you are saying." These phrases are often heard.   An employee may have been told by his teacher that he's too lazy to ever make anything of himself. His parents may have nagged him about his sloppy habits and told him that they were much better than he when they were his age. Perhaps he was never quite able to make the team. His co-workers get upset with him. Hardly anybody thinks he's important.   He isn't

too sure about it either. In fact, in his mind he
is probably the loser that everybody thinks he
is.

But, along comes a new supervisor. He looks
for strength, not weaknesses. He praises this
employee at every opportunity. Soon this "loser"
begins to feel much better about himself. Suddenly he realizes that somebody thinks of him as
special. He begins to think of himself in this
manner. That supervisor becomes someone he would
do just about anything for. He knows he is seen
as a worthwhile human being with untapped creative potential. And he intends to prove that
supervisor right!

Leader Gets Full Involvement

A leader should be encouraged to strive for
the involvement of all members at each and every
meeting--not once, but several times.

Circle size may be the most significant factor.
If it is too large, everyone is cheated! It
is a fact that large Circles have the highest
dropout rate; because involvement is lacking.
There are just too many members for the leader to
handle.

Involvement techniques include: brainstorming,
asking questions, group discussions, giving
assignments, and participation in management
presentations.

Developing An Involvement Checklist!

If a list of members' names is made up,
and a check mark is placed behind each when
involvement occurs, the outcome can be surprising. Despite the most sincere desire to involve
members equally, the majority of leaders do not;
and they are normally unaware of their failure to

do so. The check sheet helps to avoid this
shortcoming. It can be maintained by either the
leader or an assistant leader.

The Management Presentation Develops Confidence

The management presentation represents an
unusual vote of confidence to Circle members.
True, it is a nerve-wracking ordeal to be uninit-
iated. But its accomplishment can bring the
flush of victory. It has everything. As a
recognition device, and as a way to communicate,
it is unexcelled.

The growth of confidence in members who are
involved in these presentations is important.

TEAMWORK

Win-Win

Human beings are very competitive. They like
to win; but winning can be of questionable value.
Who will be the losers? How soon will the victor
have to deal with the vanquished again? How
durable will any victory really be?

The objectives should be to achieve win-win
situations, not win-lose ones. Each party involved should feel that he or she has won.
Research has proven that win-win solutions are
preferable to win-lose situations where someone
suffers defeat.

One facilitator's experience will help
illustrate this approach. George was a facilitator for a large group of Circles. He knew that
one of the Circle leaders was about to put on a
management presentation--his first. An industrial
engineer working in that area had been posing
problems for the Circle; and George was trying to

determine if there was a way to overcome this
difficulty. George approached the Circle leader
and asked, "Tom, have you invited Jim (the industrial engineer) to the management presentation?"
Tom stiffened and snapped, "Hell,no!   He hasn't
done anything to help us!   Why should he be
there?" George replied, "He is the industrial
engineer in your area. I know how you feel about
him; but he probably thinks the Circle is infring-
ing in his personal territory as the official
problem solver."   Tom shook his head and said,
"If you want him there, I'll invite him, but he
isn't going to like what he hears!" George smiled
and shook his head, "Tom, isn't there anything
he's done that's good?   There must be something
positive that you can say about him."   "Not a
thing, believe me," was Tom's quick reply.   "But,
I understand what you are getting at. Let me talk
to the Circle members and see what they say."   Tom
talked it over with his Circle members.   They had
the same reaction as he, but agreed to give it
a try--to invite the engineer.

On the morning the Circle presentation took
place, Jim was the last person to enter the room.
The presentation started when the leader introduced the first speaker, a young woman.   At one
point she looked directly at Jim, a smile came to
her face, and she said, "And, thanks to Jim, we
got the data we needed to solve the problem."
Everybody in the room, including Jim, was surprised.   Jim's reputation was well known.   People
turned to look at him with some degree of amaze-
ment.   "Had this person really changed?"   They
wondered.   Jim appeared to be quite puzzled by
what was happening.

During the next 20 minutes, the time it took
to complete the presentation, Jim was complimented
a total of four times; these were the only compliments he had received from anybody during the
three years he had been in the department!

The Circle in this instance experienced a
WIN, a gigantic one! But, so did Jim. The Circle
members would have had a win anyway. But, if they
had caused Jim to lose, he would have been a
continuing source of trouble and an obstacle to
their progress from then on. Three weeks later
George asked the members of the Circle how they
felt about what they had done. It was unanimous.
"Best thing we could have done. You can't believe
the change in that man." George knew that Jim had
not completely changed; but he did agree with the
members that there had been a substantial change
for the better. It even extended over into an
improved relationship between Jim and other
employees. Truly, this was a win-win situation.

Synergism

Synergism is defined as the "Total being
greater than the sum of the individual parts!"
The coach who develops an "esprit de corps" among
team players kindles a fire that can inspire a
united effort of startling proportions. The
incredible victory of the U.S. Olympic Hockey Team
(mostly college players) over world hockey powers
such as the Russians, the Czechoslovaks, Swedes,
and Fins in the 1980 Winter Olympic Games is such
an example.

Other things, in addition to enthusiasm, had
to be in place as well, of course. Each team
member had to exercise his particular specialty
in the most heroic and spectacular way--giving
until there was nothing left to give, then reaching down and finding something more to give.

CODE OF CONDUCT

To assure win-win relationships, a Circle
should develop a code of conduct by which to
operate. This is the set of rules that governs
that Circle's operation. This extraordinary

technique, simple and quick to put together, effectively transforms the theories of group dynamics in communication into a practical reality.

Each Circle creates its own code of conduct as a customized venture. A standard code of conduct shaped by the steering committee certainly would save time and uniformity would be assured; but if the steering committee fashioned the code of conduct, it would surely be viewed by Circle members as "Management trying to tell us how to behave--just like we're a bunch of children." If the Circle members do it, it's theirs. They are the authors. They have pride of ownership and commitment to make it work.

Additionally, experience clearly shows that Circle members adopt stricter guidelines for themselves than management normally requires.

Examples of code of conduct items selected by Circles are listed below. Of these, most will select approximately ten:

* Attend all meetings and be on time

* Listen to, and show respect for the views of other members

* Make others feel a part of the group

* Criticize ideas, not persons

* Take responsibility to help other members participate more fully

* Be open to, and encourage the ideas of others

* Every member is responsible for the team's progress

* Maintain a friendly attitude

* Strive to assure enthusiasm

* Everyone is equal during meetings

* Give others a chance to express themselves more, even if it means less personal participation

* The only stupid question is the one that isn't asked

* Participate according to the golden rule

* Keep an open mind and look for merit in the ideas of others

* Listen carefully to the ideas and contributions of others

* Pay attention -- avoid disruptive behavior

* Attend meetings regularly and partici- pate in discussions

* Avoid actions that delay progress

* Carry out assignments on schedule

* Ensure that credit is given to those to whom it is due

* Show thanks and appreciation to non-members who give assistance

* Avoid conflict during meetings

* Avoid criticism and sarcasm toward the ideas of others

* No disruptive side conversations

* Maintain a friendly atmosphere at all times

* Speak up and express ideas

* Always strive for win-win situations

* Don't lecture unless you are an expert

* Don't give solutions -- find causes first

* Don't belittle the ideas or opinions of others -- you are not the judge

* Before you criticize, give praise and honest appreciation

* Ask questions instead of giving orders

* Help others to save face

* Praise every improvement no matter how little

* Use encouragement

Preferred time to develop a code of conduct is during the second training session, right after the Circle has studied Brainstorming.

Brainstorming is the technique they use to formulate their code of conduct. The leader will have discussed the subject with them at their first meeting and will have asked them to think about ideas for it.

The facilitator may give the leader printed examples of code of conduct rules to distribute to the members shortly before the meeting.

Advantages of doing it this way:

-It helps trigger additional ideas

-It speeds the formation of the code of conduct, allowing it to be done in half the usual time

-Assures greater uniformity of codes of conduct between different Circles

-Members will likely decide to adopt many
    ideas right from the example sheet; but the
    decision to do so will be theirs

The facilitator should be sure the leader
posts the code of conduct chart in the Circle
meeting room.   It serves as a constant reminder
to Circle members and alerts visitors in a quiet
way that the group has a code of desired behavior
for members and guests.

BEHAVIOR MODIFICATION

Simply stated, behavior of an individual
is determined by the rewards he receives. If the
reward is a desired one, it serves to reinforce
the behavior and the behavior will be repeated.
Otherwise it will not.

The reward should be given only when the
behavior is positive; and, preferably, it should
be given as quickly as possible.

Research in the shipyard industry disclosed
existence of both negative and positive reinforcement.   Some companies made the decision to drop
negative censure of behavior almost entirely in
favor of positive reinforcement. The results were
immediate and occasionally miraculous.

Behavior Modification Example.   Joe, the Circle
leader, was frustrated by the continual late
arrival of Helen, one of the members.   It was
disruptive; and it was also in violation of the
Circle's code of conduct.   Joe's frustration and
anger was obvious, even though he tried his best
to hide it. He would get Helen aside and talk to
her either during or after the meeting.

Joe talked to the facilitator about Helen;
and it was clear that he was about to decide that
someone had to go--either he or Helen.   The

facilitator explained that possibly Helen's need for attention was so great that she was willing to provoke negative attention rather than none at all. "Try something new," urged the facilitator. "Don't react in any way to her negative behavior. Wait until you see something positive and then tell her about it!" Joe agreed.

Helen seemed surprised when she could not disturb Joe by being late. She came in even later. No reaction. One day, she took an active part in a discussion. That was Joe's opening-- what he had been waiting for. He thanked her for her help. Helen seemed surprised, but pleased.

This was repeated several times and brought about dramatic changes in Helen. No longer late, she took assignments with enthusiasm as she strove toward actions that brought the desired reinforcement--attention. Positive attention, that is.

COUNSELING TECHNIQUES

There will be occasions when it is necessary for the facilitator to give advice and counsel. Often this is because of negative behavior that cannot be handled during Circle meetings. The services of a professional counselor would be welcome on such occasions; but, unfortunately, such help is usually not available.

The facilitator must meet this challenge. There will also be times when the leader may have to do the same--with or without the help of the facilitator.

Counseling Guidelines

* __Be a good listener.__ One must work hard at being a good listener so as to thoroughly understand the member's viewpoint. To

encourage the member to open up, frequent use
of non-committal statements such as, "I see,"
can aid. Statements such as, "I understand,"
should be avoided, as they could be mistaken
for agreement. Interject skilled questions
that cannot be answered in a word or two. It
is better to illicit answers that provide the
member with a chance to vent feelings and
attitudes.

*   Make certain the member knows he or she
    is understood. Counseling sessions fre-
    quently fail because the member assumes,
    rightly or wrongly, "They didn't even under-
    stand what I said!" This can be avoided if
    the facilitator says something like, "I want
    to be certain I understand you completely.
    Let me try to repeat it to you." After doing
    so, the question should be asked, "Is that
    what you said?" The exchange should not
    proceed further until the member agrees that
    the facilitator or leader knows exactly what
    he or she has said, even if it means going
    back and forth on the statements made several
    times.

*   Do not argue. The facilitator must resist
    the temptation to argue. It is doubtful
    that anyone wins. More likely, the member
    will become entrenched and inflexible in the
    stance he or she has taken.

*   The facilitator should clearly explain his or
    her concern. The concern, often being
    negative, can frequently be preceded with an
    observation that is positive and complimen-
    tary. This strengthens the member's sense of
    self worth at a time when he or she may feel
    no better about himself or herself than he or
    she senses the facilitator does. Counseling
    sessions are a kind of negotiation. A good
    negotiation is when one party does not feel
    he has been defeated. It is preferable
    that both emerge satisfied that they have

gained something. The member's gain may be that he or she has been understood or has achieved a new prospective.

As soon as a member gives a signal that a change is possible, attention must be placed on getting his or her involvement and a declared commitment. Thus, that member will be party to effecting the desired change. The facilitator may even desire to explore a variety of alternatives. Hopefully, most of these alternatives will be suggested by the member.

CONDUCTING MEETINGS

Circle meetings can be efficient and pleasant or they can be the opposite. The purpose of the following is to provide some suggestions for the facilitator to use in working with leaders.

What Not To Do During Meetings

* Don't lecture--you're not necessarily an expert

* Don't give answers--the purpose of the discussion is to search for ideas

* Don't belittle the ideas or opinions of others

* Don't argue with group members. Their ideas are important

What To Do To Assure Good Meetings

* Prepare in advance for the meeting

* Open the meeting--give a brief introduction so people will have a chance to settle down and adjust their thinking to the subject

* Stay in the background, listen to the responses, be a "facilitator"

* Keep the discussion moving--have questions ready to ask if the discussion lags

* Encourage participation--try to bring out the quiet members

   Don't let one or a few members dominate-- call on people when you know they are trying to speak

* Summarize--from time to time sum up what has been said, and show the group where they have been and where they are going

* Allow time for a summary statement before the meeting concludes

* End the meeting on time or ahead of time

Good meetings require work.   The leader plays an important role in making sure that meetings are an enjoyable and productive experience for all.

Don't make the group decisions for them.   Some- times the group leans on the leader to provide answers or solutions.   When this happens, the leader should turn the questions back to the group for discussion.

Don't accept solutions too quickly, without adequate discussion.   Suggest that the Circle generate as many alternatives as possible before getting into the evaluation phase.

Don't mistake silence for agreement.   It   is frequently assumed that the quiet member is in agreement.   Commitment is vital to carrying out the group decision. Verify that each person is in agreement.

Encourage minority viewpoints.   Do not allow the majority to block discussion of minority views. These may stimulate new ideas.

Provide frequent summaries.   This   assures   that
everyone is on the same track.   Maintain minutes
of the meeting.

Maintaining Control

Occasionally, side discussions may prove
distracting.   The group may get into an argument
that is wasting everyone's time; or a serious
breach of harmony might be building up. The leader
can regain control by the use of any of a variety
of techniques.   Some examples include:

* Rising to a standing position

* Walking around the room while talking

* Raising the volume of his or her voice to
  attract attention

* Picking up some object such as a piece of
  chalk or a pointer. (Strangely, group members
  are attracted to an item the leader holds in
  his or her hand or waves around in some
  way.)

* Flipping the light switch on and off two or
  three times

* Tapping on the table or a glass to gain
  everyone's attention

* Changing the seating arrangement for members
  to reduce the likelihood of unnecessary
  chatter

* Posting the Circle's code of conduct where it
  is visible to all members

* If a code of conduct already exists, drawing
  attention to it

* Asking questions using the first names of

members. One's name is like a "magic bell,"
the way it can focus attention

*   Tell a joke or a story. Everyone likes to
    hear a good joke and will readily give
    attention

How To Handle Special Situations

Quiet person. The use of brainstorming techniques, and in seeking members' opinions by going
in rotation, is an excellent way of "bringing out"
the quiet member. Sometimes it is necessary to use
that person's first name in directing a question
to him or her. The quiet person might accept
responsibilities, such as: keeping the minutes of
the meeting, recording ideas for a brainstorming
session, and taking on various assignments.

The talkative person. There is often one member
who is constantly talking. His or her ideas might
be good; but unless the excessive talkativeness
can be eliminated, the other members may become
frustrated and lose interest because they can't
express themselves. This individual may be an
excellent contributor; but something has to be
done. Perhaps he or she can be given assignments
which will make it more difficult to talk and work
at the same time, such as keeping the minutes of
the meeting. Also, he or she might find it
difficult to talk much if writing down the ideas
during a brainstorming session. The leader can
address questions to specific members, rather
than ask them so that anyone could feel free to
answer. The leader might even say, "You've given
us some good ideas. Let's hear what some of the
other members have to say." Sometimes, a special
assignment given to the talkative member can be
fruitful--such as using his or her assistance in
getting more involvement on the part of the other
members.

Negative person.   In some Circles there are
members who disagree with nearly every suggestion
made.   When this happens, the other members soon
become discouraged and, typically, will threaten
to drop out unless this problem is brought under
control.

A danger here is that negativism is contagious.   The best way to counter negativism is with
enthusiasm and a positive outlook.   It may be
frustrating or difficult for the leader to be
enthusiastic in the face of negative comments; but
he or she must remember that enthusiasm is just as
contagious, or more so, than negativism.

Ask the negative person, "What would you
do?" He or she is then forced into a position of
"put up" or "shut up."   If he or she does make a
suggestion it may evoke the same treatment that he
or she has been giving to others.   One or more
experiences of this sort may result in improvement.

Paraphrase the negative comments he or she
makes.   The shock of hearing how badly it sounds
may cause a change.

Give the negative member additional assignments to carry out. Often this type of person is
an energy source who feels that his or her capabilities are being underutilized.   If this is
the case, the leader has nothing to lose and
everything to gain by making this person a hard
working contributing member of the group through
increasing his or her responsibilities and workload.   There have been instances where the negative person has been given a responsible job such
as that of assistant Circle leader and has learned
to perform well after going through leader training.   When all else fails, the leader should have
a private counseling session with the negative
person.

The playboy or playgirl.   The playboy or playgirl
flaunts his or her disinterest in the group with
nonchalance, horseplay, "cute" cynical remarks,
jokes, etc.

    The leader can direct attention away from
this person by failing to reward him or her with
attention.   This kind of person may also benefit
by receiving assignments that will keep him or her
occupied.   As with the other types of negative
behavior, the leader may have a private counseling
session with him or her to determine the cause of
the disruptive behavior.

Recognition seeker.   This individual likes to
let the Circle know how great he or she is by
boasting and by telling of his or her personal
achievements.   The braggart can be an annoying
disruptive force in the Circle. The leader should
also recognize that he or she is probably an
energy source who is waiting to be challenged.
The member's need for recognition can be used to
the advantage of both the individual and the
Circle.   A Circle rarely has a shortage of
assignments!

BE FRIENDLY--SMILE!

    The   book,   HOW TO WIN FRIENDS AND INFLUENCE
PEOPLE, by Dale Carnegie, has a chapter explaining
the importance of smiling. It is good advice; but
unfortunately, too few people do it. Watching a
crowd go by can illustrate the scarcity of smiles,
even though most of the individuals in it realize
the value of smiling.

    A survey showed that men smiled at other men
12% of the time; but, they smiled 70% of the time
at women! That suggests that people tend to smile
when they are trying to impress someone else.   It
also suggests that they know it works.

<u>Smiling has a positive effect on others.</u> Be-
havioral scientists tell us that people are more
likely to answer positively when asked something
with a smile.

One study discovered that department store
sales increased as much as 20% after a campaign
to teach salespeople to smile at the customers
was conducted.

One huge hotel chain launched a "smile"
campaign among all of its employees including
the maids and janitors. This not only affected the
quality of the work being done by the hotel staff
but also changed customer comment cards from a
negative 30 to 1 ratio to a positive 30 to 1
ratio. A smile is one of the best ways to insure
good human relations between members of the Circle
and those who interface with them. It gets one
through the tense moments. It helps people to
accept constructive criticism. A smile is so
powerful that it goes a long way to assuring
that people feel that they have been in a win-win
situation.

When one smiles at another, he or she is
likely to smile, too. Perhaps it's a way of
saying, "Thanks for helping make it a better day
for me!"

COMMUNICATION

"It was a NICE day."

These words, as part of someone's story, could be interpreted in many ways.

It could mean the sun was shining--or that it was hot! To a farmer suffering through a drought, rain would make a day nice--just as snow would to a ski lodge operator. "Nice" could also mean the stormy, miserable day on which one learned of an important and long-sought promotion.

The interpretations could go on and on. More precision in word selection is needed to assure accurate and easy communication.

THE NEWSPAPER--A FORMAT THAT COMMUNICATES

Few things are more aggravating than listening to the person who rambles on for 20 minutes to say what could have been said in 20 words.

The key to conveying the maximum information in the minimum amount of time is to state the crux of the matter as succinctly as possible first.

78

An excellent guide is found in the way newspapers report the news. The headlines give 80 per cent of the basic story. If one reads further, the first paragraph provides most of the essential generalities. Succeeding paragraphs simply give details of progressively less importance. To fit a story into available space, the editor merely cuts off paragraphs from the bottom. He knows that little if any of importance will be lost. This practice might be a wise example for Circle members, leaders, and facilitators to follow, presenting their information in the order of importance, as if they might be cut off without warning.

WAYS A CIRCLE COMMUNICATES

Three broad categories describe the techniques by which the Circle communicates: (1) Oral (2) Body English, and (3) Written.

Oral

There are eleven million meetings every working day in the U.S. alone! The human race is talkative! But, apparently it takes a great deal of talking to attain adequate levels of communications. Could it be better? Of course. Some of the principles described herein may be helpful.

Face-to-face is best. Face-to-face communication is vastly superior to written communication when a Circle is proposing a change. Change can be threatening and the listener may be filled with questions about what is "really" meant. In face-to-face communications, he or she can observe the expression on the speaker's face, note tonal qualities in the voice, and watch for clues from body movements. Best of all, he or she can interrupt to ask, "Do you mean....?"

The management presentation is face-to-face
communication at its best. The Circle may be
recommending a change. The likelihood of its
proposal being understood and accepted is enormously enhanced when the manager can ask questions.

All Circle members usually take part in the
presentation to management. Two-way communication
is important because the manager may be quite
unfamiliar with background details surrounding the
recommendation.

The facilitator and leaders are well advised
to do as much of their communicating as possible
on a direct face-to-face basis. As a general
rule, when a choice exists, employ personal
contact over written communication.

KISS Principle   KISS (Keep It Sweet and
Simple) means exactly what it says.

Cultivate the ability to break matters down
to their simplest terms. Some individuals seem
disposed to interject confusion; and this is easy
to avoid. It helps if one can mentally retreat to
a more remote vantage point to observe and evaluate. This procedure aids in placing a mass of
facts in their proper perspective.

One should make it a practice to integrate,
condense, summarize, and simplify facts rather
than to expand and complicate them.

Many meetings go nowhere until someone
finally says something like, "It all boils down
to this. . ." or, "The essential fact is. . ."

A successful corporation executive was
renowned for his brilliance in making winning
presentations to top level industrial and governmental groups. He confided that after carefully

preparing and arranging his materials he would conduct a dry run using one of his several children. The selected child would be approximately 8 to 10 years old. He would then make his presentation; and two results were necessary. One, the presentation had to be interesting and entertaining enough to hold the child's attention. Two, the child had to be able to grasp the crux of the concept and to discuss it with him.

If these two requirements were met, he felt confident that his message would be clearly understood by those he would be addressing. Demeaning? "Not at all," he explained, "I often deal with complex technical material and if non-engineers are to understand, it must be reduced to basic concepts."

Circle members can use the KISS Principle when making a presentation to management. KISS aids can also include charts, photos, and actual hardware or paperwork.

Quality Circle Familiarization Presentation

The facilitator should make numerous Quality Circle presentations to familiarize potential members and leaders, management, staff groups, and union officers with the concept. Do not retreat from this by distributing written descriptions of Quality Circles.

Often an organization purchases an audio-visual module, usually 35mm slides, that provides a general introduction and overview of Quality Circles. If possible, it should be customized by including slides that "personalize" it to the organization and its location. For example, the first slide might be a view of the organization's headquarters or plant sight. Another slide might be of the chief executive officer. Others could include scenes of the office and production areas, and personnel.   This causes it to be viewed as "ours," and a major step is established in winning new support.

   The Voice.   The voice can directly influence communications. If a Circle member, upset with another member, angrily strikes out verbally, it is almost a certainty that the response will be expressed in anger. In other words, anger begets anger.   The result is frequently that walls or barriers are erected and positions become inflexible. The adage, "You reap what you sow" is quite true.   On the other hand, if some restraint had been exercised, a smile and a kidding remark might have avoided the unpleasantness.

Body English (Non-Verbal)

   Anyone who has observed the conversation between persons who are deaf can appreciate the value of "body English" in communications.   Their hands spell out key words and phrases.   This, combined with facial expressions, body posturing, and touch, achieves a communications speed equal to that which is without the handicap of deafness.

   Facial expression. Careful scrutiny of a speaker's face is bound to provide clues that will enhance understanding of the message being transmitted. Examples include: excitement, happiness, irritation, anger, and boredom.

   Equally important are the emotions being registered on the face of the listener. A skilled speaker watches carefully for indications that allow him or her to "read" the listener.

   The management presentation is an arena where firsthand observation of facial expressions creates a valuable extra dimension in communications.

Body expression provides clues to both the sender and receiver. Something may be wrong if the listener ceases to look at the speaker. A lowering of the eyes, looking at the door, gazing out the window, or reading reports conveys a disturbing message. Perhaps this is the wrong time and place. Maybe it should move along faster. That could be the signal to the speaker to ask, "Any questions?" Feedback might be very much in order at such a time.

A listener who keeps checking his watch is also sending a message. That message is just as clear as the one the "yawner" sends out; or, the person who does a tappety-tap routine with his fingers. If one is unclear about the message-- one should ask.

One company directed that professional employees be work-sampled. Personnel doing the sampling were not always in a position to be able to evaluate whether they were observing work or non-work items. Body English signals of the most elementary nature became the vehicle to convey this information. The samplers would observe an individual and record either, (1) Work, or (2) Idle.

Signals to portray work or idleness included:

*   Talking on the telephone--Work

*   Talking on the telephone and smiling or laughing--Idle

*   Talking to another employee--Work

*   Talking to another employee and smiling or laughing--Idle

*   Sitting at desk, not moving, but holding a pencil--Work

    * Sitting at desk, not moving, without a
    pencil--Idle

    Needless to say these signals and many others
that were used were loaded with potential for
error.   But, rudimentary as these body English
signals were, the overall results were reported
by the organization doing the sampling to have an
accuracy level of 95%.

Written

    Written communications definitely have a
place in conducting Circle activities. They are
essential to rounding out methods by which facilitators, leaders, and members communicate.   The
spoken word exists for a fleeting moment.   The
written word lingers on as a permanent record.
The written message can even exert "impact." This
was the crux of the Western Union ad campaign to
promote greater use of its telegraph services.

    The organization's newspaper.   It would be
ideal if face-to-face communications were possible
with all employees--ideal, but impractical.
Sometimes the message must be "broadcast" via the
organization's newspaper. It will undoubtedly miss
many, but only because some fail to read it.   If
an attractive heading is included, and perhaps a
photograph, it will catch the eyes of more
readers.   Use of the in-house newspaper minimizes
the likelihood of, "Nobody told me!" This is
important.

    The organization's newspaper serves to do
more than simply inform--it provides a powerful
but low cost way to provide recognition.

    Quality Circle newsletter. Circles at some
organizations use their own special "newspaper" to
communicate.   Often assembled by the facilitator
from inputs primarily provided by leaders and

members, it is distributed to all Circle members
and others who are interested. Items are usually
typed with illustrations inserted and photos to
add interest. One such Quality Circle newsletter
is issued monthly and consists of one regular-size
sheet typed on both sides.

Activity reports. The facilitator can use
the activity report both as a communication tool
and to put things on record. Distribution of
copies should include Circle leaders, managers
with Circles, steering committee members, and
anyone else who wishes to be informed.

Items in a facilitator's activity report can
provide information which can prevent or minimize
overlap in Circle projects. Commitments to do
a management presentation are documented. Once
in print, there is less likelihood of postpone-
ments. Recommended solutions and subsequent
follow-up can be recorded.

The frequency of facilitator activity reports
varies between weekly and monthly. Occasionally
a summary activity report can be issued semi-
annually or annually.

Leaders normally prepare weekly activity
reports. By all means, Quality Circle items should
be a regular feature. "Keep the boss informed!"

Facilitators should encourage steering
committee members and other executives to also
include Quality Circle items in the activity
reports they prepare.

Minutes of meetings. Anyone who is interested should have access to the minutes of Circle
meetings.

Normally, these are typed. Copies are
duplicated and distributed.

A shortcut taken by some Circles involves bypassing a formal distribution. Handwritten minutes are contained in a binder. No distribution is made, but access to the binder is easy and available to all.

Minutes of steering committee meetings are likewise maintained and distributed.

Agendas that have been distributed prior to a Circle meeting communicate to participants what should be prepared for to assure a more productive session.

Schedules and Action Plans are used to communicate goals, milestones, responsibility, and progress. Posted where Circle members, management, and others can see, they serve to "tell the world" where they are going.

GENERAL

Golden Rule

Every time the principle behind the Golden Rule is violated, the potential for a breakdown in communications is created.

The majority of people want others to think well of them. Every person likes to feel that his or her job is important in some way to others. No one wants to be looked down upon or made to feel like the fool, particularly in the presence of others.

Man has a constant struggle for security, human dignity, and to be "somebody." When this perfectly normal human feeling is challenged, there is likely to be a breakdown in communications.

Be Aware Of How Suggestions May Be Perceived

A suggestion given by Circle members to their leader or a recommendation from the Circle to the manager may be perceived in a number of ways. On one hand it may be interpreted as a positive action that demonstrates loyalty and willingness to building a stronger, more competitive organization. On the other hand, it might be seen as a "cheap shot" to draw attention to what might be thought of as incompetence on the part of the superior for not having thought of it himself.

The way suggestions are presented largely determines the way they are interpreted. It is important to assure that a win-win partnership exists for all.

Same stimuli--different reactions. Two employees who are observed smiling about something during working hours may convey different messages to different observers. The insecure supervisor might feel he is the butt of some joke. The supervisor who is convinced that work is basically distasteful would likely assume his employees are "goofing off," or don't have enough to do. Otherwise, why would they be smiling?

The boss who thinks work is as essential as play and rest might see the smiles as evidence that the employees are happy and content.

Halo effect. The halo effect can distort communication. The expression, "He can do no wrong," may cause problems, because obviously, he can do wrong.

Fred was the best club treasurer a certain group had had for years. The membership was convinced these virtues applied across the board. This "halo effect" resulted in his election as club president, where he proceeded to fail disastrously.

Past or present performance (the halo effect) is nothing more than a guide. It should be used that way. One should keep all options open. To avoid "halo effect entrapment," other opinions should be sought. One should operate on short-term commitments, and "inspect what you expect."

"Inspect what you expect." Years ago the author saw these words printed in the upper righthand corner of an office blackboard. For example, a facilitator expects that each Circle leader is maintaining minutes of meetings. He or she tells the leaders to be certain to do it; but, later discovers, with embarrassment, that some leaders are not. The solution is simple. "Inspect what you expect."

Do not mislead. Written reports are often turned in full of errors and omissions, and they may mislead and trigger decisions that should never be made. Circle leaders and facilitators should be sure of their facts ahead of time. If questions are asked and the answers are not apparent, guesses should not be made. A wrong answer is worse than no answer. If one doesn't know, he or she should say so; but add, "I'll find out." Facts should never be distorted. Someone higher up in the organization may have to act on what is reported as fact.

Charts can communicate misleading information by the mere arrangement of data. It can happen accidentally; but the audience may not be amiable about it. A dry run with the facilitator present may bring out irregularities before it is too late.

FEEDBACK

Communications are clearest when feedback is used to insure the clarity of the messages.

One should develop the practice of asking questions to see if the listeners have understood what is intended, and should ask to have instructions repeated.

Misunderstandings are inevitable. Therefore, an atmosphere that encourages people to ask questions when they do not clearly understand must be created.

Communications Feedback Game

The following describes two entertaining exercises that illustrate the importance of feedback during the process of communicating. Two volunteers are needed. One takes exercise #1; and the other handles exercise #2.

With rare exception, the results are dramatically improved in exercise #2 because of feedback.

COMMUNICATION EXERCISE #1

VOLUNTEER NUMBER 1

1.   Your job is to get each of the participants in the group to accurately and quickly reproduce the following diagram.

2.   You are to do this by describing, telling, and/or instructing with your back to the group.

3.   The group will not be allowed to ask any questions or to comment on your presentation. You will not be allowed to solicit such information from the group.

4.   Assume that all rectangles are equal in size, that they touch at sensible places (i.e. corners or mid-points), and that they form either 45 or 90 degree angles.

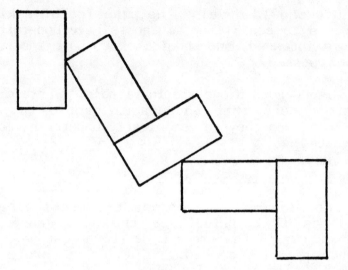

Instructor: At conclusion, ask Volunteer #1
and other Circle members to describe
their feelings during the exercise.
NOTE: Do not show diagram until
Volunteer #2 has completed
the second portion of this
exercise.

COMMUNICATION EXERCISE #2

VOLUNTEER NUMBER 2

1. Your job is to get each of the participants
    in the group to accurately and quickly
    reproduce the following diagram.

2. You are to do this by describing, telling,
    and/or instructing while standing or sitting
    and facing the group.

3. The group will be allowed to ask questions
    and comment on your presentation. You will
    be allowed to solicit information from
    the group.

4. Assume that all the rectangles are equal
    in size, that they touch at sensible places
    (i.e. corners or mid-points), and that
    they form either 45 or 90 degree angles.

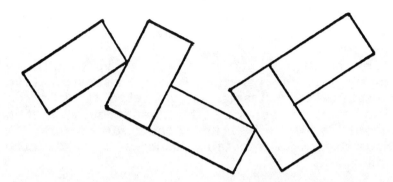

Instructor: At conclusion, ask Volunteer #2 and
             other Circle members to describe
             their feelings during the exercise.

Teaching And Feedback

Program-learning textbooks teach in a highly
organized manner with or without an instructor.
They provide a series of questions. Each is related to the previous question but slightly more
difficult. The answers are usually to the right.
These are concealed by the student, but are exposed as he wishes to check answers.

The fundamentals of effective teaching are
incorporated in the above learning process. To
state it another way, the basics of good instructional practice include:

1. New learning should be broken into
    a series of small increments, a piece
    at a time. Each question provides a
    tiny advance in the total learning.

2. Immediate feedback. This takes place
    by a quick look at the answer.

3. Reward and reinforcement. This is
    provided when one sees that he or she has
    the correct answer.

This approach is effective for a facilitator
who is teaching a class of leaders or for a leader
who is teaching his or her Circle members. It is
essential to go slowly and in a logical sequence,
to ask questions constantly, and to provide a
constant flow of answers. It is counterproductive
to wait until a lesson is completed to do these
things. To do so could be disastrous, as the
students could be either "lost" or asleep. A
constant flow of questions assures a steady flow
of feedback.

Practice sessions often precede the actual
management presentation. Members are encouraged
to anticipate questions likely to be asked, so
that they will be more confident in their ability
to respond when doing the actual presentation.

Feedback On Circle Projects

Circles use goals and milestones to schedule
their projects. But, that is not enough. Managers rightfully insist on visibility for projects
they are responsible for. A Circle should do no
less. Therefore, each schedule must reflect
current progress (feedback) against scheduled
commitment.

A golfer can predict his score on each of the
18 holes. That is analogous to a schedule. The
scorecard is the feedback system. Without the
score--few golfers would play the game. Feedback
informs! Feedback inspires! Without it the game
is not interesting--not just golf, but any game.

COMMUNICATIONS SUMMARY

The following essentials should be kept
in mind and are restated here for emphasis:

*   The tone of voice is more important than one is likely to realize. Put a smile in one's voice, and it is amazing what can be said without provoking the other person.

*   Do not expect anyone to change his or her mind by being asked to, told to, or argued with.

*   It is often a good idea, after a person has stated a complaint, to ask him or her to describe it again, "So I can be sure I understand." Repeating it sometimes makes it seem less important.

*   Use every opportunity to make the other person feel better or more important.

*   Attempt to control one's desire to gain the upper hand when pointing up weaknesses in the other person's point of view. Do it in a way that the other person's ego is not unnecessarily damaged.

*   When disagreement occurs, get each party to paraphrase the other person's position to the satisfaction of the other.

*   Remember, <u>as the other person sees the situation</u>, he is probably right.

*   Where disagreements have arisen, stay on the problem rather than the personalities.

*   Ask questions to see if your listeners have understood your message. Have them repeat it to assure that you are getting through.

    At this time it would be wise to review the code of conduct. Each Circle should have its own code to enhance group dynamics and communication.

USING GOALS TO MAXIMIZE RESULTS

Does the New Year's resolution qualify as a productive way to set goals? "I am going to lose weight," for example?

Such a resolution falls short in several ways.

It is not attainable simply because no measurement goal has been established.

It is not measurable because no measurable goal has been established to measure against.

There is no target date. A definite date should always be included.

There is no challenge. The resolution is, "I am going to lose weight." Because it doesn't say how much, by definition, any weight loss could be considered to be a success. More likely, the absence of a challenge makes it unworthy of pursuit. A better way to state it would be, "I will lose 40 pounds."

It is difficult to imagine any organization operating without schedules. In fact, it is inconceivable! With no schedules, little would happen and the organization would soon find its

economic muscles faltering and collapsing. What
is a schedule, and how does it relate to using
goals to maximize results? That is the subject of
this chapter.

WHAT GOALS?

For what kind of problems could Circles
be setting goals?

The temptation is to "go for the big one."
Therein lie several dangers. Management is
always aware of the big problem. If aware,
and if management has not solved it, why should
the Circle (with more limited experience and
resources) attempt it? Besides, if it is a big
problem it likely involves other organizations.
That may remove it from the Circle's area of
expertise--another reason to stay away from
it.

As a general rule, Circles should concentrate
on the small problems. Several small solvable
ones from the area of the Circle's expertise can
easily outweigh a big one. In addition, there
always seems to be an abundance of small problems. Perhaps this is because management and
other professional problem solvers are too busy to
bother with them. Or, maybe it is because
they are simply unaware of them. Often the
only persons conscious of the small problems are
the people doing the work. If ignored even by
Circle members, no one will try to solve them.
It is possible, too, that--added together--
these small problems may comprise a very significant barrier to the success of an organization, or
of a department in it.

WHO SETS THE GOALS?

Those charged with fulfilling the goals
must be involved in their establishment. This
is an essential ingredient to building commit-

ment. It should be noted that the word "involved"
is used--involved totally or in part. If the
goals are established by management without
Circle involvement, then the commitment will
belong to management.

ESTABLISHING CIRCLE GOALS

There is an array of factors involved in
setting Circle goals. These factors are listed
below.

Goals Should Be Properly Stated

"Improved morale" is an example of a vague
and unclear goal--it is almost as bad as the
typical New Year's resolution.

Goals Should Be Stated Objectively

In the example above, "improved morale" is
too subjective, too difficult to measure. Because
morale and turnover are related, the goal might be
better stated as, "reduced turnover," or, "reduced
turnover in the keypunching department." Turnover
is a definite quantity that can be measured.

Goals Should Be Clarified With Times And Dates

For example, "reduced turnover in the keypunching department by June 30." There is an
awesome power in stating a date. It is most
powerful when the person charged with meeting the
deadline participates in selecting it. That adds
an additional ingredient--commitment.

Goals Should Be Challenging

"Make them reach." If a goal is easily
attainable, it may be deemed not worth wasting
time on. Or, it may be left to the last moment.

Of course that approach could have merit. At least the last minute panic provides some degree of challenge! An excellent way to build in challenge is to ask those doing the task to participate in the goal setting process. People tend to be harder on themselves than others are. This can strengthen the vital factor of "commitment."

Goals Should Be Attainable

A goal should have challenge; but it must be realistic. It is non-productive to build in a future failure by being unrealistic. "We are going to knock the error rate from 40% to zero in 3 months," could be an example of an unrealistic goal. If the error rate has been historically high, there is little likelihood that it will tumble dramatically in a short period of time.

A key point--Circle goals will become more attainable when the scope of a project is entirely within the purview of the Circle.

Goals Should Be Measurable

"I am going to lose 40 pounds within the next 6 months." A weight scale can be used to measure one's progress.

"Let's improve morale," is not easily attainable because it is difficult to measure. It would become measurable if more accurate gauges of morale were used. For example, attendance, punctuality, grievances, or turnover are measurable.

The Quality Control department could provide a manufacturing Circle with information on scrap and rework; and engineering might provide efficiency reports for the area of the Circle's operations for example.

Milestones Should Be Included

A goal of an around-the-world sight-seeing trip by ship, rail and auto in 40 days could easily be imagined. Of course, it is attainable; but it might be wise to break it into a series of smaller goals, usually termed "milestones." Starting in Liverpool, England, the first milestone could be to journey by ship to New York in 8 days. The second milestone might be to travel by train to Los Angeles in 3 days, and so on throughout the journey.

(a) Victories Are Important

When a Circle goal is attained, the members get the thrill of victory. But they need not settle for just one victory. The goal can be divided into a series of milestones. As each is attained, there is a new victory--as many as there are milestones!

Milestones help a Circle to advance a step at a time toward the attainment of its goal. They help to prevent slow and relaxed starts that usually result in a frantic effort as the scheduled completion date nears.

(b) Responsibility Should Be Assigned For Each Milestone

Otherwise, everyone may wait for "someone else" to take care of it.

(c) Milestones Should Be Measurable

Just as the overall goal should be measurable, so should each milestone be measurable. "If you don't know where you are going, you won't know when you have arrived."

COMMITMENT

A person might say to himself or herself, "I am going to go to next Saturday's game." On Saturday morning, the intention to go may still be strong; but as time passes, it may begin to fade; and the decision may be altered to, "I'll watch it on TV, instead."

What's lacking is commitment.

Commitment would have been established if a ticket had been purchased ahead of time. Or, if the statement had been made to a friend, "Let's go to the game together." Or, "Let's meet at the game."

Visibility

A chart portraying a Circle goal becomes a strong commitment if posted in the work area for everyone to see. An activity report can describe the same goal in words. In effect, it says for all to read, that the Circle is committed. And indeed it is!

FEEDBACK

Status On Goals And Milestones Must Be Provided

Feedback is vital to assure achievement of goals and milestones. For example, if one determines to lose 40 pounds in 6 months, but access to a scale during this time is denied, there is little likelihood that the goal will be attained.

Feedback informs. Feedback inspires. One might hear the expression, "I love to bowl." But suppose a curtain were dropped after the ball is released and the view of the pins is obscured. Nothing is changed except there is no longer any feedback. It is extremely doubtful whether the love of bowling would keep the person playing very long after the loss of the feedback.

Every game, and virtually every action that people take, has a feedback system integral to it.

Circle goals must have built-in feedback systems. Feedback is practically synonymous with success.

Feedback Should Be Rapid

Optimum results cannot be expected when feedback is supplied on a delayed basis. Immediate feedback allows for immediate reaction and readjustments to the operation. It also furnishes the fuel that drives the Circle toward a continuing pursuit of its goals.

Sources Of Feedback Data

Feedback may be supplied by accounting, engineering, manufacturing, or quality control. Or, it may come from observations made by the Circle itself. It may be posted to Circle charts either by the organization supplying it, or by the Circle members. It is likely to garner more attention and commitment from the Circle members if they are involved.

FORMATS TO USE

Three format variations can be used depending on the preferences of the Circle members and its intended application. These are:

*   Schedules

*   Milestone charts

*   Action logs

SUGGESTED FORMAT FOR LEADERS TEACHING GOAL SETTING TO MEMBERS.

Tell the group that it is about to take on a most challenging assignment -- that of preparing a schedule for carrying out the project selected by them. This comment may evoke reasons why it can't be done at this time because there is not yet adequate information to permit doing it right. However, it is essential to keep in mind that all organizations live by schedules - schedules that were often constructed with sketchy and fragmented pieces of information. The point is, do the best with what is available -- <u>but do it!</u>

Conditions are seldom static! Changes do occur! What if the realities of the schedule are altered? No problem! Simply make the appropriate changes; but label the revised schedule with a number and the date of revision.

Three different schedule formats will be described below. Any one of them can be used, depending on its intended application and on the preference of the members. The first illustration is of the milestone schedule, which is a simplified version of the milestone chart. It can, under certain circumstances, become considerably more complex as it reflects the totality of the situation it is portraying.

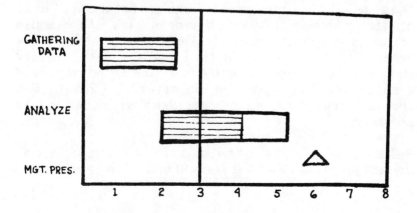

Next is the line graph schedule, wherein the solid line depicts the plan as perceived when the schedule was conceived, and the dotted line reflects the feedback of results actually being achieved.

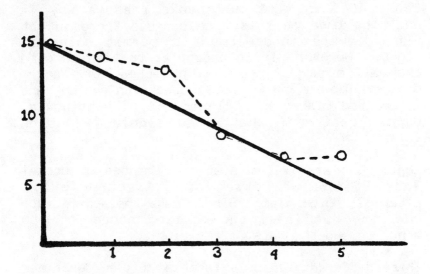

The third one is an action plan log, which is basically a schedule. It differs from the two types listed above in that the use of words greatly exceeds the use of graphics. Also, responsibility is more likely to be indicated with this approach.

Each goal (or problem) must be clearly stated. This is very important! Vague statements will hinder progress or make it impossible. An example of an inadequate goal statement might be, "decrease errors." It fails to state specifically what kind of errors and by how much. An improved version is, "decrease typing errors by 20%." Get the members involved in arriving at clear goals statements.

Seldom is a goal attained in a single step. Usually, several Action Steps are required.

Involve members in determining what the steps will be. A first step might be, "determine the present error rate." A possible second step could be, "design a check sheet to tally and categorize errors." Subsequent steps might be considered to be solution steps. As with other formats described herein, it is essential to be prepared to revise the action steps as the solution unfolds.

Responsibility must be fixed. Each step in the action plan is assigned to a specific member. If more than one member is needed to be responsible for a particular step, the name of each person must be noted on the log. Occasionally, more than one action step will be assigned to a single member.

If someone outside of the team is identified to help with an action step, the name of the one member who will provide the coordinating link to the assisting non-member must also be listed on the log.

ACTION ITEMS

| Item | Action | Who | Date | |
			Target	Actual

Targeted <u>completion</u> <u>dates</u> are included in the action plan, but they must be agreed to by the persons assigned to carry out the action steps. If you establish the dates, then you own the commitment to meet them rather than the persons assigned to carry out those steps. Target completion dates may change as new facts and circumstances unfold; and the action plan log must be appropriately up-dated to reflect these changes. The historical value of the log is improved when obsolete dates are lined through rather than erased.

Have the members select the type of schedule they prefer to use and proceed with the scheduling operation.

TRAINING

Too many problem analysis programs have failed because the "analysts" were not adequately equipped to analyze. There are tools to increase one's effectiveness. The extent of the demand for improvement in this area is indicated by the number of consulting organizations that exist to service those who recognize the necessity to sharpen these skills.

Quality Circle training takes place at a variety of levels in the organization as the following outline indicates:

FACILITATOR TRAINING

The facilitator is most often a university graduate. Whatever his or her degree, it is a certainty that problem analysis skills were acquired. As an example, small differences, mostly in terminology, separate the problem analysis skills of the industrial engineer from those of the accountant.

The beauty of the Quality Circle problem analysis skills is that they emerge as the "universal language" that _everyone_ involved with Circles understands.

The facilitators must be capable of shaping the many pieces that must fit together to assure that the Quality Circle philosophy be allowed to embrace all segments of the organization. The kind of training contained in this handbook brings about this capability.

LEADER TRAINING

The men and women who lead the Quality Circles are the key links in successful Quality Circle activities. These individuals are on the wave crest as the concept is carried into the operating organizations. That is where signs of success and failure will first be noted. It is not an easy burden to be charged with such responsibility.

What kind of training? The closer the leader comes to knowing as much as the facilitator, the better. Because it takes time to acquire this knowledge, most leaders concentrate on the essentials: the analytical techniques, the basics of group dynamics, motivation, communication, and operating successful Circle meetings. The acquisition of these skills provides the basics that, with backup from the facilitator as required, will enable the leader to develop a strong and healthy Circle. As proof positive that the Quality Circle philosophy is a people-building one, the leader provides the training to the Circle members!

MEMBER TRAINING

Some worker-participation programs equip supervisory personnel with problem analysis skills. They are supposed to be the problem solvers. In Quality Circles, a quantum jump takes place, in that those most knowledgeable about the job are trained in problem analysis techniques so that they, too, can truly become involved.

TRAINING FOR THE LEADER

Supervisors and others selected for leader training will be assigned to attend a course designed to prepare them for their new roles as Circle leaders.

This raises several questions.

How Many Hours Of Training?

The majority of organizations provide approximately twenty course hours, give or take five hours. The actual number of hours should be a function of the educational level of attendees and other company training courses they have completed. The course can be conducted on three consecutive days, or one day for each of three weeks, or some other combination.

Who Does The Instructing?

The facilitator usually assumes the role of chief instructor. In fact, the facilitator may be the only one. Where professional training personnel is available, it is recommended that they work with the facilitator to assure the best possible teaching combination.

Another valuable--and often willing--source of assistance is the organization's experienced Circle leaders, if any. They provide a high degree of "believability"; and their involvement as part-time instructors can provide another personal "people-building" experience.

Student Participation

Students gain more knowledge and confidence if they participate by helping the instructor present some of the course materials.

This is absolutely essential! The fact that some will become alarmed and concerned when told that they will handle some of the instruction is a clear indication that they need this experience before attempting to teach Circle members. (Leader training graduates are unanimous in their opinions that this experience is helpful.) The degree of participation in the instruction is determined by the facilitator. If the class is large, for example, two students might work together to present one of the training techniques.

What Is The Course Content?

The course is built around the various problem analysis techniques used by Circles, such as brainstorming, decision analysis, problem analysis, etc.

But, in addition, there are the Quality Circle leadership skills that must be acquired and honed before successful Circle operation can result.

The following is a suggested schedule for a leader training course, which may be used as a guide.

SUGGESTED
3-DAY LEADER
TRAINING COURSE

1st Day   Selected management and staff personnel should be invited to morning session.

8:00 AM   Kickoff by key company executive.

8:15   Facilitator provides status of Quality Circle activities.

8:30   What is it? Objectives. How does it operate?

9:30	BREAK

9:45   Elements of successful Quality Circle activities.

10:30   Roles of the steering committee, facilitator, and leader.

11:00   Training preview.

11:30   Students prepare for their upcoming Quality Circle presentations.

12:00   LUNCH

1:00 PM   Facilitator presents Quality Circle (Q-C) technique, "Case Study and Problem Prevention Techniques."

2:00   BREAK

2:15   Motivation.

3:00   Questions & answers session with one or more experienced Quality Circle leaders, if available.

4:00   ADJOURN

2nd Day

8:00 AM   Questions & answers.

8:30   Q-C Technique, "Brainstorming." (Include a practical example.)

9:30   BREAK

9:45   Q-C Technique, "Data Collection Techniques."

10:30   Communications.

11:00   Q-C Technique, "Data Collection Formats,
             Plus Graphs."

11:45   Questions & answers.

12:00   LUNCH

 1:00 PM   Using schedules and/or action logs to
             maximize results.

 1:30   Q-C Technique, "Decision Analysis
             Using Pareto."

 2:15   BREAK

 2:30   Group Dynamics.

 3:00   Q-C Technique, "Basic C-&-E Problem
             Analysis."   (Include a practical
             example.)

 4:00   ADJOURN

3rd Day

 8:00 AM   Q-C Technique, "Process C-&-E Problem
             Analysis."   (Include a practical
             example.)

 9:00   Q-C Technique, "The Management
             Presentation."

 9:45   BREAK

10:00   Q-C Themes--examples.

10:30   Potential problems.

11:00   Records to be maintained.

11:15   Measurement techniques.

12:00   LUNCH

1:00 PM   Discussion: "Starting Your Circle."

1:30   Leader examination.

2:15   BREAK

2:30   Critique of Leader examination.

4:00   ADJOURN

THE LEADER EXAMINATION

Few people like to be tested, even if it is to their advantage. When Circle leader candidates are first told they will be given an examination, the usual comment is: "Why us? We never get tested on company courses." This reluctance on the part of company training departments to administer examinations is considered by many to be a mistake. Naturally, students would just as soon dispense with the examination. It is a nuisance to have to worry about it and to study the material in preparation for the exam. However, those who complete the test will normally agree it was beneficial. The examination, while helpful in itself, can become a valuable learning experience, if time is taken for a thorough critique.

The following questions are typical of those normally administered in a leader examination. This number of questions given can be answered by most leader candidates in 15 minutes or less. The critique and discussion of these same questions will usually require another 30 minutes.

Standardized, constantly up-dated leader examination packets containing over 100 questions are available from the Quality Circle Institute.

Quality Circle
Leader Examination

1. Who selects the problem the Circle will analyze?

    a) Management or technical staff
    b) Steering committee
    c) Facilitator
    d) Circle leader
    e) Circle members

2. Problem solving has always proven more productive than problem prevention.

    True_____   False_____

3. The Quality Circle techniques must be modified before being used by office employees?

    True_____   False_____

4. The 4 M's are often used in cause-&-effect problem analysis. Name as many as you can.

    _____

    _____

    _____

    _____

5. It is <u>not necessary</u> to write down every idea that is suggested in a brainstorming session.

    True_____   False_____

6. During brainstorming, a member should suggest only one idea per turn.

    True_____   False_____

7. The subject to be brainstormed should first receive the approval of the facilitator.

   True_____   False_____

8. The first step in a brainstorming session is to clearly define the subject.

   True_____   False_____

9. Which Quality Circle technique(s) is likely to immediately follow the use of a check sheet?

   a) Cause-&-effect problem analysis
   b) Pareto chart
   c) Histogram
   d) Brainstorming

10. The facilitator has the responsibility to collect the data for the Circle.

   True_____   False_____

11. Normally, what Quality Circle technique precedes constructing a Pareto chart?

   a) Cause-&-effect problem analysis
   b) A histogram
   c) A check sheet

12. Normally, what Quality Circle technique is employed after the Pareto chart has been constructed?

   a) Cause-&-effect problem analysis
   b) A histogram
   c) A control chart

13. The verification step in cause-&-effect problem analysis is:

   a) Mandatory

b) Recommended
c) Rarely used

14. When circling the most likely causes, what should you be looking for?

a) Changes
b) Differences
c) Notable distinctions
d) All of the above

15. In cause-&-effect analysis, the problem to be analyzed should be kept somewhat general in scope so as to encourage a broad range of possible causes to be suggested.

True_____   False_____

16. A column graph, line graph, or pie graph can portray the exact same data.

True_____   False_____

17. Charts used in the management presentation:

a) Must be prepared by the art department
b) May be prepared by the Circle members

18. A Circle should give a presentation to:

a) Provide status on current activities
b) Make recommendations
c) Describe completed projects
d) All of the above are correct

19. Management presentations should emphasize:

a) Improvements in quality
b) Reduction of costs
c) Improvement in working conditions
d) All of the above

20. To assure maximum effectiveness and to serve as a "safe" learning experience for members, the first Circle presentation should be done solely by the Circle leader.

    True_____   False_____

21. It is quite common for two or more Circles to hold a combined meeting.

    True_____   False_____

22. The concept of "similar work" often needs clarification. Does this mean that an inspector could probably be a member of a manufacturing Circle?

    Yes_____   No_____

23. When conducting member training, the leader should:

    a) Act as "back-up" to the facilitator who will take the lead
    b) Take the lead with back-up from the facilitator

24. A written report of a Circle recommendation is often an adequate substitution for the management presentation.

    True_____   False_____

25. Establishing and maintaining a "win-win" philosophy in Circle operations is the responsibility of the:

    a) Steering committee
    b) Management
    c) Facilitator
    d) Leader
    e) Member
    f) All of the above

ANSWERS TO LEADER EXAMINATION

1. Circle members. They know better than anyone else the impediments and obstacles they are encountering in achieving the kind of quality, cost, and schedule being demanded of them.

2. False. A Circle will get into problem solving initially. After they have put out some of the obvious and apparent fires they will assume the most valuable Circle role--that of preventing problems before they occur.

3. False. Quality Circle techniques are applicable wherever people are involved. They are just as correct for office employees as they are in the production shop.

4. The 4 M's are normally referred to as:

   Manpower
   Materials
   Methods
   Machines

5. False. Every idea is recorded during the brainstorming without evaluation of any kind. To evaluate whether an idea is worthy of being recorded is to dampen the spontaneity, creativity, and enthusiasm of the Circle members.

.6. True. A member may have several ideas that he would like to voice. It is preferable to limit that individual to one idea in order to maximize the overall effectiveness of the group. He will have plenty of opportunity to come up with other ideas.

7. False. The leader and members will make this decision. If, for some reason, the

facilitator feels it is inappropriate, he will strive to make the leader aware of this outside of the Circle meeting.

.8. True.   A clearly defined brainstorming topic will keep everybody on the subject and bring forth ideas that are directly pertinent to the matter at hand.   It increases the effectiveness of the Circle.

9. Two answers are correct. Both the Pareto chart and histogram are constructed after data has been collected on a check sheet.

10. False.   The facilitator may make suggestions on how and where the data may be best collected, but it will be gathered by members of the Circle, or by somebody brought in to give them temporary assistance.

11. A check sheet is used to gather the information necessary to construct the Pareto chart.

12. A cause-&-effect problem analysis normally follows a construction of a Pareto chart. A Pareto chart identifies the number 1 problem to be subjected to problem analysis.

13. The verification step in cause-&-effect problem analysis is mandatory.   It may be quite obvious how to do the verification or it may be extremely puzzling. Nevertheless, it is always done.

14. All of the above.

15. False. The problem should be as specifically defined as possible to more successfully concentrate the problem solving energies of the group and to maximize effectiveness.

16. True.

17. Charts used in the management presentation, may be, and usually are prepared by the Circle members.

18. A Circle should give a management presentation to provide status on current activities, to make recommendations, and to describe completed projects.

19. Management presentations should emphasize improvements in quality, reduction in costs, and improvements in working conditions.

20. False. Not only is it rare that the Circle presentation is done solely by the Circle leader, it is also unnecessary. The Circle members will do quite well in participating in this exciting event.

21. False. It is actually quite rare for two or more Circles to hold a combined meeting. It has been done and occasionally quite successfully. Normally, it becomes rather difficult for a large number of people to be effective. A better way is to invite a single member or a small delegation from one Circle to visit another.

22. Yes. This is especially true when the inspector works in the area where the manufacturing employees are involved. Thus, he should be familiar with the work being done by the manufacturing group.

23. When conducting member training, the leader should take the lead with backup from the facilitator. The facilitator is normally present during the member training meetings and will provide the necessary backup to the leader if needed.

24. False. The written report does not begin to approach the management presentation

in effectiveness.   Nor does it have the recognition value provided by the presentation.

25. Establishing and maintaining "win-win" philosophy in Circle operations is the responsibility of the steering committee, management, facilitator, leader, and members.   Everybody must work together in a cooperative way to assure that everybody wins.

MEMBER TRAINING

Management certainly understands quite clearly the value of education and training.   That is evident by the courses, seminars, and conferences they attend and those in which they encourage their people to enroll.   This enthusiasm usually wanes when it comes to extending that training on a wide scale to lower levels in the organization.   Partly, it is an awareness of the very significant cost factor because the numbers of people are enormous.   Unfortunately, it may also be to some degree due to other factors, such as: "Those people don't care about the organization's need, so why waste our money training them"; or, "They aren't capable of any good ideas." Crass as these opinions are, they are held by some management people.

TRAINING PRODUCES RESULTS

Quality Circles has performed its magic at several levels, but none more dramatically than at the member level.   It is the sensational achievements of Circle groups that have influenced a turnabout of management thinking concerning the cost of training them.   No longer viewed as the cost of training, it has become, "our <u>investment</u> in training."

THE TECHNIQUES

The basic analytical building blocks are the Quality Circle techniques. They are:

*   Case Study & Problem Prevention Techniques

*   Brainstorming

*   Data Collection Techniques

*   Data Collection Formats, Plus Graphs

*   Decision Analysis Using Pareto

*   Basic Cause-&-Effect Problem Analysis

*   Process Cause-&-Effect Problem Analysis

*   The Management Presentation

These are covered in detail in the "Quality Circle Member Manual."

Work sheet problems following the description of each technique provide an opportunity for hands-on experience in a way that is definitely non-threatening to products or processes. The quiz concludes the learning process and brings everything together in an easily comprehended manner.

TRAINING PAYS OFF IN MANY WAYS

Members not only enjoy the training sessions, but are eager to attend, once they see what is involved. The skills they learn serve them both on and off the job.

ADVANCED TRAINING TECHNIQUES FOR QUALITY CIRCLES

The old adage "training never ends" is as applicable for Quality Circle members as it is for anyone.

The basic training techniques as described
in this book give Quality Circle members the
foundation upon which problems can be analyzed
and solved. Nevertheless, there will be instances
where a Circle should acquire knowledge of additional analytical techniques. In the Western
World, as well as Japan, most Circles can operate
well with the basic techniques. But when the need
arises, the additional advanced techniques should
be provided.

Four techniques will be briefly described.
These are only a sample of what could be considered necessary for a particular Circle. There is
actually no limit to the variety of training that
might be acquired by a specific group of members.

Histograms

A histogram is simply a normal distribution
curve displayed in graph form. It is a series of
columns, side by side, that normally would take on
a bell shape. The height of each column represents
the number of occurences a specific item represents within the normal distribution curve.

Items lending themselves to analysis through
histograms include variable data, such as:
absenteeism, error rates, voltages, weights, and
other measurements.

Circles interpret the shape of the bell to
arrive at conclusions. When the bell takes on
an abnormal shape described by a term such as
bimodel or skewed, clues are provided as to the
root of the problem.

Scatter Diagrams

If two different sets of data are plotted on
the same graph, the resulting series of plot
points will take on a shape. That shape is useful

in determining if a problem exists and what the possible cause might be.

One example of two sets of data is when the heights and weights of people are plotted. The vertical scale might represent heights and the horizontal scale indicate weights. A plot point is recorded on the graph where these two intersect for each person. After a group of people have been so plotted, a pattern emerges that can be interpreted.

If an office brought in all new electronic typewriters to reduce errors, the effect could be plotted on a scatter diagram. If the new typewriters did result in the desired goals, it could be stated that a positive correlation exists. On the other hand, if an increase in the number of errors occurred, then it would be a negative correlation.

Control Charts

There are few differences between a line graph and a control chart. The control chart has upper and lower dotted lines which are referred to as control limit lines. Their location is mathematically determined; and they are placed so that if the line being posted crosses one of them, it is a definite indication of trouble.

A common example of an informal control chart is one maintained by the person who wishes to maintain his weight at a fairly constant level: neither too heavy nor too light. He plots his weight on a daily basis. He also has a dotted upper control limit line, above which he does not want to go. In addition there is a lower control limit line, below which he does not want to drop.

Control charts can often be maintained by Circle members and should be displayed in the work area so that constant feedback is provided.

Stratification

Stratification occurs when one sorts a large amount of data into groups or categories. It brings life to the admonition, "divide and conquer."

Quality Circles are most likely to use the stratification technique in areas concerning histograms, control charts, and Pareto diagrams.

Stratification by itself does not solve problems; but it does make it possible to gain insight that will aid in the solutions.

THE ORGANIZATION

There is no "Circle organization" in the true sense of the word. There is only the normal management hierarchy and its relationship to the entire organization.

The Circle simply fits into it in a most complementary manner.

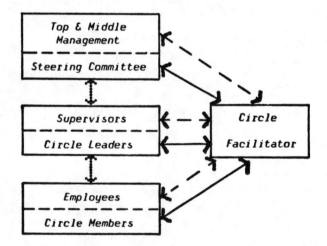

The management personnel provide the support and guidance for Circle activities. This is done

through their participation on the steering
committee.   A great number more have Circles
in their organizations.

The supervisor is the Circle leader, at least
when the Circle is new.

The members are the employees in the area who
desire to participate in the Circle activities.

Bringing it all together is the function of
the facilitator who coordinates all aspects of the
operation.

THE STEERING COMMITTEE

The steering committee is a group of people who lead the Quality Circle activity in an organization. The name "steering committee" happens to be the one commonly given to the group charged with this responsibility; but it may be called any of several others. Advisory committee, task force, program team, and quality council are examples. The name is not important; but how well it functions is! This group is the board of directors of the Quality Circle activities.

What Is The Steering Committee?

Fundamentally, the steering committee must set goals and objectives for the program. It establishes operational guidelines and controls the rate of expansion. It should be presided over by a chairman; and decisions should be reached through the democratic process--one person, one vote.

Why This Committee Is Essential

The steering committee is charged with the responsibility to create successful Quality Circle activities. Its success depends on im-

126

plementing Quality Circles within the framework of the five most important principles of good management: setting objectives, planning, staffing and scheduling, operation (directing), and control.

The degree of success can be quite another matter. That will be shaped by the committee's attention to detail and its commitment to thoroughness.

The steering committee is the policy making group. Management should not simply "pull together" a group of people and consider that this essential committee exists. Its membership should be carefully selected. The fate of the entire program depends upon how well this committee functions.

The entire steering committee must have a clear understanding of Quality Circles. Few things are more dangerous than the committee member who wants to modify Quality Circles before comprehending its basic features.

The steering committee, when organized and functioning in the manner described herein, is an essential first step toward launching any organization's Quality Circle activities.

Steering Committee Membership

The membership of the steering committee should be made up of individuals selected from a variety of sub-organizations within the whole, so that no one feels left out. While Circle activity often starts in production areas, it normally spreads to other organizations. Steering committee membership is therefore comprised of personnel from such functions as: operations, quality control, personnel, education and training, engineering, finance, office operations, mar-

keting, and the union. Of course the facilitator
should also be a member.

The Level Of Personnel On The Committee

There is a tendency to use several approaches. Some say the membership should be made
up of middle management people. Others feel that
it should be staff only. Still others favor
having only line management as members. The
author's work with a variety of steering committees leads him to recommend that it be comprised
almost entirely of top-level management personnel.
Often, this includes the chief executive officer,
such as the organization's president, the plant
manager, or other highly placed executives. Some
of the most successful steering committees include
not only the chief executive officer but his or
her executive staff. Once selected for service on
the steering committee, a member should be discouraged from selecting a subordinate to take his
or her place; except, perhaps, when that subordinate has a high degree of commitment to the
concept. The general rule is that the steering
committee should be comprised of personnel with a
strong goal to make the Circle program succeed.

Leaders And Members As Committee Members

The author suggests that both leaders and
members be included on the committee perhaps on a
rotating basis. One method is to have the leaders
serve three months and the members one month. The
selection of these committee members is often made
with an election or a drawing. Both the leaders
and members value the recognition; and everyone
involved benefits from the increased understanding
and direct flow of communication that ensues.

The Ideal Number Of Committee Members

Involvement and participation is just as
important at steering committee level as it is at

Circle level; therefore, the membership should be restricted to a maximum of fifteen. The minimum should be five. Committee members should actively participate at every meeting.

Union Representation. It was mentioned in a preceding paragraph that the union should be represented on the steering committee. The union president and his executive staff should be apprised of the planned Quality Circle activities and of what it means to the organization, to the employees, and to the union. This kind of information is absolutely essential to ward off any apprehension regarding possible organization moves to subordinate the role of the union. It should also be emphasized that while the subjects of quality, cost, and attitudes are primary candidates for Circle activities, in no way should matters that normally fall under the jurisdiction of the union be taken up by the Circle. Examples of topics outside of the Circle's charter would be: wage and salary policies, personnel matters and grievances. Union representation on the steering committee has, on occasion, given rise to apprehension by some who fear any form of management partnership with the union. While such fears are understandable, it is regrettable that Circle activities be jeopardized because of them. In practice, the entire experience of such management-union cooperation tends to prove a pleasant surprise to both parties. Adversary roles disappear, replaced by cooperation and teamwork.

Even though a union receives an invitation to participate on the steering committee, it may not accept. Experience has shown that over half of the unions prefer to watch from the sidelines rather than take active leadership roles through steering committee participation.

Nevertheless, in essentially all cases, the union is active in Quality Circles through participation by union stewards--who, typically, are the first to accept Circle responsibilities.

The Chairman Of The Steering Committee   must be one who encourages an open exchange of ideas and adheres to a philosophy of "one person, one vote."   This is particularly important when the chairman carries a high rank in the organiza- tion.   Others may feel intimidated and permit themselves to be dominated by such an individual.

Philosophy Must Be Communicated

Every organization has a philosophy--often one that was largely shaped by its founders.   That philosophy usually encompasses a belief in its people and in the importance of their role as part of the organization team.   The author first discovered the prevalence of such a philosophy when investigating Quality Circles in Japan during 1973.   Workers generally knew about it and took pride in talking about it.   It has been a pleasure and a surprise to discover that many Western World organizations also have philosophies.   Even more interesting is that when such philosophies are communicated to the workers, they are touched and impressed; and they respond.

Quality Circle activity is the most natural vehicle available to make an organization's philosophy something real, something more than mere words.   It is nothing short of putting words into action.

Building Support

This involves "selling" others on the merits of implementing Quality Circles.   Attention must be concentrated on winning support from various levels of the management structure.

Getting Involvement

The most effective way in which this essential support is gained is through a dual approach.
First the Quality Circle concept is explained to
the appropriate management people; then their
involvement is encouraged. The latter is most
easily accomplished by asking such questions as:
"What can we do in our organization to make this
concept work best?" Or, "What can we do to attain
this objective in your area of our organization?"
This method tends to reduce resistance based on
"not invented here," and to foster "ownership"
among all levels and areas of management.

Establishing Relations With Competing Programs Or Organizations

Implementation must not be undertaken until
all groups are identified which might currently be
operating (or should be--having the charter to do
so) in the same areas as Quality Circles. While
on the surface it may appear that none are, this
may not be the case. The suggestion committee
management should be contacted, as well as the
people responsible for the education and training
department, the safety committees, labor relations, production committees, the union, quality
committees, and those involved with organizational
development, for example. There is a high probability that one (or more) of them is already doing
something. Their experience and interest can
represent valuable resources; and their involvement in Quality Circles should be encouraged.

Establishing Circle Objectives

This is the process of identifying general
areas where improvement is possible. There has to
be a reason for an organization to become involved

in Quality Circles; and this reason, or reasons, should be identified.

It could be as simple as one objective, or as many as a dozen. Several organizations have identified only one objective; and in almost every case that objective has been to improve quality. The words "improved quality" are general in nature and usually mean product quality, quality of the service, and quality of the working life.

The following is a list of objectives that might be considered for adoption by the steering committee:

* Reduce errors and enhance quality

* Inspire more effective teamwork

* Promote job involvement

* Increase employee motivation

* Create a problem-solving capability

* Build an attitude of "problem prevention"

* Improve company communications

* Develop harmonious manager/worker relationships

* Promote personal and leadership development

* Develop a greater safety awareness

The objective--to improve quality--seems to be common to all Quality Circle activities; undoubtedly because a higher level of quality will result in happier customers and thus promote repeat business. Further, a reduction in the level of defects is directly translatable into higher productivity and profits--profits that spell increased job security. And it goes beyond that. Individuals who are involved in the work itself, and in the challenge that it brings to them, are affected by attitude improvements. It can't be helped! It is a surefire spin-off of truly involving people in the work they are doing.

Determining Actions Outside The Charter Of The Circles

Experience has shown that some items should be considered outside of the charter of the Circle. These items should be identified and clearly spelled out so that Circles understand their boundaries. These generally include the following:

* Benefits and salaries

* Employment practices

* Policies on discharging employees

* Personalities

* Grievances

Note that the items identified are normally within the realm of union rights. It is a mistake to take the risk of threatening the union's position by allowing Circles to discuss these matters. Regardless of whether there is a union or not, there are channels for these matters to be discussed and the Quality Circle meeting is not the ideal time or place to do it. Quality Circles is a work-related activity; and employees will understand this and will respect it.

Identifying Funding Resources

It requires money to install and operate Quality Circles. Funding the start-up is a task for the steering committee. Cost is incurred when members attend Circle meetings--and it matters little whether these meetings are during, or after, normal working hours. When after-hours, it means payment at overtime rates. The facilitator adds slightly to that cost, as do expenditures for implementation of Circle recommendations. Questions must be answered, such as: "Do members charge to an overhead account; and, if so, to which one?" Or, "How will training costs be funded?"

This is a fundamental but vital task for the steering committee. It will be easier if the spotlight is focused on Quality Circles as an investment instead of a cost--an investment, incidentally, that will potentially result in handsome returns.

Determining If Consulting Services Are Required

No responsible executive (or committee of them) wants to inflict a "half-baked homegrown" program on an organization--one that may flounder and possibly fail. Everyone wants to back a winner! There is an adage: "The sweetness of a successful venture lingers on long after the cost is forgotten."

Quality Circles should be implemented with all factors geared for maximum success. The major cost of the Quality Circle activity is the expense of members attending Circle meetings; and the front end and one-time cost of the services of a qualified consultant is only a small fraction of that cost. Therefore, if the availability of money is not a severe problem, and if personnel

already in the organization's employ are not fully
capable of implementing Quality Circles, and if
excellent training materials are not readily
obtainable, the committee should give full consideration to making use of a provably competent
consultant to get the activity started quickly and
correctly.

Evaluating In-House Capability

The education and training department may
be a source for one or more training courses which
are applicable for Quality Circle use.   Its
management may express the desire to develop all
of the necessary training materials; but the
decision to pursue this route should await a
realistic determination of the cost compared to
that of purchasing readily available material.
(Some organizations have developed their own;
but the cost has been enormous.)

Developing The Quality Circle Policy And Procedure Document

This document stipulates the Quality Circle
policy, and defines the manner in which various
segments of the organization shall endeavor to
comply.

Chapter 18 contains a sample of this important document, and it addresses the following
matters:

- Purpose
- Objectives
- Policy
- Organization

It may be used as a guide for the development of a policy and procedure document to
fill the specific needs of any organization.

Selecting The Facilitator

The facilitator is the individual responsible
for day-to-day coordination of the Quality Circle
activities. This selection must be consummated
with the greatest care. Among other reasons, it
must be remembered that the facilitator will be a
member of the steering committee. The degree of
success of the Quality Circle activity is usually
significantly influenced by the precision with
which this selection is made.

The steering committee should carefully
review the portion of this book that deals with
the facilitator's task in detail prior to initiat-
ing the selection process.

Determining Whether The Facilitator's Should Be A Full Or Part-Time Job

As a rule of thumb, unless an organization
is quite small (under 200 employees) the facilitator should devote full time to the task.   So
called part-time facilitators in large organizations usually relate that they end up doing full-
time facilitating, even though they may officially
carry other job titles.

Deciding On The Method For Selecting The Facilitator

Three selection techniques predominate. They
are, in increasing order of preference:

1. The facilitator is commandeered by the
    "key" person involved with Quality
    Circles

2. He or she is selected from several
    individuals who have been nominated by
    steering committee members

3. Selection is from open competition
    throughout the organization

In rare instances the facilitator is chosen from outside of the organization. However, as the popularity of Quality Circles continues to develop, this approach may be used more frequently in the future.

Steering committee members should be involved in the interviewing and selection process for the facilitator; and the selection should be made as soon as possible after the formation of the steering committee.

Part-Time facilitators may be required at a later date to supplement the full-time facilitator. Each part-time facilitator may handle two or three Circles and report, on Circle activities, to the full-time facilitator. However, the appointment of these individuals is at the discretion of, and with the approval of, the steering committee.

Selecting Leaders for the Pilot Program

The steering committee has official responsibility to select the leaders for the pilot program. However, in actual practice, the leaders are usually selected by the managers of the departments where the pilot program will operate. These leader candidates usually meet with the steering committee prior to the beginning of their training. The steering committee should use this opportunity to assure these individuals that management support exists and that their participation is valued.

The input received from the potential Circle leaders can also be a valuable aid in the finalization of Circle policies, procedures, and guidelines which will give direction to the Circle activities.

At some point, the steering committee may decide the leaders be selected through election by members; but this should not be done for the pilot phase. This is because it is essential to success to have supervisors who have demonstrated not only their leadership capabilities, but who are also committed to the Quality Circle management philosophy.

The author prefers that the supervisors be the initial leaders. Later, these leaders might be encouraged to have the Circle members elect the leader. This should occur only as the Circle matures and members elect their leaders for the right reasons.

There could be considerable numbers of employees who want Circles, but who can't have them, because certain supervisors say, "I'm not interested!" Some steering committees have offered Circles to any groups that want to form them; and this approach has often caused such supervisors to become constructively involved. However, if the reluctant supervisor does not join, the leader may be selected through election by the members. A pilot Circle should never be formed in an area which is controlled by a supervisor who is not interested in or is hostile to the program.

Deciding About Rewards

This subject is dealt with elsewhere in the book, but is mentioned at this point because it is a responsibility of the steering committee. It can take the form either of cash, or of other non-monetary benefits. If a suggestion program already exists, the steering committee must make a decision as to whether there will be some kind of "marriage" of Circle activities with the suggestion program. Many organizations have done so with a significant increase in activity in the suggestion plan as a result of the fusion.

Others take the position that, because meetings are conducted during company hours or after hours on an overtime basis, that is reward enough. "After all," they reason, "Circle members benefit by not only being paid for meetings, but have the diversity of exploring other activities that challenge and stimulate."

Establishing The Method Of Recognition

There are many forms of recognition provided by Quality Circle activities; and the management presentation is probably the most significant. The power of this device as a motivator is awesome. There are many Quality Circle programs operating where there is no other form of reward or recognition. The management presentation provides an opportunity for members to communicate directly--person to person--with management, and to receive immediate feedback.

Other Forms of Recognition that the steering committee can consider using include:

* Company newspaper features

* Outside newspaper publicity

* Company bulletin board postings

* Pins, trophies, plaques

* In-house conferences

* Visits to other branches of the organization, if any

* Visits to other outside organizations using Quality Circles

* Attending and/or presenting papers at outside conferences

Setting Up A Promotion And Publicity Plan

Quality Circles must be "launched"! This begins when some kind of communication is effected

to advise all employees that these activities
are commencing. This initial notice often takes
the form of a press release in the company newspaper. At that time it is essential to avoid
enticing and exciting employees who may want to
get into Quality Circle activities before the
pilot program has had a chance to operate. It is
simply to inform before the "grapevine" takes
over and distorts the message the steering committee wants to convey.

Later forms of promotion and publicity should
include articles in both the organization's and
neighborhood newspapers, and the other activities
as described in the preceding paragraph.

Reviewing And Evaluating The Activity

The implementation process is only one part
of the management's responsibility. Quality
Circles is no different from any other activity in
that it must be managed. Further, it requires
periodic assessment to determine if it is functioning satisfactorily and according to plan.

The feedback received through the review
process frequently leads to modification of the
entire operation. Such alterations can enhance
the success of a Quality Circle activity.

Some steering committees consider that the
stimulation that is created prior to the review
and evaluation is of significant benefit to
the health of the program.

FACILITATOR

One of several key ingredients for a successful Quality Circle activity is the facilitator, who coordinates the overall program. The person occupying this position is sometimes called the "Quality Circle Coordinator." The Japanese literature occasionally refers to this individual as a "Promoter." Although usually a full time position, it may be part-time in smaller organizations.

SELECTION BY STEERING COMMITTEE

The facilitator should be selected as soon as a definite decision has been made to implement Quality Circles. The steering committee has this responsibility; in fact, sometimes, the selection of the facilitator is the first thing done by the steering committee.

It is important that this position not be established as a "dead end" one. A career path should be worked out; and the person selected should have management potential.

CHARACTERISTICS

The facilitator needs a multiplicity of characteristics and should be a combination of coach, coordinator, enthusiast, communicator, innovator, promoter, teacher, statistician, and catalyst-- all in one! While this may appear to be a very difficult role, experience shows that almost every organization already employs one or more persons with the qualifications and ability to fill it, since the necessary attributes are what are sought for management personnel.

SKILLS

The facilitator should be an individual who is achievement oriented. This orientation should be directed to making things happen through people. The facilitator must be one who relates well to others and enjoys working with them. Ability to exhibit tact and diplomacy is mandatory. Communication skills are usually developed over a long period of time prior to taking on the facilitator assignment. The facilitator must be an individual who can keep a "chin-up" attitude even when things don't look bright. The facilitator should be a persuasive individual who is effective in winning support from others. Ability to speak effectively before groups, both large and small, is not only desirable, but essential.

BACKGROUND

It is difficult to describe the kind of background a facilitator should have. There are too many examples of facilitators who have successfully operated Circle activities to say that any one formula excels. Typically, facilitators emerge from backgrounds such as industrial engineering, manufacturing engineering, quality engineering, personnel, education and training, supervision, management, and other occupations requiring close involvement with people. Where Circles are going to operate initially in the manufacturing area, there is sometimes a tendency to underrate potential facilitator candidates without manufacturing or quality backgrounds, such as those from personnel or education and training. Perhaps the concern is that these people would have difficulty in relating to production personnel. However, these facilitators, often people with no manufacturing background, have proven to be just as effective in getting things done. The key seems to be the ability to function as a facilitator--one who coordinates to make things happen through others.

EDUCATION

Again, there seems to be no single best recommendation. At a recent gathering of a large number of Quality Circle facilitators, a survey was taken to determine if one kind of educational background was preferable for Quality Circle work. Several were engineers with electrical engineers predominating. Mechanical engineers were also numerous. Other facilitators have degrees is in psychology, behavioral science, business, mathematics, and economics. The list doesn't stop there. It even includes such seemingly unrelated educational backgrounds as music and foreign languages. Several facilitators did not have any degree.

There is no evidence or research to suggest that a certain kind of degree is preferable.

HOW SELECTED

Elsewhere in this book, three general ways to make the facilitator selection are described. In summary they are:

1.   Appointment of an individual by some key management employee involved with Quality Circles.

2. Selection made from interviews among candidates nominated by various members of the steering committee.

3. Chosen as a result of interviews conducted for employees who responded to an open invitation regarding the facilitator position.

The facilitator is often required to work staggered shifts; and it is important that all candidates understand and agree to this arrangement.

FACILITATOR PAY LEVEL

In most organizations, it exceeds the scale for supervisors, and is approximately the same as for engineers. However, there is a wide variation between different organizations.

JOB DESCRIPTION

In this chapter are sample job description formats for the facilitator, to serve as a guide. If the job availability is openly posted, this approach normally produces a substantial number of candidates.

CANDIDATE APPLICATION FORM

After the job description, a typical application form is shown. It may be modified to conform to any organization's requirements.

SELECTION FORMS

A cursory examination of the applications is made to narrow the field; and written notice is sent to those eliminated because of the lack of certain attributes. These notices should state why the candidates did not qualify. Remaining candidates are normally interviewed by the steering committee. The forms shown after the typical application form can help the committee members to be objective in their final selection.

JOB DESCRIPTION FOR QUALITY CIRCLE FACILITATOR

General: To serve as coordinator for Q-C activities. A Q-C is a small group of employees who do similar work, meeting on a regular basis to identify and analyze causes of problems and recommending solutions to management. Objectives of Q-C's include improved quality of products, services, and working life; reduction of costs; enhancement of safety factors; and increased operational effectiveness that will lead to added job security through improved competitive positon.

Duties: Facilitator will initially participate with the Q-C steering committee to develop a Q-C implementation plan and establish operational guidelines. Later, facilitator will train leaders for each Circle. Facilitator will attend Circle meetings and provide backup coordination and organizational interfacing services for routine operations. Facilitator must be willing to spend time and be accessible to Circle members who will be located in office and production areas. Duties require necessity to communicate effectively with entry level employees as well as executive personnel. Must maintain records to reflect Circle achievements.

Experience: Knowledge of production and/or office areas. Teaching experience is an advantage. Experience with voluntary groups is beneficial. Leadership experience is important. Should project enthusiasm in promoting Q-C concept with management and other employees.

APPLICATION
for position as
Quality Circle Facilitator

Name	Present Position Title

Education: 10   11   12   13   14   15   16   17   18
             (Circle year completed)

Degree	Completed	School

Degree	Completed	School

OTHER TRAINING THAT YOU FEEL IS RELEVANT

1. _____

2. _____

3. _____

TEACHING OR OTHER EXPERIENCE AS AN INSTRUCTOR

Date		Organization	Subject
From	To		
___	___		
___	___	_____	_____
___	___	_____	_____
___	___	_____	_____

PARTICIPATION IN EXTRA CURRICULAR ACTIVITIES such as voluntary group or civic activities during the past ten years:

HOBBIES:

REASON FOR DESIRING THIS POSITION:

STEERING COMMITTEE INTERVIEWS
with
QUALITY CIRCLE FACILITATOR CANDIDATES

RATED BY: C. Orr

Date: 7/1/80

RATINGS
9 - 10 Excellent
7 - 8 Very Satisfactory
4 - 6 Satisfactory
1 - 3 Unacceptable

CANDIDATES

	Grant Indus Eng	Smith Personnel	Richards Line Supt
Years of Company Service	4	3	16
Years as Hourly Employee	0	0	5
Years as Supervisor	0	1	11
Education (Years)	17	16	14
Special Skills	24yrs I.E.	M.S. Teacher 3yrs	AA Deg LIM óuses

RATING SCORES

Communicates well at all levels	9	7	7
Admin./Organizational Skills	8	7	7
Training Skills	6	10	7
Dependability	7	5	7
Initiative & Persistence	8	7	8
Personality	9	7	8
Persuasiveness	7	7	8
Knowledge of Operations	8	6	8
Enthusiasm	9	7	6
Past Performance Rating	8	6	9
Overall rating	9	7	8

POSITION ANALYSIS

Job No._____

Resultant
Salary Level_____

(Names of Incumbants)   Div/Sub_____

Position
Title_QUALITY CIRCLE COORDINATOR_____   Dept._____
Supervisor's
Title___V. P., Manufacturing_____   Date_____

Number and Titles of Persons Supervised:

Basic Func. of Position: The Quality Circle Coordinator is responsible for
research, design, and implementation of the Quality Circle philosophy in the
organization. Once implemented, his/her role is that of a catalyst that insures
the success of the program by monitoring the Quality Circle program operation,
working with the steering committee, training members and circle leaders,
interfacing between circles and top management, and maintaining records.

Description of Duties:	% OF TIME
1. Program Operation	45%
A. Promotion - The Quality Circle Coordinator is responsible for promotional activities to provide awareness of the existence of Quality Circle operations both within and outside of the organization, and to furnish recognition to the participants.	
B. Quality Circle Meetings - Attend and monitor Quality Circle meetings; Quality Circle Coordinator takes role of counselor and teacher to see that meetings are organized and productive, without taking control from Quality Circle Leader.	
C. Quality Circle Problems - Assist Quality Circle Leaders in problem identification and appropriateness to group capabilities.	
D. Problem Solutions - Assist Quality Circle Leaders and Quality Circle members in preparation of Management Presentations of problem solutions.	
E. Measurement - Assist Quality Circle Leaders and Quality Circle members to channel measurement criteria into quality cost, or attitude improvements that are consistent with the goals of the organization.	
2. Steering Committee Duties	5%
A. Quality Circle Coordinator is a member of the Steering Committee.	
B. Interface with Quality Circle and Steering Committee to provide guidance and direction.	
C. Quality Circle Coordinator sees that Steering Committee meets on a regular basis.	

IR - 107 (FRONT)

Description of Duties (Con't)	% of Time

3. Training   **35%**

   A. Provide for and assist in the training of Quality Circle members in Group Dynamics and process techniques.

   B. Provide for and assist in the training of Quality Circle Leaders.

   C. Provide for and assist in training of non-members (to assist in the success of Quality Circles by providing an awareness of the Quality Circle philosophy to non-members).

4.ˈ Coordinate Circle Operations   **5%**

   A. Communicate and coordinates activities between circles in the organization.

   B. Assists and counsels Quality Circle as to resources available.

5. Interface between circles and other organizations   **5%**

   A. Communicate circle activities to non-member departments in the organization.

   B. Communicate circle activities to management.

   C. Maintain Records

      1. Document circle activities.
      2. Document before and after results of circle operations.

6. Quality Circle Development   **5%**

   A. Attend outside meeting and seminars on Quality Circles.

   B. Membership in local and national Quality Circle organizations.

Date   **Prepared by:**

H - 107 (BACK)

POSITION FACT SHEET
IR-109

Div/Sub ___T.M.D.___

Dept. ___101___

Position ___Quality Circle Coordinator___   Incumbent _____

Spec. Knowledge Req'd: In depth knowledge and understanding of Quality Circle concept, history and philosophy. Must be able to communicate effectively at extreme levels in the organization from bargaining unit employees to top management. Must have comprehensive knowledge of Human Relations, Group Dynamics, and Problem Solving Techniques; must have training, Human Resource development and sales expertise. (See additional comments on back).

Experience Req'd: Two to three years experience as production supervisor; three to five years as Training Manager or supervisor in a manufacturing environment, with expertise in the following areas: Management and supervisory training, sales, group dynamics, group process and problem solving.

Orientation Time Req'd: Three to six months

Analytical Ability Req'd: Must possess high degree of analytical ability and creativity in the areas of Problem Solving and Group Dynamics. Must have a high degree of initiative.

Contacts w/others: Very important contact with all levels of the organization. Limited important contact with corporate staff and outside consultants. Contact with any level is extremely motivational in nature.

Judgment Req'd: High degree of judgement required due to contact with all functional areas of the organization regarding problem solving, solution implementation and process change within the organization.

Knowledge of Oper. Req'd: Knowledge of manufacturing organization is required to include familiarity of responsibilities of both line and staff departments.

Responsibility – Co. Prop.: Routine office equipment, audio-visual equipment including video-tape recorder, cameras, film, overhead, and slide projectors.

Physical Effort Req'd: Little physical effort, mostly sitting, but considerable walking and standing.

Working Cond.: Private office with availability of private conference rooms.

Risk: Slight

Equipment used: (Indicate (R) Regularly: (O) Occasionally)

Video-tape equipment - (R)

Movie and slide projectors - (R)

Flip charts and overhead projectors (R)

Additional Comments:

Educational Requirements:

Undergraduate degree in management or related field required. Post graduate degree not required but extremely beneficial.

Incumbent's Signature

Prepared by: **Date**

Approved by: **Date**

MEMBER OF STEERING COMMITTEE

The facilitator is always a member of the steering committee. In cases where the steering committee consists of high level management executives, the facilitator forms an important link connecting this executive group to the realities of what is happening at the Circle operating level.   It is common for the facilitator to operate as the executive officer for the steering committee in that most of the day-to-day policies of the steering committee are conveyed to the Circles by this individual.   The facilitator has a responsibility not to dominate steering committee activities.   Because of close proximity to Circle operations, it is easy for the facilitator's job to evolve into a dominant role. The facilitator may have to work at making certain other members of the steering committee continue to be involved. As a general recommendation, the facilitator should not assume the role of committee chairman, because this tends to cause a reduction in involvement by the other members.

REPORTS TO A HIGH LEVEL

In a manufacturing organization, the facilitator usually reports to either the director of manufacturing, the director of quality control, or the director of industrial relations.   Of the three just mentioned, the most common is the director of manufacturing. This is often deliberately arranged by the quality organization, which normally "discovered" Quality Circles.   This assures manufacturing involvement rather than just thinking of it as another quality control program.   Other reporting relationships include to a vice-president level, and to the chief executive officer.   Sometimes this is a plant manager, sometimes it is the president of the organization The objective is to have the facilitator report to a high enough level of management, regardless of the type of organization with which he or she is associated, to provide the position a degree of respect and power.

MAY BE FULL OR PART-TIME

As a general rule, the facilitator's job should be full time; although there are exceptions to this recommendation. Some organizations are too small to justify having a full-time facilitator. The facilitator who is part-time should be free, initially, to operate in a full time capacity. Or, the main job assignment should be as a facilitator, and the secondary assignment at whatever other duties are to be performed. Otherwise, it is possible for the facilitating tasks to be subordinated and not given the proper attention. In other words, the individual who serves as facilitator must have as his or her prime responsibility the requirement to facilitate Circle activities. Other duties, relating to non-Circle activities, are handled on a time-available basis.

However, because of its cost effectiveness, as related to both productivity and quality, one company with which the author is acquainted has a full-time facilitator with only 120 employees. Experience indicates that part-time facilitators in larger organizations usually devote full time to the Quality Circle activity regardless of the titles they may carry.

THE OPTIMUM NUMBER OF CIRCLES PER FACILITATOR

How Many Circles Can A Facilitator Handle? In general, one facilitator should be able to successfully handle 20 mature Circles; however, there are wide differences of opinion on this. Some organizations have them operating more, and some less. There are many organizations which consider that a ratio of ten to one is ideal for

optimum cost effectiveness. The key factor is
how well the facilitator performs. It is difficult to successfully operate a substantial number
of Circles if the facilitator falls into the trap
of doing the jobs of the leaders. The facilitator
must always keep in mind that the leader's job is
to lead; and the facilitator's is--as the name
implies--to facilitate and to coordinate.

COORDINATES CIRCLE ACTIVITIES

Start-up

Initial steps to initiate Quality Circles
involve contacting various individuals who could
serve as Quality Circle leaders. Personnel usually
identified for this activity include foremen
or supervisors. The facilitator, particularly if
well acquainted with the area where Circles will
start, plays an important role in the selection of
leaders best suited for this kind of assignment.

After the leader has been trained, and is
ready to talk to the members of the work group
to identify those who are interested in Quality
Circle participation, the facilitator is usually
able to assist.

Typically, the manager of a department calls
the meeting of potential Circle members and the
facilitator is usually one of those who explains
the general workings of Quality Circles. Normally, this is done with the use of charts or
slides; although the facilitator is but one of
two or three speakers at such an orientation.
The kind of information dispensed is usually quite
meaningful and can go a long way in helping to
shape potential member attitudes at this critical
time. The question and answer session that always
follows is another opportunity for the facilitator
to serve by giving the proper perspective to
employees.

Coordinator

        As a coordinator, the facilitator must do
whatever is necessary to provide for a smooth-
running operation; but this must be a diminishing
role if the facilitator's workload is not to
become too heavy. It is common for facilitators
to "over-facilitate." As a Circle begins to
function efficiently, the facilitator must back
off. When required, the facilitator may arrange
for engineers or staff people to meet with Circles, for example. In short, the facilitator must
do that which is not done by leaders or members.

        Win-win is the philosophy that must be
continually emphasized by the facilitator. He or
she must not permit management or staff personnel
to "use" a Circle or allow one Circle to exploit
either another Circle or any individual in order
to make itself look good.

Coach

        As coach, the facilitator must be able to
assess the strong and weak points of the Circle
leaders and members. He or she must constantly
build on the strong points of leaders and members
to create an effective and efficient Quality
Circle operation. Prior to each meeting, the
facilitator should determine that the leader has
an agenda; and afterwards, there should be a
discussion concerning the good and bad aspects of
the leader's method of conducting the meeting.

Shift Operations

        The majority of industrial and business firms
conduct their activities on more than one shift.
Circles will operate on each shift. In addition,
it is common to occasionally combine their first
and second shift personnel into one Quality
Circle. An example is when only two or three

people do a certain operation on each shift.
While it would be inadequate to operate a Circle
on either first or second shift alone, it works
well doing it together. In such a case, the
meeting takes place somewhere toward the end of
the first shift or beginning of the second shift,
or possibly overlapping both shifts. Where Circles
are operating on more than one shift, it becomes
more necessary to provide them with the coordination that will assist them in selecting Circle
projects that have not been taken up by others.
On occasion, a Circle may deliberately take on a
project which is also being worked on by another
Circle; because, perhaps, they believe that their
approach is superior.

Management Presentations

The management presentation is a special
event for a Circle. It provides recognition to
the Circle and allows the members to communicate
in a most direct and effective manner. However,
many Circle members, while intrigued and excited
by the magnitude of this event, are nevertheless
somewhat freightened at the prospect of having to
stand before their manager and make a presentation. It simply isn't part of their usual
experience. The facilitator must understand
that the management presentation is something they
want, but that they will be likely to procrastinate about--"We are going to do the management
presentation, but in a few more weeks." That kind
of postponement can continue for some time. The
facilitator must encourage the Circle to set a
date and stick to it. Special training may be
advisable at that time as provided by the training module, "The Management Presentation."

The leader and members decide who should
attend the management presentation, with help and
advice, if required, from the facilitator. The
presentation is made to the manager to whom the

Circle leader reports; but it is normal that other managerial, executive, and staff personnel may attend also. In such cases, the facilitator assists the leader in making the necessary arrangements.

The facilitator must also assist the leader in making arrangements for an appropriate place in which to make the presentation.

Experience

A background as an instructor certainly helps; but it is not mandatory. Teaching skills can be acquired. In lieu of any teaching experience on a formal basis, involvement as a teacher for volunteer groups can be helpful. Examples could be teaching music, a Sunday school class, working with boy scouts, etc.

Another partial substitute for a training background is experience as a public speaker. Public speaking tends to be one-way communication; but it can be quite beneficial.

In-Plant Conferences

Several organizations have periodically arranged in-plant conferences that all Circle members attend. The word "conference" is perhaps misleading, because this event may last only one hour. The format may be something like this: The members gather in a large room or auditorium. The meeting is usually chaired by the facilitator, who introduces one or more key executives. Some may speak for a minute or two each to set the tone for what is to follow. Then three or four previously selected Circles will make short presentations before the audience. This may be followed by some kind of award ceremony whereby congratulations, certificates or other types of recognition are provided to the Circles. In one

case, each Circle received a certificate certi-
fying their formal existence as a Quality Circle.
In other cases each member of every Circle received some kind of certificate. The variations
are limitless.

The Circles selected to make presentations
are normally picked on the basis of special
performance during the year.   They are not
selected on the basis of how many dollars were
saved as a result of one of their projects.   The
logic behind that is that some projects result
in large dollar savings with very little effort,
while other projects may have a small payoff
despite being well engineered and effectively
executed by the Circle. Another method of choosing
the Circles is with some kind of nondiscriminatory
selection process.   Yet another way is to have the
manager of a certain area in the company play an
important role in selecting the Circle that will
represent his or her area.   Still other selections
are made by Circle members themselves--they decide
who represents their section of the company.

The role of the facilitator in all of this is
to operate behind the scenes, and to assist,
guide, and counsel to help make this special event
a success. It is a tremendous motivator for the
Circle members, and management as well.

Outside Conferences

Outside conferences such as those presented
by the International Association of Quality
Circles on an international, national, regional,
or chapter basis represent something in which
Circle members may be able to take part.   Chapter
level conferences are often attended by the
entire membership of a Circle; and they may make a
presentation.   This could be done all the way up
to the level of an international conference; and

while it is not to be expected that it would be done on an international basis in the early stages of Quality Circle activities in a company, it is possible as a long-range goal.

Again, the facilitator is the coordinating force that ties together all the loose ends that help to make such things occur. Indeed, the facilitator's role may be more than simply a coordinator.

Organizations consider this experience to be not only a developmental one for Circle members and leaders, but also one in which the company itself receives recognition and prestige.

COMMUNICATES EFFECTIVELY WITH ALL LEVELS

In-Person Communication

Talking to people not only has to be easy for a facilitator, it must also be fun--an enjoyable activity; because there will be a lot of it.

But will it be easy when one has to discuss Circle functions with a highly placed executive? That kind of experience may not have been previously gained. On the other hand, depending on the prior background of the facilitator, talking to entry level personnel may be an uncomfortable duty if one is not accustomed to it.

The facilitator must develop effective communication techniques with personnel at all levels. That's right, develop them! No matter how good one is at the start, skills should be subjected to continuous improvement.

How much time should be devoted to communications? A simple rule can be stated: "Enough; but not too much." In practice, it may not be so easy to

apply.   Establishing schedules, discussing them
with those involved, and working out modifications
is an initial responsibility. Example schedules
are:

*   Steering committee: One hour per month

*   Meeting with facilitator's superior:
    30-60 minutes per week

*   Meeting with each manager who has Circles
    in his or her organization (e.g. Pur-
    chasing): 30-60 minutes per month

*   Meeting with each department manager with
    Circles in his or her department: 30
    minutes every two weeks

*   Meetings with each Circle leader: Before,
    during, and after each meeting until
    training is complete and the major prob-
    lems have been taken care of. Thereafter,
    quick contacts on a formal or informal
    basis at least once each week

*   Contact with members: Most communication
    with members occurs during Circle meet-
    ings.   Also, by establishing some visi-
    bility in the work area, members who want
    to talk to the facilitator will have a
    better opportunity

In addition, there will be occasional meetings with various other individuals as required.

Presentations

Time considerations will occasionally require
the facilitator to put on presentations for
groups. Prior experience and knowledge in doing
this will help ease time constraints for everyone.
Presentation aids such as: charts, slides, view

foils, and flip-charts can be invaluable in speeding the communication process. Also, by careful and thoughtful planning the facilitator may be able to drastically reduce the time required without losing clarity. Most important, questions should be encouraged during the presentation; and time at the end of these meetings should always be allowed for questions and answers.

The subject of communication is dealt with in considerable detail in Chapter F16 and elsewhere in this handbook.

Activity Reports

The facilitator's effectiveness as a communicator can be increased through the publication of a weekly activity report; and it is normally from the facilitator to his immediate supervisor. Sometimes it is from the facilitator to the steering committee. Copies should be routed to all who have an interest in Quality Circles, such as steering committee members, managers with Circles, and leaders. It is frequently beneficial to send copies to individuals who are "just curious"; because their interest may be aroused to the point where they become proponents or even actively involved.

TEACHES LEADERS

The facilitator is responsible for the leader training. This involves a whole series of responsibilities, some of which are listed below.

Recruiting The Leaders

Designing The Training Curriculum

The training materials used by most organizations have been purchased; and this is the most cost-effective approach. Other organizations feel the need to make some minor modifications. It is highly recommended that modifications be minimized until at least a few months of operating experience has been gained. One should always learn the system before trying to modify it.

Duration of the course will vary depending on how it is organized. Some companies prefer to hold it on a three-day continuous basis. Others do not want the supervisors away from the work area for that length of time, and so schedule one day for three consecutive weeks. Another popular variation is a full day on Monday, a full day on Wednesday, and a full day on Friday.

Arrange For Instructor Assistants

The facilitator may do all of the instruction; but it may be beneficial to seek the help of others. Examples are: instructors from the education and training department, the assistant facilitator, managers with special expertise on specific subjects needed in Quality Circle training, and experienced leaders who are willing to participate.

Arrange For Teaching Facilities And Equipment

The classroom facilities, audio-visual equipment, and other aids for the instructor should be on hand, and ready for use. It is always a good idea for the facilitator to be sure that everything is ready ahead of time so that no unpleasant surprises occur after the students have arrived and the class is ready to begin.

Have Required Handouts Ready For Distribution

Most classes will have a variety of handouts to aid in the instruction and training process; and, each leader should have a Quality Circle manual.

It may seem obvious, but arrangements should always be made to have paper on hand so that the leaders may make notes, if needed.

Teaching The Class

The material should be presented to the students in the most interesting manner possible.

While it is important to adhere to the curriculum as much as possible, it is also necessary to be flexible at times. The routines may be altered, as needed. Questions should be encouraged throughout the training period; and an examination should always be given at the end to maximize the benefits gained from the course.

In some cases the examination is used as a learning experience rather than as a method of determining which of the attendees will pass and which will fail. (It would be exceedingly rare for a leader to fail to pass the course.)

The examination should be followed by a critique of all of the questions; and this may consume twice as much time as the examination itself. It is common, after the critique is completed, to hear leaders comment, "This examination and critique really brought it all together for me."

Certificates Of Completion

A certificate of completion is normally awarded to each person finishing the course. The educational training department probably does this as a routine matter and will be glad to cooperate. Further, it is important that copies of these completion certificates get into the personnel folders of the students who have completed the course.

MAINTAIN RECORDS

Sooner or later, someone is going to raise the question, "What kind of improvements have resulted from our Quality Circle activities?" This is a fair question and one that should be asked. The person with the responsibility to have the facts and figures for the overall Circle activities is the facilitator. This individual has to either see that others are maintaining records or do it himself or herself.

Records should be maintained on improvements in quality, reduction of costs, scheduled improvements, energy conservation, achievements, safety improvements, as well as attitude improvements. Most of these can be translated into dollar savings. Dollars represent a very understandable common denominator.

The following pages show examples of some of the records that must be maintained.

LEADER FEEDBACK FORM AND INSTRUCTIONS FOR USE

The content of this evaluation may be provided either in written or verbal form. It is not necessary to give the completed form to the leader.

This form provides a record that indicates whether or not progress is being made.

The facilitator should always be as positive as possible, and should avoid writing only negative comments. Sometimes it is possible to put a negative comment in the space allotted for positive comments. For example, suppose a leader has a history of interrupting members when they are speaking. The facilitator might be able to write under "Positive Comments," "Less interruptions today. I think it is helping. Members seemed more involved. Keep working on it, though. You have made great progress."

It should be kept in mind that the leader really wants feedback; and it can help effect improvements.   New leaders need and deserve feedback on a weekly basis. Experienced ones may require it less often.

If possible, it is a good idea to have another facilitator provide the feedback on occasion. This aids by presenting another point of view to the leader.

A leader may inquire, "Can you tell me how I compare with ____?" The facilitator can respond in generalities--never in specifics.

QUALITY CIRCLE

LEADER FEEDBACK

(To be prepared by the facilitator)

_____   _____   _____
          Leader   Dep't.   Circle Name

_____   _____
  Meeting Date   Subject of Meeting

_____
Positive Comments:

_____
Suggestions for Improvement

_____   _____
 Date Communicated to Leader   Facilitator

QUALITY CIRCLE

FACILITATOR QUARTERLY STATUS REPORT
TO STEERING COMMITTEE

A. General Status

	Shift		
	1st	2nd	3rd
Number of Active Circles	—	—	—
Number of Circles Dropped During Quarter	—	—	—
Number of Inactive Circles	—	—	—

Circles Dropped During Quarter:

Leader	Org'n	Reason
_____	_____	_____
_____	_____	_____
_____	_____	_____

Circles Inactive (List regardless of when Circle became inactive)

Leader	Org'n	Date	Reason
_____	_____	_____	_____
_____	_____	_____	_____
_____	_____	_____	_____
_____	_____	_____	_____
_____	_____	_____	_____

B. Membership Status as % of Total Employees:

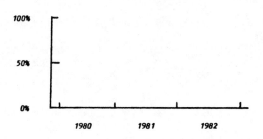

C. *Project Status*

   Number of projects started this quarter   _____

   Number of projects dropped this quarter   _____

   Number of projects resulting in management presentations   _____

   Percentage of accepted recommendations   _____

   Number of accepted recommendations that have been verified   _____

   Average number of work days from acceptance to verification   _____

D. *Evaluation*

   Organization Support:
   1. Positive Support - Specific Examples

      2. Lack of Support - Specific Examples

E. *Goals*

Instructions

   This report can serve as a guide to the facilitator in preparing a quarterly report to the Steering Committee.
   Once approved by the Steering Committee, copies can be routed to executive (and other) level management for informational purposes.

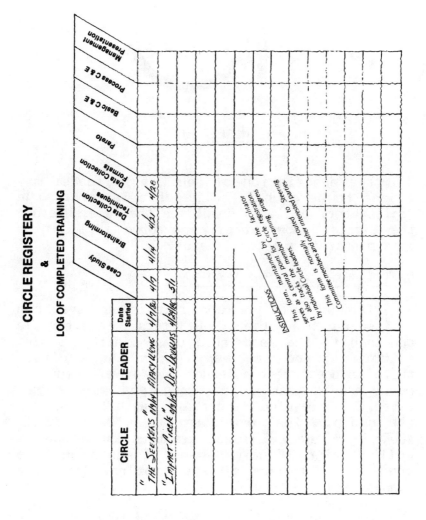

THE LEADER

The description of the Circle leader may appear to be much like the description of the facilitator; and this should be the case; because the Circle leader ideally performs in much the same manner as the facilitator.

WHAT IS EXPECTED OF A LEADER?

Thousands of books and articles have been written on this subject. Of course, this text is confined to the leadership of a Quality Circle. Although there are many "do's and don'ts," there is one that the leader must never forget if he or she is to build a strong team, meet objectives, and develop leadership capability within the group. That one item is: "DON'T DO IT YOURSELF!" Many Circles have been led astray by well meaning, "one-man-band" leaders who are completely unaware of the problems they are causing for the future.

No successful leader ever gets to the top and stays there by doing other people's work for them. Assuredly, it seems simpler, sometimes, to "do it yourself" rather than to delegate responsibility and risk failure; but, that is a trap into which leaders must not fall.

The successful leaders build for the future. They involve other members of the Circle in carrying out assignments even though they know that they could do the jobs better. If the leader considers some of the members to be weak and deficient, that is all the more reason for them to get experience while he or she is available to help them, if necessary.

It is well worth repeating: "DON'T DO IT YOURSELF!"

The Supervisor As The Circle Leader

Experience demonstrates that Circle activities will have a greater degree of success when the supervisor is the initial leader. The Quality Circle concept gains quicker acceptance when it steps into the existing organizational structure. The supervisor is already designated to perform a leadership role in the organization. If the Quality Circle does not operate within the existing organizational setup, it might be viewed by some as a competing organization. Although this may be considered to be highly unlikely to some, it has happened in several organizations and must be dealt with.

Ways To Select Circle Leaders

There are a variety of methods that can be used to select the leader of a Circle. Some of them are outlined below:

*   Some steering committees conduct a competition for the position of facilitator. They realize that some candidates, although not selected, may wish to become Circle leaders. This works well, particularly when the candidates for the facilitator position are supervisors. This approach has produced highly motivated leaders who are generally

outstanding examples for subsequent generations of leaders.

* Leaders may be nominated by either the
steering committee members or by a panel of
managers. The credentials of those nominated
are reviewed and the successful candidates
are selected for participation in the Quality
Circle pilot program.

* Volunteers are encouraged by simply putting
out the word that Circle leaders will be
needed. This gives everyone an opportunity
to respond. Further, the sense of democratic
selection is sometimes enhanced by selecting
the winning candidates through a random
process such as drawing names from a hat.

* Leaders are frequently drafted. The manager
of a department that is going to have Quality
Circles may identify the supervisors he
or she wants to lead Circles during the pilot
phase. This works out effectively except in
instances where the leaders selected do not
have the required commitment or belief in the
Circle program.

Non-supervisors As Leaders

This condition normally evolves in the
following manner. The supervisor becomes the
first leader. After the Circle has been in
operation for some time, he or she identifies
another individual, usually a lead person, to act
as an assistant leader. After that individual has
received leader training and has had an opportunity to demonstrate effectiveness in the role as
assistant leader, promotion to full Circle leader
usually occurs.

Leaders Found Through Election

Eventually, the operation of the Circle
becomes smooth and efficient; and the supervisor

can feel relaxed about not being personally in
personal command. It is at this stage that the
Circle may consider electing its leader. By this
time, the members understand what is needed to
operate effectively, and they will choose their
leader for the right reasons. The Circle will
likely be one or two years old when, and if, this
occurs.

There are organizations that have elected
Circle leaders at an earlier date than described
above. There are even those which started their
Circle activities by electing the leaders. A
major danger in electing the intitial leader
is that Circle members do not know enough about
the operation to know what the important characteristics of a leader are. Therefore, the wrong
person may be elected for the wrong reasons. It
is also a fact that the supervisor in the area
may feel threatened and possibly withdraw his
support of the Circle activities.

The Leader Is Responsible For His Or Her Circle

The leader alone is responsible for the
smooth and effective operation of the Circle. It
is not the job of a facilitator. Leaders vary in
the amount of support that they require from the
facilitator, but that need should continually
diminish.

There is little question that Circles dominated by the facilitator will get off to a faster
start. But, it is the on-going, day-to-day
operation, that eventually evolves that will slow
the progress of the Circles led by the facilitator. There just is not enough time for the
facilitator to provide leadership to a number of
Circles. Even though progress may be a bit slower
initially, the leader should take as active a role
as possible. Leaders learn far better by doing
than they do by observing how others perform.

The Circle Leader Selected Must be Committed To The Process

The leader should be convinced that the attempt at this kind of activity is worth the time and effort. He or she may be skeptical of the results, but must be committed to the process.

TRAINING

Training for Quality Circle leaders comprises more than just learning what the Quality Circle techniques include. There is theoretical information, but it is supplemented by practical examples. The leader must learn how to handle the Circle members. To do this, it is necessary to receive training in group dynamics and communications. Of course, understanding the overall Circle organization within the company is important, so that the Circle can operate at maximum effectiveness. Teaching techniques assist the leader in getting his or her message across. Learning what kinds of themes, projects, and problems should be adopted also proves helpful when the Circle is initiated. Working with a Quality Circle is similar in many respects to working with any volunteer group. A volunteer group is different--the members are not required to remain members. It is not a captive audience. Poor leadership may result in Circle members wanting to drop out. After a Circle has completed a project, it should determine what kind of savings resulted. Part of the leader's training is to learn how to do this important task; and it is vital that he or she know who can be of assistance with it when needed.

The Facilitator Trains The Leaders

The facilitator is responsible for providing training to the Circle leaders. The facilitator may be assisted in this task by individuals from

the education and training department. Sometimes
a manager or staff person with special expertise
also assists.   There are Circle programs where
experienced Circle leaders also take part in
helping to train the new ones.

The Leaders Train The Members

After the leader has received training, the
Circle is organized, and training is provided to
the members.   The teacher is the leader.   As a
backup only, the facilitator is present during
the first few training sessions.

Some leaders have surveyed members of their
Circles to determine if there are members who wish
to take part in the training process.   Occasionally a surprise will occur.   Members have all
kinds of interesting backgrounds; and occasionally
they may form an important resource in helping to
handle some part of the training of other Circle
members.

Provide Quality Circle Training For All Super-
visors Whether Or Not They Are Circle Leaders

This approach has been used successfully by
several organizations.   It has been found that
some supervisors will procrastinate about getting
their Quality Circles started. If, however, they
are routinely scheduled through leader training
courses, they may initiate Circles much more
quickly than otherwise.

Occasionally, an excessive number of supervisors will emerge with a desire to launch Circle
activities before the facilitator is able to
provide the proper assistance. It is a mistake to
train a supervisor in the art of leading a Quality
Circle; and then to say, "I'm sorry, you'll have
to wait. We are not ready for you to start your
Circle."

INCENTIVES TO BECOME A CIRCLE LEADER

Leader Training

Study Quality Circle problem analysis skills.
These techniques are aids for Circle use in
solving problems. Initially, the leader acquires a
sequence of skills that are basic in nature and
common to most Circle activities. Advanced skills
in problem analysis are appropriate only occasionally, and only for some Circles; therefore, they
are not included in the training of every Circle.
They are normally studied only if their use is
indicated by special circumstances.

These problem-solving skills are taught by
the leader to the members during the first few
weeks after the Circle has been formed.

Acquire new leadership skills.   As the name
implies, the leader must lead.   Skills acquired
through training enhance this ability.   Leaders
study subjects such as motivation: communication,
group dynamics, leadership of volunteer groups,
and teaching techniques.   The learning of these
subjects is often enhanced through role playing
and experiential exercises.

These skills, while applicable to Circle
activities, will carry over into, and benefit, the
normal work routine. Best of all, they are not the
typical classroom skills which are learned, but
which often do not apply.   The Circle setting
provides a forum where the leader is encouraged
to transform theory into practice.

Training credits accrue at most organizations for
successful completion of Quality Circle training
courses.   While this should never be the primary
reason for undertaking leader training, it nevertheless is a consideration that should not be
overlooked.

Open New Channels For Communications

The informal setting afforded by Quality Circles either facilitates the flow of information between the leader and the members, or it opens totally new avenues that did not exist before. Just as important are the opportunities for new or broadened communication channels with management. The management presentation is the obvious vehicle to make this a reality. More than that, sheer weight of numbers (Circle size) tends to add a note of authenticity and believability to their recommendations.

A third and general area for improved communications is with staff personnel. This benefits both them and the Circles which interface with them.

Circles communicating with other Circles is yet another powerful way to effect change. It becomes a case of peers talking to peers, a method which is frequently superior to depending solely on the formal management structure.

Opportunity To Possibly Become A Part-Time Facilitator

As the number of Circles grows, it becomes increasingly difficult for the facilitator to handle all of them. Many companies provide support for the facilitator by using a network of several part-time facilitators. Each facilitates two or three Circles on a part-time basis. In some organizations, the supervisor who has Circle experience may have the opportunity to do this. An example is the supervisor with 25 people. Twenty-five employees are enough to establish 3 operating Circles. An assistant leader is then appointed to run each. The supervisor should be thought of as the overall leader, or could be considered to be a part-time facilitator.

Experience as a part-time facilitator further equips that individual to assume responsibilities as a full-time facilitator, if the opening occurs and the desire is there to fill it.

LEADER DUTIES

Acquire Necessary Training

Prior to the formation of the Circle the prospective leader must acquire skills in the Quality Circle techniques dealing with problem solving.

Recruit Members

At the conclusion of leader training, potential members are contacted and asked to join. Several approaches may be taken at this time. The recommended approach is for the manager to hold a briefing session for those who can join the Circle. He may be assisted by the facilitator and an organization executive. The leader also takes a part in this kind of briefing. The leader usually does not ask for volunteers at this time but defers it until he has had a chance to talk in person with each individual. This one-on-one follow-up should occur within a day or so of the briefing.

Schedule Circle Meetings

Scheduling the Circle meetings is usually accomplished with the help of Circle members. Will they be held during normal working hours? Or, will they be on overtime? Regardless, they should be on a regular basis, whether weekly or at some other frequency.

When Circle meetings take place, the leaders should provide an agenda so that the time allotted is used with maximum efficiency.

Insure That Meetings Are Job Oriented

It is easy for Circle meetings to drift into general "bull sessions." Worse, they may move onto topics that are not within the Circle charter, such as wages and salaries, personnel matters, or grievances. The leader must constantly be aware of this possibility, and be ready to get the group back on course.

Encourage Involvement By Voicing Opinions On Various Aspects Of The Problem Analysis

The best Circles are those that provide an opportunity for all members to be heard. The leader makes this happen by using several of the Quality Circle techniques, and employing the leadership skills learned in training sessions.

The leader can assist by restating important parts of the Circle conversation to redirect attention. The leader must be prepared to stimulate group discussion by injecting appropriate inputs and giving encouragement.

The leader opens and closes the meeting at the scheduled time. Opening late virtually insures that members will soon catch on, and the meetings will become later and later. Not ending on time will likely cause difficulties with management because of excessive time being devoted to Circle activities. Prior to each meeting, Circle members should be notified if the normal starting time is altered in any way.

Conclude each meeting with responsibilities and assignments clearly defined. If individual assignments need clarification, it can be done outside of the meeting, to avoid taking the time of all members of the Circle.

At the conclusion of each meeting the leader must be sure that Circle minutes are properly

prepared. These minutes may be distributed; or
some other arrangement may be made for their
availability, such as leaving them in a central
place in the work area where they are accessible
to the manager, the facilitator, or any Circle
member. The management presentation is an all-
important responsibility of the leader. Although
the leader involves most of the members in this
activity, he is responsible for its occurrence.
This function is so important to the success of
the Circle that the leader must be held accountable for its execution on a regular and timely
basis.

The leader must maintain close communications
with the facilitator. Talking with the facilitator prior to the Circle meeting will help to
assure that the planned agenda is meaningful, and
not in conflict with something taking place
elsewhere. After the meeting, the leader and
facilitator should discuss those points that were
particularly well done, and those that need
improvement.

People building is the leader's responsibility. This includes making members better than
they already are by giving assignments, encouraging participation in management presentations,
and training. The leader should also promote
new Circles in his or her area. Although he or
she may have started with only one Circle, eventually there will be an opportunity to expand to
include other members of the work group. Occasionally the leader is approached by potential
members who want to organize Circles; but, if
the leader is being truly effective, he or she
will take the initiative and let other groups
know that Circle opportunities are available for
the asking.

Management by objectives is a primary function of the Circle leader. It is not enough to
say, "We will improve the Quality." That is much

too vague. It is much better to say, "We will improve the Quality by 10% within the next 4 months." Goals must be measurable if they are to be meaningful and attainable. Further, a feedback system must be established to let members know how well they are doing toward achieving stated objectives. The Circle that operates with the concept of management by objectives is the Circle that excels--the one that is always in the lead.

REPORTS THAT MUST BE MADE AND FORMS TO MAINTAIN

Minutes of each meeting are maintained, usually by a member; and the leader must check these over at the conclusion of each Circle meeting. A suggested format will be found on Page 408 of the Leader Manual.

A weekly activity report is normally maintained for on-going communication between the supervisor and the manager. Circle activities should be included in this weekly activities report. (This report is not illustrated herein.)

The member attendance log is maintained by the leader, or some designated member of the Circle, to keep a record of which members are attending the meetings on a regular basis. If a succession of absences becomes apparent, this should be the signal for the leader to make inquiries as to why. A suggested attendance Log form is shown on Page 409 of the Leader Manual.

A member training status record is also maintained by the leader; and a suggested form is shown on Page 411 of the Leader Manual.

LEADER CIRCLE

Circle leaders usually band together to form a leaders' Circle that meets approximately once

a month.   Whatever the meeting frequency, the
schedule established should be maintained.   The
leaders' Circle meetings work best when topics
of general interest to all of the attendees are
discussed.   It is a serious mistake to deal with
a specific Circle.   If this precaution is not
heeded, the leaders of the other Circles are
likely to "turn off" and discontinue attendance.

THE MEMBER

The member is that part of the Quality Circle that makes it all worthwhile. This is the individual, often drawn from entry level ranks from any portion of the organization, whose participation as part of a team, can truly affect an organization's quality and competitive image. It is at this level that ideas are being sought. Exploratory probes for ideas have rarely considered this massive resource in almost all organizations. Since the advent of Quality Circles, this tremendous resource is being permitted to contribute to both organizational and individual success; and the excitement it is causing is unprecedented!

WHO IS THE MEMBER?

The question is often asked, "What group of people should have Quality Circles. Assembly? Fabrication?" The answer to this question may seem too all-encompassing, but it is, "Wherever people are involved."

Production

This is where 85% of the members come from at the present time. It was in the factory that

the Quality Circle concept was first applied in
Japan. The factory worker was too long considered
to be just another cog in the wheel, and certainly
not a source for ideas. "Besides," it was rea-
soned, "these jobs have been planned by experts to
the minutest detail. What is left?"

Office

A fast-growing recognition, becoming increasingly evident, is that the office setting also
represents a fertile area for Circle growth.
Presently at the 15% level, this percentage is
growing.

The name, Quality Control Circles, or Q C
Circles, tended to deter formation of Circles in
offices. Dropping the word "control" has removed
much of the misconception that it is all about
"inspectors"; and that means the shop.

Where is it used outside of production? The
list is long. Again, if one looks for a common
denominator, people is likely to be the only one
to emerge:

* Hospitals

* Merchandising

* Banks

* Power companies

* Telephone companies

* Insurance firms

* Engineering

* Clerical/engineering
    support in factories

* And countless others

Management

Even management personnel can benefit by involvement in Quality Circle activity. Several organizations report success at this level. However, little is shown about the actual practice of Quality Circle principles at such Circle meetings.

A variation of the management level Circle is the leader's Circle. Leader Circles usually meet once a month. They are effective if they avoid trying to solve the problems supervisors are encountering--e.g. a leader Circle comprised of leaders from each of: machine shop, assembly line, janitorial, accounting, and secretarial. If they work on a problem in the machine shop, the Circle deteriorates--people are bored, and they begin to miss meetings. They must work on common problems such as, "How do we train the new member who has just joined the organization? All of our existing members have completed training and we do not want to make the others sit through it again."

The Outsider As A Member

Sometimes the Circle picks up an individual from another department as a member. An example is the inspector who joins the manufacturing Circle in the area he or she is assigned.

The key is, "Does the outsider understand the processes involved in the regular work assignments?"

NON-MEMBER

Just because an individual elects to drop out, or not to join a Circle, it doesn't mean that he or she does not believe in the value of worker participation. It may simply mean that Circle participation isn't of interest to him or her. In one survey, Circle dropouts were queried, "Should

Circle activities be continued and extended
to others?" Approximately two-thirds said,
"Yes!"

The lines of communication should be kept
open to the non-member. Non-members should be
encouraged to submit ideas to the Circle. And
they do! One clique of three non-members proposed
an idea to a Circle member. She persuaded them to
come to the next Circle meeting to discuss it.
They liked it and remained.

A good relationship with the non-members is
important for another reason. Circle ideas, when
implemented, may affect them. Their acceptance of
change will be smoothed if they can influence the
change recommendations. The opportunity to do
so should be built into the process.

TEMPORARY MEMBER

Occasionally a Circle adopts a project that
calls for it to work closely with another organization. This borders on danger because of,
"telling those other people how to solve their
problems."

This can be handled by getting a representative from "that other area" to become a temporary Circle member until the problem is solved.

Their own people will be much more likely to
be receptive to change when they influence the
direction of that change.

TRAINING

An in-depth exposure to the Quality Circle
techniques comprises the bulk of the Quality
Circle training that is done. This is thoroughly
covered in the "Member Manual" which each member
receives. Well-illustrated instructions, work

sheets, and quizzes make for a rounded training program.

The training goes beyond simply learning the analytical techniques during formal instruction sessions. The Quality Circle operation is a process that is learned by doing. The code of conduct, a marvelous exercise in practical group dynamics is something "learned-by-doing." That, in turn, encourages member teamwork, and an emphasis on people building whereby they work more constructively with other Circle members as well as those outside of the Circles. Their expertise in the art of communication is the result of putting into practice what they have learned through the training module: "The Management Presentation."

SUGGESTED FORMAT FOR INITIAL MEETING WITH POTENTIAL MEMBERS

This meeting should be attended by those employees in whose area there will be a Quality Circle.

In addition to the group supervisor (who will be the first leader of the Circle), it should include the supervisor's manager, the facilitator, and perhaps an executive.

FORMAT

Welcome everyone.

Introduce any guests.

Answer the question, "What is it?"

Tell what your organization's objectives are for this activity: improved quality, safety, better communication, cost reduction, improvement of competitive position, job security, etc.

State what is <u>not</u> within the charter of Quality Circles, such as involvement with pay rates, grievances, personnel matters, etc.   Point out that there are other channels for dealing with such matters.

Briefly describe the details of how this activity operates. Point out that members will receive training in problem analysis techniques, they will be involved in selecting the problems in their work area that will be taken up as team projects, they will work out the solutions to problems they select for attention, and that they will be directly involved in presenting recommendations to management.

Name various organizations that have installed this type of employee participation activity. Examples are: General Electric, Xerox, Lincoln National Life, Reynolds Tobacco, Uniroyal, Firestone, The Singer Company, F.A.A., U.S. Navy, U.S. Air Force, U.S. Army, Ampex, RCA, Hewlett-Packard, Lockheed, Boeing, Armstrong World Industries, Bendix, Michigan Bell Telephone, Coors, Northrup, Hughes, Martin-Marietta, TRW, J.C. Penney's Catalog Centers, and hundreds of others.

Tell them that Japan initiated the first teams (called Quality Control Circles or QC Circles) in 1962 and that it was not until the mid 1970's that they were first adopted in the Western World.

Let them know that there is an International Association of Quality Circles which was founded in late 1977, for the purpose of furthering the Quality Circle concept world-wide, and they may join, if they wish. It publishes a quarterly magazine which will prove to be of interest to them.

Describe how your organization got started in this activity, explain the role of the steering committee and name its members.

Explain how the facilitator provides support and assistance to the members and others.

If it has not already come from someone in the group, ask the question "What's in it for me?" Some of the answers you can provide include:

* Training in problem analysis.

* The opportunity to identify the problems you have been living with and no one seems to care about.

* Being recognized as the "expert" in your area.

* Being allowed to select the problems to be analyzed.

* Having the chance to actually analyze the selected problem.

* The opportunity to present recommended problem solutions directly to management.

* The chance to contribute to enhancing the organization's quality reputation, to make it more competitive, and to assure greater job security.

Introduce the training course. List the subjects that will be covered: Case Study & Problem Prevention Techniques, Brainstorming, Data Collecting Techniques, Data Collecting Formats Plus Graphs, Decision Analysis Using Pareto, Basic Cause-&-Effect Problem Analysis, Process C-&-E Problem Analysis, and The Management Presentation.

Encourage a lively question and answer session.

Conclude by asking members to give it some further thought. Tell them they will be contacted later so that any additional questions can be answered.

Thank them for their time and adjourn the meeting.

FOLLOW-ON ACTION

Within a day or two, the supervisor should
check with each employee who was at the meeting,
to ask if he or she has further questions.
Usually it is not necessary to inquire if an
individual wants to join. Typically, the employee
says, "I want in!"

CHARACTERISTICS TO ASSURE SUCCESSFUL QUALITY CIRCLE ACTIVITIES

Successful Quality Circle activities are rarely due to chance. They result because certain essential elements are present.

The absence of one or more basic elements will impair the degree of success. They may not topple Quality Circle activities; but they will surely limit the degree of attainment.

The steering committee should be aware that, as a body, it can contribute immensely toward assuring that these basic foundation blocks are in place.

These essential elements are as follows:

*   Management is supportive
*   Participation is voluntary
*   There is a people-building attitude
*   Training is provided
*   Teamwork is encouraged
*   Recognition is provided
*   Members select problems in their
      area of expertise
*   Circles solve problems, not just identify
      them.

191

MANAGEMENT SUPPORT

Management support is but one of the several elements that play an important role in the success of Quality Circle activities. But it is unique in the sense that it must come first. That is, if management support is non-existent, then none of the others matter; because the Quality Circle activities are doomed to failure.

Kind of Support

The program must have management support. But it must be of a particular kind. The support must have three qualities.

It must be within or under the control of the organization using Quality Circles. Often, the initial enthusiasm for the program comes from quality control managers. The fact that they believe in Quality Circles is important. Nevertheless, their support by itself is not enough. They must convince their counterparts in other organizations that the program is to their best interests. After all, it is usually other than quality control employees who will be members of the Circles.

It should be at the highest possible level in the organization. In the example just given of the manufacturing organization, the support would be sufficient if it included the manufacturing manager and the quality control manager. The program will have a greater chance of maximizing its effectiveness if, say, a vice-president is a key backer. But the company president, a plant manager, or a chief executive officer will do even more to assure every possible advantage for the Circle activity if they are known to support it.

Depth of management support is also a factor. It is important that as many people in the management structure as possible be supporters--including those on the manager's level, those that he or she reports to, as well as those who report to the manager. The support for the Quality Circle program should not be limited to one or two managers.

Make management support visible. The fact that management support exists is reassuring and is vital to the success of the program. But it must be more than that. Management must convey to all people in the organization that the support is there, particularly to those individuals who are members of the Circles. This support is conveyed by what management says and what is written about its support. The manager must realize that what is done will do more to convince people than what is said. An excellent way for a manager to demonstrate support is to drop in on a regular Circle meeting. The fact that such a visit may be of very short duration is not a detriment. The Circle members understand that the manager is a very busy person; and the fact that he or she cared enough to stop in says more than words could ever convey.

Circles must be encouraged to make their own presentations to management. Encourage management presentations by the Circles in the organization. They must not send substitutes. The members want to see their managers there in person. The management presentation happens to be an exciting event that goes a long way in communicating that management is supportive.

Managers often have the opportunity to present papers within the company or to organizations on the outside. The mention, in these papers, of Quality Circle activities is a sure way to convince members that their managers care.

Managers also have the opportunity to include Quality Circle items in their organizations'objectives. Obviously, if the manager really believes that the Circles are worthwhile and are paying their way, he or she should be willing to include them as part of the overall objectives.

The management presentation is an opportunity for the manager to build additional management support. Other managers, perhaps those who are not convinced as to the merits of Quality Circles, may witness the presentations. They may leave with a changed point of view after seeing the enthusiasm and improved attitudes of those who had an opportunity to do something worthwhile for their organizations beyond their regular duties.

PARTICIPATION IS VOLUNTARY

History shows that few churches have gained permanent members when attendance was mandatory. In fact, mandatory attendance may have built longlasting resistance. Another example of voluntarism is the marriage contract. Those who go into marriage without really wanting to are not likely to enjoy wedded bliss for long.

People should join Quality Circles because they want to do so--not because someone told them they had to join. Of course, it is just as important for management to allow those who want to volunteer to do so.

It should be understood that not everyone wants to be a member of a Quality Circle, just as not everyone wants to be a member of other groups that abound in all communities. Some people, in a work area where a Circle operates, may prefer to remain at their work stations during meetings because they are not interested in the activity.

Expected Percentage Of Volunteers

The percentage of individuals who have a chance to become Circle members, and volunteer to

do so, extends from a low of 30% to a high of
100%. The average seems to be around 70%. The
presence of a labor union does not seem to be a
factor. For example, one large company in the
eastern United States, with no union, experienced
a 70% volunteer rate. Another plant in the same
company, with a strong labor union, had a volunteer rate of 95%.

Method of recruitment can influence the
number of volunteers. Some leaders have their
Circles ready to go before they receive their
leader training; because they enthusiastically
"talk it up" in advance. Usually, however, the
leaders say little about the program until after
their training is complete.

The most usual way that members are recruited
is to have an informational briefing presided over
by the department manager and attended by an
executive, the facilitator, and the leader. After
the session is over the leader can ask for volunteers; but is more likely to get an increased
participation if he or she suggests, "Think about
it and I'll get back with you." Members need time
to incubate this new concept. The leader can then
talk to them on a one-to-one basis within a day or
so, and handle it as simply as, "What do you think
about having a Quality Circle in this area?" He
or she will soon find out what questions may have
been left unanswered, and if there are any misunderstandings that must be handled.

Effect Of Attitude Of Management On Subordinates

Employees will look up to leadership. If
they see a manager who is enthusiastic about the
Quality Circle concept, who has a belief that his
or her people can make a worthwhile contribution,
and that their ideas are encouraged and welcomed,
they are likely to have similarly positive attitudes and will want to participate. If the

reverse is true, employees cannot be expected to become excited about it.

One manager destroyed the enthusiasm of one of his supervisors who was making plans to get a Circle started. He commented, "You want my opinion? Quality Circles make me want to vomit!" The stunned supervisor later decided, "Why waste my time if that's the way he feels."

Degree Of Volunteerism When Meetings Are Held Outside Of Regular Working Hours

No accurate record is available; however, fewer people can volunteer when meetings are held after work hours because of carpool arrangements, bus schedules, or personal schedules. Thus, the percentage of volunteers will ordinarily be less than if the meetings are held during the normal working hours.

Meetings Held Outside Normal Working Hours At No Pay

Although unusual, there are some surprises in this area. About 15% of the companies who schedule meetings outside the normal working hours indicate that employees receive no pay for their participation.

There is a company in the United States, with well over 50 Circles in operation, wherein all Circles meet during their 30-minute lunch time each week, without pay! There is a strong union operating at that plant; and some of their greatest support comes from the active participation and leadership of union stewards in the Circle activities.

Will There Be Drifters In And Out?

There will be some who drop out of the Circle, just as others will refuse to join at

first, but will later decide to give it a try.
One hard-working young lady decided that Quality
Circle membership was not for her.   "I've seen
programs come and go and this one isn't going to
be any different.   It will fall flat on it's
face, like most of the others did after 3 or 4
months."   She stayed at her regular assignment
during Circle meetings.   After 4 months her
attitude had changed dramatically.   "Things are
really happening.   It is hard to believe, but
things we have wanted to do for years are finally
getting done."   She joined, and became an enthusiastic and contributing member.

Volunteerism Can Act As A Safety Valve

If someone is hostile and negative about
Circle activities, it is preferable that he or she
not join.   And it is best to allow a member of a
Circle to quit if he or she desires to do so.
Naturally, the leader will endeavor to discover
and correct the causes of such occurrences.

Voluntary At The Supervisor And Management Level?

A survey indicates that 97% of the companies
with Quality Circles report that member participation is voluntary.

Supervisory and management personnel are not
treated quite the same.   Eighty-one percent of
the companies say that supervisory involvement is
voluntary if the people want to start a Quality
Circle.

Management participation is voluntary in 76%
of the organizations that have Quality Circle
activities.

The fact that supervisors and managers are
less likely to be able to determine if the Circles
will be able to operate in their areas is not a
problem; because they always have the option of

getting other individuals to participate in their
stead. As an example, the supervisor can start
as the Circle leader, and, as soon as practical
he or she can appoint an assistant who can serve
as the Circle leader. In the case of the manager,
he doesn't really have to be much more involved
than to take part in the management presentations
Some managers have attended their first management
presentations and become converts. Experience
indicates that it is a common mistake to underestimate the ability of the Circle to be cost
effective.

A "Twist" To The Concept Of Volunteerism

Some organizations have built in a slight
alteration to the concept of volunteerism; and it
has been successful. An example will illustrate.
A supervisor is ready to start a Circle. He or
she has 10 people in his or her group. After
explaining Quality Circles to them and hearing all
of their questions, he or she announces, "You are
all members of the Quality Circle. You will be
involved in training and working on actual problems during the first several weeks. Because it
is a voluntary activity after the training is
complete, you can drop out if you wish." That
does it? And it isn't. What often happens is
that several individuals who normally would not
have given it a try will find that Quality Circles
are fulfilling many of their needs and is indeed
an enjoyable experience. It's like, "I tried it
and I like it."

Union objection? Not one union has objected
to date. Certainly, the temporary feature of the
mandatory involvement has had something to do with
that lack of opposition.

THERE IS A PEOPLE-BUILDING ATTITUDE

Quality Circle activities built around a
people-building philosophy will succeed. If a

people-using philosophy operates, then it is but a matter of time until it will fail, or, management will change its attitude as a result of what it sees happening.

The concept of people-building is integral to the philosophy of Quality Circles. It is based on trust and respect for others and a willingness to take the time to help to develop each person to his or her full potential.

Pygmalion Effect

"Expect a lot, and you'll get a lot!" People try to live up to the expectations of those they respect as a Circle leader, manager, or facilitator. The facilitator will play an important part in shaping their attitudes about themselves and what they feel they can do.

A high expectation can be a self-fulfilling prophecy. Most people have been handed assignments that cause them to say to themselves, "I can't do it!" But then, they tend to think, "The boss thinks I can; and he ought to know—he's the boss!" "Besides, if he thinks I can do it, I'm not about to change his mind!" So they rise to the occasion and produce the expected results.

On the other hand, a low expectation can also be a self-fulfilling prophecy. "If the boss thinks I'm a loser, then why try to change his mind. Maybe I am a loser, and anyway even if I'm not, who cares?"

One newly-trained Circle leader was pleased that all 25 people in her group wanted to join her Circle. However, for the pilot program she was to have only one Circle. Other Circle leaders told her she had no problem. All she had to do was to select the top seven or eight people and she would have a single fantastic Circle. She wisely said, "No, I don't want to give the message to those who are not picked that they were not good enough to be part of the Circle." She decided to select the Circle members on a nondiscriminatory basis. She accomplished that by putting all 25 names into a hat and drawing out eight of them for her first Circle.

Under her positive leadership, based on high expectations, she had a top flight Circle that produced tremendous results.

Ways that people building takes place

People building can be accomplished in a variety of ways. Here are a few examples:

*   Members receiving assignments

*   Leaders making sure that every person is involved at all meetings

*   Members being given the chance to take part in brainstorming sessions

*   Members leading brainstorming sessions

*   Assistant leaders running portions of, or entire meetings

*   Assistant leaders attending leader-training classes

*   Members receiving training

*   Members taking part in management presentations

*   Members participating in problem analysis

TRAINING IS PROVIDED

Training Or No Training

This was the problem faced by one major U.S. company when it first started Quality Circles.

Its management was divided as to the value or the necessity of training. They did an interesting thing. They established two pilot programs that ran side by side. In one, the leaders received no training at all. They simply organized Circles and started identifying and solving problems. The other group went through the normal Quality Circle training. Five months later the two groups were compared and the differences were dramatic. The results convinced management to go with training.

It is possible to assemble a group of people, sit them around a table, and ask them to identify problems; they will. More than that, they will find solutions to some of these problems. The difference is, with Quality Circle training they will solve those problems faster than they otherwise would; and they will handle problems they otherwise would not have been able to consider.

The above only confirms a statement attributed to Dr. Ishikawa, commonly noted as the "Father of QC Circles" in Japan. He stated, "A ton of enthusiasm is worthless unless backed by an ounce of scientific knowledge."

Management Training

Ideally, managers should receive at least one day of training. As a compromise, it is often done in 4 hours. As an absolute minimum, it should not be attempted under a 2-hour period. Naturally, in such short periods of time, only an overview can be provided. But at least it supplies the manager with enough information so that he can provide the necessary coordination and support.

Leader Training

Leader training usually is done on a 3-day basis. The majority of companies supply approximately 20 hours of leader training. Leader training includes an understanding of the various Quality Circle techniques. In addition, it includes training in interpersonal relations, communications, motivation, group dynamics, and a variety of other skills that must be acquired for successful Quality Circles operation.

Member Training

Member training is generally limited to a study of the Quality Circle problem-solving techniques.

Member training takes place during the first several weeks. It is a combination of receiving training in the problem-analysis techniques; but the Circle members are also given the opportunity to apply what they are learning to actual problems they have undertaken to solve in their work areas.

The details of the training program are contained elsewhere in this handbook.

Who Trains the Leaders?

The basic responsibility for training Circle leaders is that of the facilitator. In some companies the facilitator alone does this. In other companies the facilitator works jointly with the education and training departments to assure that Circle leaders are properly trained.

What about the supervisors as students? They are excellent students; because they know that as soon as they have completed the training, they will be organizing their Circles, and they will be the teachers for the members of their Circles!

Most supervisors do an excellent job of training employees one at a time. Few can teach groups well; but the training they receive from the facilitator equips them to effectively train numbers of people at one time.

Who Trains The Members?

Member training is performed by the Circle leader. Rather, it should be stated that the leader is the proper person to do it. Possibly a facilitator might do it more successfully, but as a people-building technique at the leader level, it is superb. Further, it clearly establishes the Circle leader as a person who is in charge and knowledgeable. A facilitator attends these training sessions, but only as an observer. Periodically, depending on the ability of the leader, the facilitator may get involved. The facilitator will be more effective if he or she minimizes involvement during Circle training sessions, and instead spends time with the leader prior to and following the meetings. The leader (with possibly some occasional help from the facilitator) provides the training in about two-thirds of the cases. One third of the time the training for Circle members is provided solely by the facilitator.

TEAMWORK IS ENCOURAGED

Destructive Competition

Human beings are competitive. They like to win. But if one individual or a group must always win in a way that results in others being losers, the spirit of teamwork and cooperation quickly disappears. No one likes to be on the losing side of a win-lose situation.

Establishing "Win-Win" Relationships

The Circle has to deal with other Circles, other supervisors, engineers, etc. That relationship should always be one that is "win-win."

Establishing a "win-win" relationship can be just as important within the Circle itself. One member cannot "win" at the expense of another member.

Code of Conduct

To make certain that one member does not win at the expense of others, an effective device is employed called the "code of conduct." It is relatively simple, and will do more than any number of textbooks on the subject of group dynamics and commnications--which Circle members ordinarily will not have the time or inclination to read. The code of conduct is most effective when devised by the Circle members themselves. On Page 62 of the Leader Manual are examples taken from various codes of conduct that have been established by different Circles. Typically, the code of conduct established by a given Circle will be prominently displayed in the meeting area so as to advise the members, and anyone else who happens to be in attendance, that there are certain rules they have prescribed for themselves to operate by. Additional information on the code of conduct is contained in Chapter F6 of this handbook.

RECOGNITION IS PROVIDED

There are many ways that the Circle can receive recognition for its efforts.

The Management Presentation

The management presentation is a major reward factor to Circle members. Here they have the opportunity, perhaps for the first time in their working careers, to communicate directly with the manager of their departments. They can explain the projects they have identified and analyzed. They can make recommendations as to how the problems should be solved and how they feel the changes can be implemented in their departments.

The management presentation is an exciting moment in the entire process. It provides a substantial reward and recognition for the members of a Quality Circle. The facilitator is cautioned not to underestimate its importance as a motivating force within an organization. As stated earlier, there are successful Quality Circle programs that provide no other form of reward or recognition other than the management presentation. That's how powerful it is. There are many examples of the importance of this feature. One example was a young woman whose last day was Friday because of having been surplused due to a union bumping situation. She talked to the supervisor about the management presentation that was scheduled for the following week. He was surprised and pleased, but worried about her desire to take part. Despite his efforts to discourage her, she showed up and was allowed to do a portion of the presentation. It is common for members, as well as leaders, to come in from a vacation, on their own time and without pay, to participate in a management presentation.

Other Forms of Reward and Recognition

Here is a partial list of some of the recognition techniques employed:

* Articles in the company newspaper

* Articles in the community newspaper

* Photos of participating members on bulletin boards

* Stories in the Quality Circle newsletter

* Activity reports

* Intra-Circle visits

* Visits by guests

* Member attendance at seminars

* Member attendance at conferences

* Attendance at in-house conferences

* Membership in the International Association of Quality Circles

MEMBERS SELECT PROBLEMS IN THEIR AREAS OF EXPERTISE

The Circle that selects problems from its own area of expertise has a much higher probability of success. In their own area, the members are the experts. They know the job better than anyone else. If they stay in this area of greatest expertise, they will have a much greater chance of success. Once they decide that they are going to solve problems in someone else's area, they are likely to run into difficulties with which they cannot cope. Usually, the only thing that will extricate them at that point is for management to step in and solve the problem for them. But that's not what Quality Circles are for. Quality Circles are designed to have people who are the experts in a given area solve the problems that most of the others in the organization are not aware of, or feel that they don't have the time or inclination to become involved with. Why does one go to an expert instead of just anybody? For example, we go to a dentist when we have a toothache, not to a physician. The reason is obvious. We know that we are going to get the best results when we deal with the person who is an expert in a certain area. It is the same in solving office or production problems. We must go to the area where the expertise exists. Circle members who remember that they should solve the problems in their own areas will get the best results.

CIRCLES SOLVE PROBLEMS, NOT JUST IDENTIFY THEM

This has been discussed in other parts of this book; but it is important enough for further emphasis.

Most working people have become accustomed to the idea that they will occasionally identify problems in their own working areas, but that the solutions to them are someone else's responsibility.

It is possible for a Circle to perpetuate this type of thinking, if members fall into the trap of expecting the organization's experts to solve the problems they identify. It is important that as much emphasis be placed on finding solutions as on discovering problems.

Select Easy Problems To Start With

A new Circle should be advised to select problems that are relatively simple, so that it can solve them with a minimum amount of frustration and get a quick victory under its belt. Nothing will build enthusiasm as fast as having successfully solved a problem. Once actual experience has been gained in using the problem-solving techniques successfully, the Circle can move on to more difficult assignments.

SELLING THE CONCEPT

DOING THE RESEARCH

"Do your homework!" One must know the product to be effective in selling others on its merits. This information can be gathered in a variety of ways.

Magazine And Newspaper Articles

Almost non-existant during the late 1970's, the media has now seized upon this new phenomenon. The Wall Street Journal, Time, Newsweek, and a host of other notable journals have discussed Quality Circles.

Conferences

The International Association of Quality Circles (IAQC) devotes its entire conference to Quality Circle papers presented by organization executives, facilitators, leaders, and members.

The American Society for Quality Control (ASQC) was the pioneer in promoting Quality Circles in the U.S. Its national, regional, and sectional conferences have included Quality Circle papers even during the early 1970's.

The American Institute of Industrial Engineers (AIIE), recognizing the productivity potential of Quality Circles, regularly includes papers on the subject at its many conferences.

The American Society For Performance Improvement (ASPI) sponsored the first of several Quality Circle papers at its annual conference in 1975.

The American Society for Training and Development (ASTD), a natural for a subject such as Quality Circles, is also involved and becoming more so.

These, and a growing number of other professional societies are joining in bringing their members to an awareness of a concept that brings many benefits with it.

Conference Transactions

Personal attendance at conferences is desirable, but certainly not always possible. The organizations cited in the preceding paragraphs bind together in book form all of the papers presented at each of their conferences. These transactions books can be purchased at nominal prices. Addresses of such organizations can be obtained from the local library.

Books

Other than books published by Quality Circle Institute, P.O. Box Q, Red Bluff, California 96080, U.S.A., there are few available at this time unless one is willing to also contract for consulting services.

Seminars

The perfect seminar at this early stage is the introductory one that provides an overview of Quality Circles. It is ideal for the busy execu-

tive, or the person who wants to learn enough to
be able to make intelligent decisions about the
subject. Usually presented during a one-day
program, it is occasionally enlarged to a two-day
session. If the intent is to provide an overview,
it is the author's firm belief that the one-day
seminar is entirely adequate.

RESEARCH OTHER COMPANIES

What Companies Are Doing It?

Information concerning what organizations
have Quality Circles can be obtained from the
Quality Circle Institute (QCI) or the International Association of Quality Circles (IAQC).
These lists usually contain the name of a contact
and a telephone number. The search should be
directed toward particular categories, such
as: area, type of product or service, organization
size, etc.

Telephone

An enormously cost-effective way to proceed
with the research is to talk directly with the
contact at each of the several organizations.
That person is typically the facilitator. Not
only can a great deal of information be transferred via the telephone, but written material
is often volunteered by the organization with
operating Quality Circles. An invitation to visit
might be forthcoming, too.

Written Materials

Every organization with Quality Circles
accumulates some general data that it might be
willing to share. With luck, one might even be
able to obtain information useful for training
purposes. The most useful information is any data
describing results. This is the most important

factor when one is trying to sell others on the merits of Quality Circles.

Visits

Seeing is believing! If possible, one should "go where the action is" to gain a full appreciation of Quality Circles. Visits are not easy to arrange. Many organizations that are amenable to receiving telephone inquiries will not extend that courtesy to allow visits. For some, it is for proprietary considerations. For others, visits are simply too time consuming.

WRITE A REPORT

Putting one's knowledge, evaluations, and proposals on paper is a time consuming task. But, experience indicates that it pays off handsomely.

Management's Language Should Be Used

The person who does his or her homework, and uses proven presentation techniques that management understands, is the one who is likely to get the approval he or she seeks. What are those presentation techniques? Business leaders respond favorably to "the five principles of good management," because they have become familiar with them through frequent use. These are: (1) setting objectives, (2) planning, (3) organization, (4) directing, and (5) controlling.

The proposal structured in such a format will stand out and should receive the consideration desired.

Advantages Should Be Highlighted

Members should be instructed to "talk the other person's language." That's good advice.

What interests most managers? The answer comes
back, "quality, productivity, and motivation."
Look for ways to express how these concerns can be
responded to in a positive way. Rest assured, few
managers will be moved by statements like:
"We should do this to make our people happier,"
or, "It is the human thing to do." It is essential to translate into dollars how items like
fewer errors, increased production, reduced
turnover, etc., are going to effect the organization.   This might be the right time to briefly
review some of these benefits:

What are the objectives of Quality Circles?

*   Reduce errors and enhance quality

*   Inspire more effective teamwork

*   Promote job involvement

*   Increase employee motivation

*   Create a problem-solving capability

*   Build an attitude of "problem prevention"

*   Improve company communications

*   Develop harmonious manager/worker relation-
     ships

*   Promote personal and leadership development

*   Develop a greater safety awareness

It Should Be Made In The Form Of A Proposal

Simply writing a report is not enough. The
extra steps should be taken to make it a proposal
complete with milestones. That's the general

equivalent of the salesman asking for the order. Those who receive copies of such a report/proposal will clearly understand that more is being asked for than a brief note with something like, "Nice report, Jones." It calls for further discussion, and moves the entire issue closer to the action stage.

THE SELLING JOB

Selling an idea can sometimes be difficult. It may be time consuming. It is not likely to happen overnight.

Resistance To Change

People tend to fear change. It implies that established patterns will be altered; and that often signals a threat to their security. "Does this mean someone is saying I haven't been doing my job?" Or, "Will I be thought less of because I didn't think of it myself?"

History is replete with examples of how change was resisted. When the steam-powered railroad train was first proposed, opponents objected on the grounds that speeds in excess of 30 miles per hour (48 kilometers per hour) would cause nose bleeds! This always seems to be the case. Vehement opposition occurred when dynamite, electricity, automobiles, airplanes, and lazer beams were proposed.

The point is, change is a fact of life. Change does bring progress in the form of new processes, technology, and ideas. One should not fight change--rather, it should be used to effect gains.

One should strive to be part of the answer, not part of the problem.

Incubation

The author consistantly hears, "I can't understand why no one feels as I do. I'm not making any progress." This is followed by, "Can you give me some ideas on how to sell Quality Circles in my organization?" The advice given always contains the admonition to be patient. Change usually takes time. There is an incubation period. After the first exposure it may take months. In one company the president told how it took him two years to turn attitudes around. He entered what he described as a "troubled" firm as its new chief executive officer. He made progress; but it was a combination of planting new ways of thinking and allowing them to incubate.

Another example was cited by a man attending a one-day public orientation seminar given by the author. "I told the boss about Quality Circles eight months ago. I felt he hardly heard me. Two weeks ago, while in his office, he shoved a seminar advertisement over to me and said, 'I've been reading about a thing called 'Quality Circles.' Why don't you go to this seminar and find out what it's all about.'" The man telling the story was stunned; but he realized his boss was serious. He decided that it was prudent, at that point, to remain silent. He realized that there had been an incubation period; and the seed that he had planted had slowly blossomed.

Enthusiasm

Enthusiasm is a trait common to successful people. It is like a smile--very contagious! One's audience is not going to be enthusiastic unless it clearly senses it in the speaker. If it does--watch out! So, when one feels enthusiasm; let it show; let it glow!

Management's Involvement Is Essential

The Quality Circle idea should not be presented as something that must be done 100% by the
book. There are plenty of variations in use.
True, they are not major ones; but the Quality
Circle philosophy is flexible enough to be accom-
modating.

The involvement of management and other
personnel is vital; and one sure way to get it is
to ask for their advice, and their suggestions
on how to customize Quality Circles to make them
work better in their organizations.

Involvement will come from management's
participation as members of the steering committee. It will also come when Circles in the
manager's organization make management presentations to them. The manager may also have the
opportunity for involvement by exercising influence in the selection of part-time facilitators
for his organization.

Differences From Other "Programs" Should Be Emphasized

Ability to sell others on the advantages
of Quality Circles requires that one be in a
position to respond to questions like, "Is it any
different than the TEAM program we had five years
ago?" The summary of differences listed below
will help the facilitator to supply a proper
response.

The features that make Quality Circles
different from other "programs" should be pointed
out by the facilitator, whether or not he or
she is asked about them.

How Quality Circles is different:

* Problems selected from area of Circles' expertise

* Members select the problem or project

* Members analyze the problem or project

* Quality Circles has its own "Board of Directors" of management personnel

* The Circle uses the management presentation to communicate

* A trained facilitator coordinates all Circle activities

* Leaders receive training in problem analysis

* Leaders train members in problem analysis

* Participation is voluntary

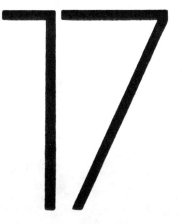

IMPLEMENTATION TIMETABLE GUIDELINE

One question that is often asked is, "After we decide we <u>are</u> going to implement Quality Circles, how long does it take to get the activity going?"

The following implementation timetable is intended as a guide to help answer that question.

It is broken into four phases. In each instance the action item is indicated and the time requirement stated. The time spans appear to be tight. However, the author has observed instances where progress is faster than that shown in the guidelines.

Phases 1 and 2 are based on the assumption that the services of a qualified Quality Circle consultant will be obtained. However, there is an alternative in which the facilitator completes an outside training course, after which he or she can then implement the program. Obviously, Phase 1 must be appropriately modified if a consultant is not used. Although it raises the cost, a consultant is sometimes brought in to assist with some portion(s) of the implementation prior to, or during, Phase 1.

PHASE I - PRE-TRAINING ACTIONS

Action	By Whom	Approx. Working Days
Decision to start	Top Level Executive	0
Contact consultant: Arrange for training materials to be sent as soon as possible:. Ask that preliminary data be rushed immediately:	Assigned individual	1

- *Familiarization A-V slide package

- *Preliminary instructions for forming the Steering Committee

- *Instructions to Steering Committee for selecting the facilitator

- *Suggested press release to be used for company newspaper to notify company personnel of up-coming Quality Circle activity

- *General orientation literature for dissemination to management and staff personnel

Main Order of Training Materials to Arrive Later

- *Quality Circle A-V Training Modules

- *Manuals for facilitator, leaders and members

Receive and review preliminary data from consultant.	*Assigned individual*	*5*
Initiate Steering Committee	*Assigned individual*	*8*
Steering Committee selects facilitator	*Steering Committee*	*18*
Finalization of Circle	*Steering Committee*	*20*
Develop the implementation plan by utilizing inputs from various sources. This step includes completion of a proposed policy/ procedure:	*Steering Committee*	*20*

> **Develop alternative courses of action*
>
> **Identify the negative conse- quences of each course of action*
>
> **Finalize the implementation plan*
>
> **Develop sequence and timing of major milestones*

The implementation plan also includes necessary funding arrangements.

Collect pre-implementation measurement data so as to later demonstrate a before and after comparison. Especially important for data not maintained in historical files such as "attitudes."	*Facilitator*	*22*

Conduct familiarization sessions among management personnel and union officials. Obtain commitments from managers who will initiate one or more pilot Circles. (This activity usually commences shortly after facilitator selection).	Facilitator	27
Distribute Quality Circle literature to pilot department managers.	Facilitator	28
Pilot department managers and supervisors read the Quality Circle literature and prepare a list of questions.	Facilitator & Pilot Department Managers	29
Pilot department managers meet with Steering Committee to discuss the questions raised in the preceeding action item.	Steering Committee & Pilot Department Managers	29
Select pilot program Circle leaders from interested supervisory volunteers.	Pilot Department Managers	29
Steering Committee meet with pilot program department managers and leaders for a question and answer session. Facilitator will distribute manuals to leaders for familiarization prior to start of consultant training.	Steering Committee Pilot Managers and Leaders	30
Publish information on the upcoming Quality Circle pilot program for release to all employees. This is done through the organization newspaper, handouts, letters, or via bulletin boards.	Steering Committee	30

Phase 2 involves a four-day implementation schedule which the author has frequently used. However, on many occasions, a schedule is custom designed to fit a particular organization's unique requirements. The schedule in Phase 2 can be expanded; but it should not be shortened. Different consultants may introduce what they consider to be helpful variations.

PHASE 2--CONSULTANT TRAINING AGENDA FOR FACILITATOR(S) AND LEADERS PLUS MEETINGS WITH STEERING COMMITTEE

The primary purpose of this training is to aid an organization in the development of its Quality Circle (Q-C) activities. This is accomplished by preparing the facilitators and steering committee to do so.

The facilitator learns basic Q-C philosophy, implementation, and operation. At the successful completion of the course, the facilitator will be qualified to provide the required training for Circle leaders.

(The initial slate of leader candidates-- usually 5--receives their Q-C training in this class along with the facilitator(s). The consultant also works with management personnel who comprise the Q-C steering committee during this time.

Training room preparations: Arrange for a 35mm slide projector and screen, cassette tape player, blackboard, and flip chart. Have all training materials on hand. Use name cards for facilitators, leaders, steering committee members, and observers.

As stated earlier, this is a four-day schedule. The actual schedule should be specially tailored to fit the particular needs of the organization, and might be longer than that.

AGENDA
QUALITY CIRCLE (Q-C)
INITIAL TRAINING COURSE
FOR
FACILITATOR(S) AND LEADERS

1st Day:

8:30 AM   Consultant meets with facili-
            tator(s) and leaders to
            distribute manuals.
9:00   Quality Circles--An overview

             What is it?
             Objectives
             History
(until   *How it operates*
noon)   *Elements for success*
             Organization
              --Steering committee
              --Facilitator
              --Circle leader
             Implementation
             Training
             Results from other organizations

            Note: Steering committee mem-
            bers and other management
            personnel should be encouraged
            to attend the morning session,
            at least. Steering committee
            members should attend the en-
            tire four days, if possible.

10:15   BREAK
10:30   Continuation
12:00   LUNCH
1:00 PM   Workshop on organization,
            training, implementation, and
            operation of Quality Circles in
            your operation.
2:15   BREAK

2:30	Continuation of workshop
3:00	Consultant meets with facilita-tor(s) and leaders. Gives teaching assignments for Quality Circle techniques.
4:00	Consultant meets with steering committee.
5:00	ADJOURN

2nd Day:

8:30 AM	Facilitator(s) and leaders pre-pare for their upcoming Quality Circle presentations.
9:00	Consultant presents Quality Circle (Q-C) technique, "Case Study & Problem Prevention Techniques".
10:00	BREAK
10:15	Motivation
11:00	Q-C technique, "Brainstorming"
12:00	LUNCH
1:00 PM	Q-C technique, "Data Collection Techniques".
1:45	Communication
2:30	BREAK
2:45	Q-C technique, "Data Collection Formats Plus Graphs".
3:30	Q-C Themes — examples
4:00	Demonstration of C-&-E Analysis
4:30	Question and Answer
5:00	ADJOURN

3rd Day:

8:30 AM	Using schedules and action logs to maximize results for a pro-ject.
9:00	Q-C technique, "Decision Analy-sis Using Pareto".
9:45	BREAK

10:00	Q-C technique, "Basic C-&-E Problem Analysis".
12:00	LUNCH
1:00	Potential Problems
1:45	Measurement techniques
2:15	BREAK
2:30	Q-C technique, "Process C-&-E Problem Analysis".
3:30	Records to be maintained
4:00	Consultant meets with Steering Committee.
5:00	ADJOURN

4th Day:

8:30 AM	Q-C technique, "The Management Presentation."
9:15	Discussion: Starting Your Circle(s).
10:00	BREAK
10:15	Leader examination (facilitator(s) also take).
11:15	Score & critique of leader examination.
12:00	LUNCH
1:00 PM	Continue scoring & critique of leader examination.
2:15	BREAK (leaders adjourn)
2:30	Facilitator examination.
3:30	Scoring and critique of facilitator examination.
5:00	ADJOURN

PHASE 3 - INITIATING CIRCLES

Action	By Whom	Approx. Working Days After Training
Review policy/procedure and implementation plan and revise per recommendations from consultant	Steering Committee	1
Department managers conduct Quality Circle (Q-C) familiarization meetings with employees. Facilitator, Circle leaders, and (ideally) an executive, participate as speakers. Employees are advised they will be contacted later for a decision.	Managers	2
Leader contacts each employee to determine Circle membership.	Leader	4
Distribute member manuals to Circle leaders.	Facilitator	4
Leaders commence weekly Circle meetings and initiate member training.	Leader	5

PHASE 4 - CIRCLE OPERATION,
FOLLOW-UP, EVALUATION, AND EXPANSION

Action	Responsibility	Months after start-up of Circles
Circles conduct management presentations to make recommendations and/or present status.	Circles	As needed or at approx. 3 month intervals
Department manager arranges to attend all or part of each Circle's meetings at least once each month as an observor.	Manager	Monthly
Steering Committee finalize plans to effect increase in number of Circles.	Steering Committee	Approx. 3 months
Publicity in organization newspaper.	Steering Committee	On-going
Prepare report to Steering Committee on cost effectiveness of Circle activities.	Facilitator	Approx. 3 months

Meeting of leaders and their managers with Steering Committee. Discussion will include: *Attitudes of Circle members *Attitudes of non-members *Attitudes of all levels of management *Attitudes of Circle Leaders *Cooperativeness of staff specialists *Satisfaction regarding publicity *Rewards and recognition *Recommendation as to whether to extend the pilot program or to commence expansion.	As Listed	Approx. 3 months
Make revisions to policy/ procedure and implemen- tation program.	Steering Committee	Approx. 4 months
Make decision when numbers of Circles will be expanded.	Steering Committee	Approx. 4 months

SAMPLE FORMAT FOR A NEWS RELEASE
OR LETTER TO ALL EMPLOYEES

In the near future, you will begin to hear comments about Quality Circles; and I want to let you know what it's about.

A Quality Circle is a small group of people--anywhere from 3 to 15 at most--who voluntarily meet, on company time, to identify and analyze obstacles that make the job less enjoyable, reduce the quality, or raise the cost of our (product or services)--things that make a difference in how much we like our jobs, how well we satisfy our customers, and how we do against our competition.

Circle members receive special training that is very useful and effective for this kind of activity both on and off the job.

Quality Circles are already in action in such organizations as General Motors, Ford, Westinghouse, Singer, General Electric, Xerox, International Harvester, Hughes and Northrop. In fact, throughout the Western World, people at all levels, in companies of all sizes, are volunteering for Quality Circle activities in constantly increasing numbers.

We, in management, are fully aware that people--you--are our organization's most valuable resource; and we know how frustrating it can get sometimes when we just can't seem to pitch in and do what it takes to make our customers happy and keep the business coming our way.

Now we're taking a bold step. Quality Circles is the vehicle that will give all of us the opportunity to become as involved as we want to be.

We'll start with a small pilot phase in two weeks, with the Circle members selected strictly

at random.   What we learn will make the expansion
of the activity go more smoothly.   Then, in
approximately four months, it will begin growing
to include those of you who would like to start a
Circle in your own area.

   If you'd like to learn more about it, ask
your supervisor for a booklet that will answer
most of your questions.

POLICY & PROCEDURE
QUALITY CIRCLE ACTIVITIES

Most organizations elect to have a policy and procedure to formalize their Quality Circle activities.

The following is designed to serve as a guide to the development of a policies-&-procedures document specifically oriented to a particular organization.

POLICY AND PROCEDURE

PURPOSE AND SCOPE

To establish policies and procedures for operating Quality Circle activities. This document addresses itself to:

* Definition
* Objectives
* Organization
* Policy

DEFINITION

A Quality Circle is a group of employees, performing similar work, who meet regularly to learn about and apply basic Quality Circle techniques. They use these techniques to identify problems within their jurisdiction, analyze them, and recommend solutions to management. When possible, they will initiate the necessary action to implement the solution. Normally, circles will consist of from three to fifteen employees from the same work area.

OBJECTIVES

* Reduce errors and enhance quality

* Inspire more effective teamwork

* Promote job involvement

* Increase employee motivation

* Create a problem-solving capability

* Build an attitude of "problem prevention"

* Develop harmonious manager/worker relationships

* Promote personal and leadership development

* Develop a greater safety awareness

ORGANIZATION

4.1   A steering committee will be estab-
      lished and will consist of represen-
      tatives from major departments
      within the company.   Examples are:
      operations, quality, personnel, edu-
      cation and training, engineering,
      finance, marketing, and the union.
      The facilitator will be a member as
      well.   The steering committee will
      be presided over by a Chairman and
      decisions will be reached by demo-
      cratic process--one person, one vote.

      Steering committee members may not
      delegate others to attend meetings
      for them.

      The steering committee will meet
      monthly.

      More than half of the steering com-
      mittee members must be present to
      constitute a quorum.

      4.1.1   The primary functions of the
              steering committee will
              include:

          *   Declare specific objectives
              for Quality Circles, such
              as quality improvement, cost
              reduction, improved communi-
              cation, etc.

          *   Identify those items that do
              not fall within the charter
              of Quality Circles

* Develop an implementation plan & operational guidelines

* Control the rate of expansion

* Determine funding arrangements

* Select the facilitator

* Select Circle leaders

* Schedule orientation sessions throughout the organization

* Arrange for necessary training for facilitators and leaders

* Determine the frequency and duration of Circle meetings

* Determine whether Circle meetings will be during normal working hours or after hours on an overtime basis

* Provide publicity for Quality Circle activities

* Establish a broad base and encourage growth of Quality Circle activities to encompass all relevant areas of the organization

* Determine the tie-in, if any, with the organization's suggestion plan

* Provide guidelines for the measurement of the Quality Circle activities and monitor the cost effectiveness and progress

* Arrange, when and if necessary, for outside consulting assistance

4.2   Facilitators. The facilitator will be the individual responsible for coordinating and directing the Quality Circle activities within the organization.

The facilitator:

* Is selected by the steering committee

* Interfaces between Circles, staff organizations, and management

* Is a member of the steering committee

* Maintains appropriate records

* Executes steering committee policy

* Is responsible for providing training for new Circle leaders

4.3   Quality Circle leaders will provide leadership for the Circles, teach Circle members the Quality Circle techniques, and will be responsible for the operation of their respective Circles. The first Circle leader will normally be the supervisor in that area. The leader will provide guidance for Circle activities and assure proper communication with management through such means as minutes of Circle meetings, activity reports, and management presentations by the Circle.

POLICY

5.1   Employees will be allowed to volunteer to:

   5.1.1   Become members of Quality Circles in their areas. They will also be free to drop out if they wish

   5.1.2   Suggest problems to Circles as possibilities for analysis

5.2   Management will:

   5.2.1   Be enthusiastically supportive of Quality Circles by:

   *   Allowing Circles to meet during normal working hours. If meetings occur after hours, pay will be at overtime rates. Authorizing meetings for a maximum of one hour per week

* Encouraging formation of Circles as a way of life in the organization

* Placing a high priority on, and encouraging members to attend Circle meetings

* Allowing member(s) to attend the meetings of other Circles, when invited to work on joint projects

* Authorizing and encouraging Circle leader candidates to obtain leader training

* Providing adequate meeting areas, equipment, and supplies to assure effective meetings

* Authorizing selective leader/ member involvement at outside conferences

* Publicizing Circle activities and accomplishments

* Supporting Circle activities in speeches and presentations

* Including Circle activities as part of organizational goals

* Including Circle items in organizational activity reports

5.2.2   Be participative in Circle activities by:

* Respecting the autonomy of Circles

* Encouraging the management presentation as a vital and essential aspect of Quality Circle activities, providing communication, motivation, and recognition

* Responding expeditiously to Circle requests and recommendations. When impossible to comply, providing an explanation in detail

* Implementing approved Circle recommendations with a minimum of delay

5.2.3   Having the authority to promote and initiate management level Circles

5.2.4   Having the right and suggesting problems and projects to Circles, respecting the right of the Circles to make the final selections

5.2.5   Having the right and responsibility to verify the cost effectiveness of Circle recommendations

5.3   Circles will:

*   Direct their primary atten-
    tion to problems and projects
    under their control

*   Assure that each member has
    an equal voice: One person,
    one vote

*   Utilize the Quality Circle
    techniques   as   described   in
    their manuals

*   Set up schedules for meetings
    and   presentations   with   due
    consideration of known
    company workloads and
    commitments

*   Select and analyze any prob-
    lems or projects within the
    scope of the official objec-
    tives adopted by the steering
    committee and described
    within this document

5.4   Circles will not address
        subjects identified as being
        outside their charters.
        These are:

*   Wages and salaries

*   Benefits

*   Disciplinary policies

*   Employment policies

* Termination policies

* Grievances and other items covered under the collective bargaining agreement

* Designing new products

* Sales and marketing policies

* Personalities

5.5 Have the prerogative to accept or refuse problems or projects regardless of the source

5.6 Identify, analyze, and implement solution to problems. If management approval is necessary, the Circles will not proceed until it has been obtained

5.7 Conduct presentations to management regarding specific recommendations, accomplishments, and status

5.8 Attempt to improve communications, harmony, and involvement between all Circle members as well as between other employees

PROBLEMS THAT CIRCLES ENCOUNTER

<u>INTRODUCTION</u>

Whenever possible, one should learn from the experience of others. This chapter is designed to alert potential Quality Circle practitioners as to what problems they may encounter and how to minimize their effect.

<u>PROBLEMS AND HOW TO HANDLE THEM</u>

<u>Just "Another" Program</u>

<u>Situation</u>: Organizations that have initiated other worker-participation programs and allowed them to waste away can expect skepticism from management personnel and employees alike. They might actually resent "being used" one more time. "This isn't going to be one bit different than what happened to all the rest of them."

<u>Solution</u>: The organization should not wait for the subject to be brought up. The worst thing is that no one mentions it. That would be unfortunate because people absolutely do remember. It must be addressed. Carefully review the differences between Quality Circles and other participative activities. On the surface, Quality

Circles may appear to some to be quite similar; but a comparison chart found elsewhere in this book discloses that there are many differences. One should be willing to ask for suggestions from the skeptics that will help in averting another future failure.

"Management Pays No Attention To Our Ideas"

Situation: When employees are convinced that management doesn't listen, it usually means that previous programs have been in place before Quality Circles came along. Perhaps it may have been a suggestion program or a general call for ideas. Nevertheless, it probably resulted in only a few of these ideas being implemented. (If management was overwhelmed with ideas, it may have been nothing more than an inability to process and investigate suggestions fast enough.)

Solution: Point out that Circle members are not being asked to generate a list of problems they "turn over" to management. Yes, they will generate a list; but rather than turn it over to anyone, they will select the problems they wish to analyze first. Inform them that their recommendations will not be written on sheets of paper for the manager to read and hopefully understand. They will communicate them face-to-face in stand-up management presentations. Yes, management listens to Quality Circles. They should be told that, typically, well in excess of 80% of such recommendations are approved. Those that are not are always explained. Further, if they wish to pursue another alternative to the same problem, it is their prerogative to do so.

Selecting Problems Outside Of The Circles' Areas Of Expertise

Situation: Perhaps the number one pitfall to successful Quality Circle operations is the

selection of problems outside of the members'
areas of expertise. A new Circle completes
training in problem analysis and proceeds to
pick a problem in someone else's area. It is
like saying, "We have no problems in our area,
so we are going to straighten out the mess in
yours." Typically, that "other" organization
is resentful and uncooperative. They inform
the Circle, "You don't know what you are talking
about!" (They are probably right.) The Circle,
having made no progress, turns to management
for the kind of support that will "straighten
out those other people." Management cannot
become involved without conducting an investigation to be sure they are making the correct
decisions; and its usual response is, "We don't
have time to consider it at this time."

Solution: The solution to this is relatively
easy if the leader can provide guidance at two
crucial points during the identification and
selection of problems the Circles will work
on. The first point is when the Circle members
are about to begin brainstorming for a list of
problems they could consider. The leader cautions
them to identify problems within their own area--
where they are the experts. With those words of
advice, they will usually comply. Without them,
they do not. The second point is when the Circle
is selecting a problem from the list that has just
been brainstormed. The leader should repeat the
same advice given earlier.

Problems Too Difficult To Handle

Situation: Problems selected from outside a
Circle's area of expertise are always too complex.
Occasionally this applies to problems from within
its own area. The analysis may drag on and
on. The spirit of the Circle lags. One or
two members may dropout. Attendance at meetings
may fall off.

Solution: The facilitator may be able to assist in one or more of a variety of ways:

1.   Encouraging the Circle to call in an "expert" for temporary guidance

2.   Suggest a review of a training technique that has potential for use by the Circle at this time

3.   Ask the manager to request a management presentation for status only. This often stimulates the Circle back into action

"We Can't Start Circles Now--Meetings Will Hurt The Schedule"

Situation: This concern has been voiced by managers and supervisors to employees who want to start Circles. Facilitators will also hear excuses which, in reality, might be little more than delaying tactics or an attempt to avoid Circles altogether.

The prospect of eight to ten people sitting around for an hour can be a frightening one. The supervisor or manager can easily translate that into an added cost of two or three hundred dollars and missed schedules.

Solution: These managers or supervisors should be shown data on results that other Circles are getting. This will help demonstrate that Circle activities should be viewed as an investment, not as an added cost. Point out that no organization has ever relaxed its schedules to accommodate holding Circle meetings. Invite them to attend a Circle meeting or a management presentation, talk to a manager who has Circles, or speak with one or more Circle leaders about their feelings regarding this activity.

Too Much Publicity

Situation: Upcoming or very new Quality Circles are the most likely to suffer from too much publicity. It is not just the publicity, it is the kind of publicity. If it excites employees, there may be a greater demand to start Circles than can be properly handled.

Solution: Publicity should describe Circles in a factual, non-emotional manner. If this still results in excessive demand, let people know that expansion will follow and provide an estimate of when they will be able to have the opportunity to become involved.

Too Little Publicity

Situation: Too little or non-existant publicity may convince people that Quality Circle activities have little management support.

Solution: The facilitator should make contact with the editor of the organization's newspaper and make arrangements to furnish on-going press releases describing Quality Circle activities. The editor can suggest formats, types of photos desired, and approximate space allocations.

If the editor has priorities that place Quality Circle activities too low to receive space, an invitation to attend a steering committee session is likely to effect immediate remedial action.

Fear Of Interference From The Union

Situation: An organization is contemplating the implementation of Quality Circles, but fears interference from the union.

Solution: Unions are rarely an obstacle in any way. When they have expressed concern, it is because they think Quality Circles might take up issues such: as wage levels, personnel matters, and grievances, which are normally prerogatives of the union.

The union president should be invited to take a seat on the steering committee. Point out that union stewards will be members of Circles. Assure them that they are part of the Quality Circles; which properly nurtured, will make for a more competitive organization that will provide greater job security for all.

Union officials like to be informed prior to initiation of Circle activities in an organization.   It is embarrassing for them to have members asking for information on Quality Circles which they are not able to provide.   They also like to hear assurances that it is not a speedup technique.

Potential Conflict Between Quality Circles And The Suggestion Program

Situation: An organization has a suggestion plan. The manager of the suggestion program sees Quality Circles as a competitive threat--an invader!

Solution: Start by inviting the manager of the suggestion program to be on the Quality Circle steering committee. Try to develop a plan whereby Circle suggestions are routed through the suggestion program. It will make the suggestion program better than ever. One company did this, and the number of suggestions doubled! Circle ideas can be evaluated by the suggestion program's cost evaluation committee for their dollar impact. Thus, both win. There is no need for conflict. The suggestion program should not be cancelled. When that occurs, it raises a question, "How long before Quality Circles gets the same treatment?"

Quality Circles and suggestion programs are quite compatible.

Excessive Concern For A Quick Financial Return

Situation: The Circle program is on trial. Anticipation is running high to achieve a quick financial return.   Supervisors are reluctant to start Circles because of the danger they may fall short of expectations.

In actual fact, Circles may produce rapid break-even results. It normally occurs early in the first year of operation; but, it is not a certainty.

Solution: The facilitator should caution against expectations of quick financial gains.   The long range benefits are where the real advantages lie. Nor is people building a short range activity. It, too, is a long-term effort.

The manager who demands a fast return would have greater likelihood of success by discharging some employees. That would do it faster and help realize short range savings; but it does not assure anything of a permanent nature. We have employed such techniques for generations; and the evidence says they are grossly inadequate--that the real solution is a long range investment and commitment in people.

Lack Of Management Support

Situation: Only a few people in management support Quality Circles. The real support might exist in, say, the quality control area, but not elsewhere.   Or, the company president wants it; but he is all alone.

Solution: If either situation exists, it is preferable to hold off starting until the three following factors are in place:

1.   Support exists as high as possible. (e.g., president, plant manager, and/or chief executive officer.)

2.   Support exists in the organization that Circle members will come from.

3.   That there is depth of management support. That is, many people in management, and at various levels, are supportive.

This subject is too important to be treated briefly. The reader should review the chapters on "Selling The Concept" and "Preparing For Expansion."

Circle Progress Is Too Slow

Situation: Circles are in place. Management is supportive. There is a facilitator. All the leaders have been trained in problem analysis techniques. Meetings are held regularly. But, the original enthusiasm has waned. Circle projects are not being completed. Thus, only an occasional management presentation takes place.

Solution: Everything seems to be in place. However, one or both of two shortcomings may be the source of the trouble:

1. Circles are bogging down because they are selecting problems outside of their areas of expertise. 2. Circle projects are not being scheduled. There are no objectives, no milestones, no feedback, and no charted visibility to reflect the status to all. There are sections in this book that address these problems in greater detail.

Circles Working On The Same Problem

Situation: Two or more Circles are working on the same problem. One may not know that the other is similarly engaged. Management fears either destructive competition or wasted duplication of effort.

Solution: The facilitator should inform a Circle that the project it wants to work on has already been selected by another group. Usually, a different project is quickly selected.

Occasionally, a Circle leader responds, "We know they are; but we disagree with their approach." That's fine. However, the facilitator can be helpful to both by making arrangements for a representative of one Circle to visit the other to report on what progress is occurring. These back-and-forth visits not only are informative, they save time for both. They also help to bring the Circles closer together so that recommended solutions are quite similar. Sometimes the recommended solution is the same. It may even be presented in a joint management presentation by both Circles.

Circle Problems Solved By Others

Situation: The Circle has selected the problem it wishes to work on. One of two things happens:

1. It calls in an "expert" from another organization; or, 2. That expert somehow becomes aware of what they're working on. In either case, he solves the problem for them. Perhaps he was intrigued with the problem and couldn't resist the temptation; or maybe he was concerned that the Circle would make him look bad if they solved it. Nevertheless, the Circle is resentful that the problem was snatched from them. They may even disagree with the way it was solved, thus lessening its likelihood of being successfully implemented.

Solution: The leader or facilitator should inform outside experts what a Quality Circle is

--that working together, the Circle will make them look better than ever, and vice-versa--and that it is important for Circle members to feel an ownership in the recommended solution to assure any long-lasting success for the project and the personal growth of Circle members.

Failure To Involve Other Organizations

Situation: An example can be used to illustrate what might happen.   A Circle confronted with excessive lost time maintains logs to gather the information needed to determine how serious it is.   Their research clearly demonstrates how antiquated the formal schedules are. Scheduling is performed by a production control organization. The Circle knows this, yet does not call them in to discuss the findings.   Rather, they go ahead with the management presentation.   An uproar ensues.   Production control is enraged at the embarrassment.   Industrial engineering is likewise embarrassed and upset; because they provided the standards to the production control schedulers. It is a classic case of win-lose with the Circle temporarily in the win position.   Also tragic is that the Circle knows better.   The members are well aware that scheduling is done by the production control people, and that they should have been involved.   Therein lies one of the dangers of worker participation.   That is, the Circle's tendency to be the giant killer in a David and Goliath encounter.   "This is our chance to really show the engineers that we can think, too."

Solution: The facilitator and leader must emphasize the importance of maintaining a win-win partnership with other organizations to insure a permanent healthy relationship. A code of conduct serves as a constant reminder of this. The Circle should have invited production control and industrial engineering to participate during the analysis.   Then, during the management presentation, it should have been made clear that the solution was arrived at with the aid of these other organizations. Management would have every reason to be even more confident in the recommendation. Not only does everyone win, but the groundwork for future positive dealings is solidified.

No Measurements Being Conducted

Situation: Nobody seems able to answer questions such as: "On the average, how many projects a year does the Circle do?" "What is the savings-to-cost ratio for all Circles?" "What is the before-and-after comparison on employee turnover?"

The inability to readily answer these key questions can logically lead to a decision to eliminate Quality Circles. "If anything worthwhile is happening, it would be known and quantified."

Solution: The answer is obvious. Maintain the records that will provide the answers. The steering committee should insist on this information. The facilitator can help the Circles maintain many of their own essential records. The facilitator will maintain other records, many of them summary-type data.

Cost and savings claims are most vulnerable to skepticism. This suspicion becomes greater when management knows that the numbers are being generated by the Circles. Savings claims should be as authentic as possible. Therefore, numbers should be verified by a group officially recognized as having the qualifications to do so.

Not Enough Facilitation

Situation: Some organizations wrongly assume that the facilitator is not really required, or that a part-time facilitator can service a large number

of Circles. A variety of symptoms will soon
appear. Examples include:

*   Meetings being cancelled

*   Poor attendance at meetings

*   Meetings starting late

*   Leaders not prepared for meetings (e.g. no
     agenda)

*   Member training sessions not occurring per
     plan

*   Circle projects too difficult

*   Circle projects out of the areas of expertise

*   Lack of objectives and schedules for Circle
     projects

*   Continual postponement of management presen-
     tations

*   No record keeping

Solutions: The leader needs to have someone to
turn to for occasional guidance.   "Every teacher
has a teacher." For example, musicians, even the
great ones, typically have someone under whom they
study.

     The point is, the facilitator should always
stay in touch, ready to assist. The "handholding"
and "crutching" will vary from minimal to substantial.   For some leaders, the gradual dimin-
ishment of assistance from the facilitator
is slow because it has to be.

     Quality Circles should not be launched
without the active involvement of a facilitator.

It should not be assumed that leaders can do it by themselves. They will eventually be able to do it to a considerable degree, but not immediately. It takes time, and it takes the understanding, and the helping hand of a facilitator.

Starting In A Problem Area

Situation: "Let's try it out in Jim's shop where all the problems are. He sure needs help. Even the engineers haven't made much progress out there! That way, we will find out if it really works before spreading it to others."

If Jim, the engineers, and their bosses have not been able to get things running smoothly, it is unfair and a mistake to expect the Circle to suddenly effect a cure-all. Usually, problem areas are behind schedule, and employees are on an overtime basis anyway. Thus, the chaotic conditions could make it difficult to provide time for Circle meetings.

Solution: Remember, the Circle works best when it picks problems from its own area, where it has control, where its members are the experts. These are often small and relatively unexciting problems.

Either keep expectations realistic or, start Circles where the ground is more fertile.

Resistance To New Ideas

Situation: Every time a new idea is put into effect, it is likely to encounter trouble and resistance--from people--the enemies of new ideas, innovations, and technology from within the organization itself. It can be expected to be the same for Quality Circles.

Solution: The test of leadership is to be able to put one's attention and effort to work and press

on with patience and fortitude. Results: cold,
hard results, will, in the long run, be the
biggest convincer of those who resist change.

Lack Of Adequate Training

Situation: Circle members may not be trained.
They may not be familiar with Quality Circle
techniques such as: the cause-and-effect diagram,
the Pareto diagram, etc. Their analysis of problems is poorly executed. Results are slow in
coming. Their enthusiasm fades and management
becomes disenchanted.

Solution: The battle of Quality Circles will
never be won without the tools and art to do the
job. Or, to quote, again, a statement attributed
to Dr. Ishikawa, "A ton of enthusiasm is useless
unless it is backed by an ounce of scientific
knowledge." Training must always be emphasized to
maintain the ability of the Circle to achieve. To
do otherwise is to run the risk of destroying its
momentum and having its progress stopped.

Disillusionment After The Excitement Of Start-Up

Situation: Eventually the initial burst of
enthusiasm may dampen due to the lack of innovative new ideas. "We've solved our problems; now
what?"

Solution: This does not need to happen. Improvement is like a bottomless well; that is, it
never ends.

There are three phases a Circle goes through:

1. The new Circle operates in a fire-fight-
    ing mode, identifying and eliminating
    the obvious problems in its own area

2. Working with other organizations that are
    giving them bad parts, for example, to
    identify and solve common problems

3. Developing a problem prevention consciousness. That is, preventing the
   problems from occuring in the first
   place

The problem prevention stage may not seem
very exciting but that is where most Circles in
Japan are operating. That is why companies in
Japan are able to boast extraordinarily high-yield
rates on their products. That is why Japanese
companies have minimal warranty costs on the
products they produce.

When a Circle reaches the third phase, it
is common for a Circle project to be described as
"Increase our yield rate from 80% to 84% during
the next six months." While Circle members are
pursuing ways to increase the yield, they are
encountering problems they were never aware
existed. In addition, they are developing a keen
quality consciousness.

Leader Resistance To Change

Situation: There have been instances where the
leader resists any effort on the part of Circle
members to introduce change. He or she even
objects to any problems being identified in his
or her area. An example is a leader who has been
in one job for a number of years and feels that he
or she would be looked down on if any problems
could possibly exist after all that time. Unless
something is done, the Circle members will
become disenchanted and start dropping out.

Solution: The facilitator, or the manager, to
whom the leader reports, should explain to that
leader that it is all right to have problems in
his or her area. It should also be pointed out
that Circle members are dropping out, because
nothing is happening.

If that fails, the facilitator should urge that leader to appoint an assistant Circle leader in the interest of developing and training a backup.   The assistant Circle leader should be given as much responsibility in running the Circle as possible. This may correct the leader's resistance to change.

A further step forward might come later, if the Circle is permitted to elect its leader.

If the supervisor who is serving as leader prefers to stay active, and is unable to relax his or her resistance to change, the manager should consider rotating him or her into another area. Perhaps two supervisors can simply exchange areas. Both will be in a new situation, and will not be likely to resist change.

Ineffective Steering Committee

Situation: The steering committee is finding that many of its members are failing to attend its meetings. It is as though they have dropped out. When they do attend, there is little involvement or enthusiasm on their parts; and they seem anxious to get the meetings over with and leave.

The number one reason for this kind of situation is a steering committee chairman who dominates the activity, and does not allow for participation or involvement on the part of the various members. The meetings have become a "one man or woman show" with the chairman as the central dominating figure. The chairman spends much of the time explaining to members what is happening and what is going to happen.

Solution: It may be difficult for the facilitator to approach the chairman and point out the errors

that are occurring. If it is a serious concern to
the facilitator, some other member of the steering
committee, who has a good working relationship
with the chairman, should be asked to have a talk
with him or her.

Other members of the steering committee,
particularly those who are having a poor attendance record, should be approached and asked
why. This information can also be fed back to the
chairman. Perhaps the meetings are too frequent.
In one company the steering committee members
complained because they were being asked to meet
on a twice-weekly basis. When the meeting frequency was reduced to once every two weeks,
attendance jumped markedly.

Involvement is just as important at the
steering committee level as it is at the member
level. The chairman plays a key role in assuring
that everyone gets an opportunity to be heard.
This should be extended to voting on different
motions that are made. Discussion prior to voting
should be encouraged.

Piece Rate Problems

Situation: Employees are on a piece rate.
Management is fretting about any success a Circle
in such an area can achieve. "Improvements might
mean cutting their rate. That guarantees no
improvements from such a Circle," is a fear
frequently expressed by management.

Solution: Employees on a piece rate are normally
criticized for a disregarding quality. "Getting
the work out is all they care about." Circles in
such areas tend to address quality problems. It
may have no effect on production or their incentive earnings. But, quality improvements raise
the production of usable output. Therefore,

quality goes up, productivity goes up, and eveyone
is happier. Further, one plant manager told
Circle leaders, "Encourage them to come up with
ways to boost their incentive pay. We are not
going to take anything away from them. They win,
but believe me, we win, too!"

Concerns Of Facilitator Candidates During Training

Potential problems will be viewed differently
depending upon the organization and special circumstances. The following ranking was compiled
by a group of 14 facilitator candidates from the
same organization. The reader should keep in
mind that the company's chairman of the board had
clearly and publicly stated his commitment to
Quality Circles. The rankings are from top to
bottom in degree of seriousness and were complied
at the conclusion of facilitator training.

ITEM	(%)

1. Lack of middle management
    support including refusal
    to implement Circle rec-
    comendations   79%

    Comment: Actually, well
    over 80% of Circle recom-
    mendations are accepted
    by management.

2. Lack of monetary rewards
    for Circles   56%

    Comment: Circles do not
    need monetary rewards to
    be successful. There are
    many factors of recognition,
    principally the management
    presentation.

3. Failure to keep records
    that prove the effective-
    ness of Quality Circles   56%

    Comment: This is poten-
    tially a serious problem
    when records are not
    maintained.

4. Competition of other new
    and existing programs   49%

    Comment: Quality Circles
    coexists beautifully with
    existing programs. In
    many instances they can
    be "married" together for
    maximum effectiveness.

5. Failure of the Circle to
    develop schedules for
    selected themes   42%

    Comment: Circles that do
    not develop schedules for
    their projects will typi-
    cally achieve less
    spectacular results.

6. Steering committee not
    assuming a leadership
    position   35%

    Comment: If the steering
    committee does not guide
    the program, then the
    facilitator will assume
    this responsibility. In
    fact, there will be a
    one man steering committee--
    the facilitator. It is
    counterproductive to put

this one individual in the
position of providing the
proper guidance for all
Quality Circle activities
in his or her organization.

7. Lack of volunteers to be-
    come Circle leaders   35%

    Comment: This will not
    be a problem in the ini-
    tial stages of Quality
    Circles. Nor will it be
    difficult to secure Circle
    leaders after it has been
    running for a time.
    Eventually, as more and
    more Circles are started,
    more people will volunteer
    to lead; however, some of
    the hard-core resisters
    may not change their minds.

8. Identifying problems out-
    side of the Circle's area
    of expertise   35%

    Comment: This is poten-
    tially a serious problem.
    Leaders and facilitators
    should be especially cog-
    nizant of the possibility
    that this can occur.

9. Problems related to three-
    shift operation   28%

    Comment: Usually this per-
    tains to how Circles can
    operate on a second and
    third shift without the
    help of a facilitator.

Actually, there can be
part-time facilitators
to take care of the
second and third shifts.
Sometimes a second shift
will hold its meeting
at the beginning of the
shift so that the daytime
facilitator can provide
the necessary guidance.
Likewise, the third shift
can often hold its meet-
ings at the end of its
shift for the same reason.

Another concern is where
there are not enough people
to justify starting a
Circle on the second shift
and another on the third
shift. This is often
solved by having the second
and third shifts join to-
gether in one Circle that
meet at the juncture of
their two shifts.

10. Work schedules preventing
     Circle meetings   28%

     Comment: Circles should
     get in the habit of hold-
     ing the meetings at the
     scheduled time. Even
     when it is impossible to
     conduct the entire meeting,
     it is valuable, for disci-
     pline purposes, to gather
     together for the meeting.
     The leader can simply
     announce that, because of
     work schedules, the meet-

ing is being postponed to
another time that will be
more convenient for all.

11. Failure of staff depart-
    ments to respond to re-
    quests for assistance   28%

    Comment: The facilitator
    may have to act as an
    intermediary to coordinate
    bringing in the necessary
    help from the staff de-
    partments. Often, little
    more than explaining
    Quality Circles to them
    and how they can maximize
    effectiveness to the bene-
    fit of the Circle, as well
    as themselves, is
    necessary.

12. Lack of communication and
    feedback to Circles   21%

    Comment: The communica-
    tion links can be main-
    tained by the facilitator's
    weekly activity report,
    the organization's news-
    paper accounts of Circle
    activities, and discus-
    sions at various levels.
    Feedback includes infor-
    mation as to how success-
    ful the Circles are being
    as they work toward goals
    that they established.
    Feedback also includes
    information to the Circles
    concerning progress being
    made on the implementa-

tion of ideas that they
recommended and that were
accepted.

13.   Lack of adequate meeting
       rooms   21%

       Comment: Although meet-
       ing rooms are usually
       available, there is noth-
       ing wrong with holding
       a Circle meeting in a lunch-
       room or in the corner of
       a cafeteria. In some
       areas where Quality Circles
       is extremely widespread,
       Circles meet in their work
       areas. For example, a table
       surrounded by lockers pro-
       vides suitable meeting
       quarters as long as the
       surrounding noise level is
       not excessive.

14.   Informal "leader" dominating
       the meetings   14%

       Comment: The facilitator
       should discuss this with
       the Circle leader. Per-
       haps the leader might
       want to accept this indi-
       vidual as an assistant circle
       leader. If so, it might be
       wise to schedule him or her
       through a leader training
       course. If the informal leader
       is unacceptable to the Circle
       leader as an assistant, there
       should be discussions outside
       of the meetings to bring the
       domineering aspects of be-
       havior under control.

15. Lack of cooperation from
    non-members   7%

    <u>Comment</u>: Usually not a
    problem. Non-members know
    that they can join if they
    wish. Although there may
    not be a Circle operating
    in every area, it is us-
    ually only a matter of
    time before the nonmember
    will be able to be ac-
    tively involved in a new
    or existing Circle.

16. Negative reaction of
    union   7%

    <u>Comment</u>: Negative re-
    action from the union is
    unusual. Simply assure the
    union that Circles do not
    get into issues covered by
    the union bargaining agree-
    ment with the company.

17. Lack of follow-up by Circles
    to insure proper implemen-
    tation of accepted ideas

    <u>Comment</u>: This can be a
    problem, but it will be
    minimal if the Circle
    leader and facilitator are
    aware of this potentiality
    and can take proper action
    to pursue the matter.

18. Failure of previous pro-
    grams

    <u>Comment</u>: Carefully dis-
    cuss the differences between

Quality Circles and the
previous programs that
failed. This normally clears
up concerns on this subject.

19. Impatience of members--
     things not moving fast
     enough   7%

     Comment: When this
     occurs it is usually
     because Circle members
     have selected projects
     outside their area of
     expertise or projects
     that are too complex.

20. Rejection of Circle
     ideas   7%

     Comment: More than 80%
     of Circle suggestions are
     accepted. If the manager
     must say, "No," it is essen-
     tial to supply the reason.
     If a clear communication
     has been maintained be-
     tween the Circle leader
     and the manager during
     the Circle's investiga-
     tion and analysis, it is
     less likely that progress
     would move toward a re-
     jection. That is, the
     manager would be able to
     explain the ripple effects
     that the recommendation would
     have on other organizations
     and why he might have to
     reject it.

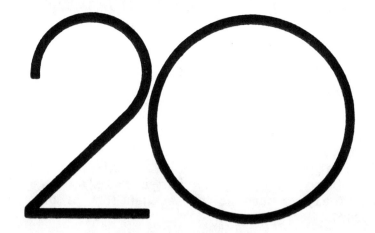

THE SUGGESTION SYSTEM
&
QUALITY CIRCLES

Many companies have an existing employee suggestion plan. It is in place to provide a communications link for ideas to get to management. In some respects there are similarities to Quality Circles. Management recognizes these similarities and raises the question, "How do we handle it?"

CAN THE SUGGESTION SYSTEM AND QUALITY CIRCLES SURVIVE SIDE-BY-SIDE?

The answer is yes. They will not only survive, but will quite likely thrive. There are a number of ways it is handled depending on the circumstances. Neither has to surrender to the other. Both can, and almost always do, retain their own separate identities. Yet there can be a marriage of sorts, if Circle ideas are routed through the suggestion system.

THE NON-PAYING SUGGESTION SYSTEM

A surprising number of companies have a suggestion system that pays no money for accepted ideas. In lieu of money, other forms of recognition are employed, such as a certificate, a

letter from a company executive, a plaque, a
dinner for two, or a photo in the organization's
newspaper.

There are few difficulties to be overcome
when Quality Circles is fused with an existing
nonpaying suggestion system. It is an over-simp-
lification, but a Circle recommendation that
has been accepted by the Circle's manager is
routinely processed by suggestion program personnel.

A shot-in-the-arm normally occurs when such a
fusion occurs. At one company, there was a
full-time suggestion program manager. No money
was given for ideas. When Quality Circles
was first suggested, he made it clear that he saw
no need--that it was unnecessary duplication. His
opposition ceased when it was proposed that,
during a five month pilot phase, accepted Circle
ideas would be routed through his suggestion
system. An amazing thing resulted. On a per-
capita basis, more than ten times as many accepted
Circle recommendations went through the suggestion
system than did suggestions originating from the
workforce as a whole. The suggestion system
indeed received a powerful shot-in-the-arm. The
appreciative suggestion systems manager designed a
Circle certificate of appreciation to award to
each Circle submitting a recommendation.

THE PAYING SUGGESTION SYSTEM

The "marriage" between Quality Circles and
the suggestion system becomes more difficult when
money is involved.

Members Share Equally

Equal distribution of money to all members of
the Circle is important. Under no circumstances

should it go to one person only. It is a team
effort all the way.

The equal distribution feature can be interesting when the total amount being distributed
is, say, $15.00. Divide that by ten members and
the amount is rather low--even embarrassingly
so! That was the problem faced by one company.
Their minimum award, frequently given, was
$15.00. They considered making the $15.00 award
to each member. Finally, they decided to split
that amount by the number of members.

An added complication is that taxes must be
withheld from each member's share.

Criteria For Dividing The Monetary Award

The amount of the award can also be quite
attractive. In some organizations it could run
into thousands of dollars. If $4,000.00 was
realized, for an example, an interesting situation
is likely to follow. That amount will have to
be equally divided. However, it may not be a
simple matter. For example, "Mary joined the
Circle only three weeks ago. Should we give her a
share, half a share, or none?" The same logic
could be applied to the following situation:

*   A member was transferred out of the Circle
     two weeks after the project was started

*   A member left the company altogether at some
     point in the analysis

*   The "expert" called in to assist briefly
     (Probably not eligible per company policy)

*   The Circle leader when he or she is the
     supervisor   (Probably not eligible per
     company policy)

*   Some assistance came from another Circle

Fear Of Idea Theft

One fear stands out among steering committee members--idea theft! What if one of
the Circle members picks up a good idea in a
Circle meeting, then secretly makes a deal with a
friend who is not in a Circle to submit it. The
goal is to covertly make a simple but relatively
attractive two-way split.

This fear is so strong that it has been
the reason why several companies have kept Circle
activities completely separate from their formal
suggestion systems!

The author certainly does not deny that
such idea theft could occur. However, he does not
know of instances where it has happened. The risk
is apparently quite low.

Staking A Claim To An Idea

Situation: The Circle selects a problem to
analyze. The facilitator informs the members that
an employee named John Smith, who is not a Circle
member, has also submitted it to the suggestion
system.

Who has the right to the idea? The Circle,
or employee John Smith?

Solution: This difficulty is easily resolved
ahead of time by establishing a policy   of
first come, first served. The minutes of the
Circle's meeting would indicate when the idea was
adopted.

Establishing A Moratorium

It is recommended practice that a moratorium
period be granted to the Circle so that no one

else can work on its idea for a fixed period of time, say, two months.

It should be possible for the Circle to extend the moratorium if the analysis is being actively pursued.

Circle In Co-Venture With An Employee

Situation: The Circle learns that the idea it wishes to pursue has already been submitted by an employee who is not a member of any Circle.

Solution: The Circle could simply drop it and move on to a different project. Or, the organizational policy could be constructed to permit the Circle to approach the employee and offer to join forces on a 50-50 basis for any reward that is received.

The employee would probably be wise to accept --the strength of the Circle's involvement would add significantly to the likelihood of the idea being perfected enough to win an award.

However, the employee could reject the alliance with the Circle. "I want it all. Why should I share with the Circle?" The Circle could decide to work on the idea anyway. However, they would know that there would be no potential for sharing in any reward.

Size Of Monetary Rewards

Already cited was the organization that had a minimum award of $15.00. Others fix the monetary reward as a percentage of the expected savings (almost always limited to 12 months). Usually that amount is either 5% or 10%. Often a ceiling is set to control the size of the reward. It varies from $500.00 to several thousand dollars.

Alternatives On Handling Monetary Awards

When the size of the monetary award is small, some Circles forego dividing it among the Circle members. Alternative ways it is handled include:

* Accumulate small awards into a fund and distribute at certain intervals, e.g. every six months

* Accumulate small awards into a fund and periodically sponsor a special function for the families of Circle members, e.g. a picnic

* Select a charity such as heart fund, cancer, crippled children, etc., and donate the award. This function is an enormously satisfying way for the members to dispose of such funds

An Example Of Monetary Rewards

A textile company in Mexico has both Quality Circle activities and a suggestion plan. They are tied together so that accepted Circle ideas are routed through the suggestion system. Members receive monetary rewards in an interesting and unusual way.

Every member of the Circle receives an award which is equal to approximately one half of one week's pay for each accepted recommendation, regardless of its value. In addition, each member shares equally in an award that equals 10% of the first month's saving.

Does it work? It certainly does! Savings-to-cost ratio is a spectacular thirteen to one.

CIRCLE IDEAS SHOULD NOT BE JUDGED BY SUGGESTION SYSTEM

It is recommended that Circle ideas not be judged by the suggestion system. The individual

best suited to decide if a Circle recommendation has merit is the manager of the department
involved. After the manager <u>accepts</u> it, the idea
is routed through the suggestion system for
determination of awards.

SEPARATING QUALITY CIRCLES & THE SUGGESTION SYSTEM

In organizations where Circle activities
are completely separate from a paying suggestion
system, it is normally due to an attempt to avoid
getting involved in some of the difficulties that
<u>might</u> be encountered when the two are fused
together.

"Can I Make More Money By Staying Out Of Circles?"

The employee might well ask such a question
when Circle ideas cannot be sent through a paying
suggestion system. If he or she comes up with a
good idea, it might pay a handsome reward if
routed through the suggestion system; however, no
rewards at all accrue for Circle suggestions.

Management personnel normally reports, "It
doesn't seem to make any difference. Most employees never seem to submit ideas to the suggestion system anyway. Some have been turned down
and won't try anymore."

RECOMMENDATION

The author does not believe in paying for
Circle suggestions if it is not currently being
done. If a paying suggestion system is operating,
then accepted Circle recommendations should be
routed through it. Monies received should be
equally divided by all Circle members.

MEASUREMENT TECHNIQUES

The introduction of Quality Circles into an organization is usually done on a pilot basis. During the pilot phase, it will be measured; and decisions made as to whether the results coming in are sufficient to warrant its continuation and expansion into other areas. The benefits of Quality Circles will be challenged by some. The only way that these challenges can be adequately handled is to have the kind of mesurement information that will show conclusively that the concept pays its way. A surprising number of new programs do not provide any measurements by which they can be evaluated. This is despite the fact that the proponents of almost every one of them claim they do. One reason why there is a reluctance is because of the cost factor. It costs money to conduct a measurement program. That's true; but it will probably cost the program if reliable measurement is not provided. Even though there are some costs involved, it is the author's opinion that these costs are cancelled out by the fact that information obtained through measurement techniques leads to better Circle performance. The second reason often stated for failure to measure is that it is too complicated. The difficulty in measuring Quality Circle activities is no more complicated than measuring any other kind of production or office activity.

Regardless of concerns expressed about measuring the concept, one can be certain that management will demand proof that Quality Circles are cost effective. Quality Circles do pay their way--in a most spectacular fashion that has been proven countless times. Measurements should be conducted so that an organization will have the information to enable it to make comparisons with other organizations. It should not be overlooked that Quality Circle members are just as anxious as management personnel to know the results of their endeavors. It becomes more than information gathering for the sake of knowing what is going on. More important, it provides the information that will allow Circle members to evaluate their achievements and to strive for even higher ones.

WAYS TO MEASURE

Much of the measurement of Quality Circles will be concentrated in three general categories. These are:

Quality improvement

Cost reduction

Attitude improvement

Who Can Help

There may be a lack of expertise on the part of the Quality Circle staff to properly initiate a measurement program. There are departments that can assist. Perhaps the most likely is industrial engineering. A second group is the finance organization. Both should be called in to help establish measurement procedures. Normally, measurement can be done without a continuing involvement on the part of outside organizations.

QUALITY IMPROVEMENT

The charge has often been levied that it is difficult or impossible to measure quality; but this is not true. Quality is measurable in many ways including the greatest common denominator of all: money!

There are a number of ways to measure levels of quality; and some are stated below:
* Yield rate (number of units reaching the end of the processing or assembly with no defects)
* Defects (errors)
* Repeated errors
* Rework costs
* Scrap levels
* Spoilage
* Defects per unit of work
* Shortages
* Delays due to errors
* Late deliveries
* Customer complaints
* Customer rejections
* Review board actions
* Repeated failures
* Design changes (sometimes due to quality problems)

Earlier, it was stated that some people claim quality improvements are difficult to measure; but the author pointed out that the use of money as the common denominator made measurement relatively easy. However, the measurement of quality defects has to be done with considerable care; because there are ways that the true level of defects can be obscured. As an example, it is well known that an inspector can find as many defects as he is determined to find. There is an additional concern in that many workers simply cover up errors they have made if they discover them themselves. This means the work was redone. It

means that additional costs were incurred. It
means that delays were involved. All of this
results in additional costs due to lower levels of
quality. Yet, nothing in the measurement of the
quantity of errors indicates that there was a
problem.

Examples Of Quality Improvement

1. Levels of lighting were increased at
    the request of a Quality Circle. Errors
    dropped 63%.

2. Two organizations within the same
    company, both doing similar work,
    tracked closely together in the number
    of workmanship errors made. One organi-
    zation installed Quality Circles, the
    other did not. Over the next 6 months,
    the organization having Quality Circles
    decreased its error rate 60%. The
    organization that elected not to put in
    Quality Circles encountered an increase
    of 25%.

3. A Circle, determined to maintain quality
    of service during its organization's
    move to another building, became heavily
    involved in planning details of the
    move. No time was lost. Telephone
    service was maintained without inter-
    ruption. This was significant because,
    at the same time, an almost identical
    organization in the same company also
    had to make the same move. Their
    Quality Circle was not involved in any
    way. Every one did exactly what they
    were told to do. The move had been
    organized and executed solely by the
    professionals normally charged with
    taking care of such matters. Many
    unanticipated problems arose causing the

department to be unavailable for service
or telephone communication for a period
of 3 days.

COST REDUCTION

Savings-To-Cost Ratio

If there is any common language in determining cost reductions, it is the savings-to-cost
ratio.   Most organizations with Quality Circle
activities include this as one of the key measures
of the success of their Quality Circles.

The chart on the following page shows how
the savings-to-cost data is normally charted.

Savings-to-cost ratios typically range from
a low of two to one up to ten to one, with the
average being approximately five to one.   Even
the company reporting the two to one ratio was
delighted with what their Quality Circle activities had brought to them.   There is a danger that
this ratio will be improperly calculated.   The
savings are normally understated.   As an example,
many of the savings that result from improvements
in the more difficult to measure areas, such as
attitude improvement and moral enhancement, are
ignored.   The reason for not including them is a
feeling on the part of the person doing the
measurement that it is impossible to establish a
dollar figure for this category.   In many instances, that is not a correct assumption.

Calculation Of Savings

Savings include everything that happens
regardless of whether it pertains to labor,
materials, or other factors.   Savings are generally projected for a maximum of 12 months into
the future.   An organization could decide to do it
for an entire contract, which might extend over a

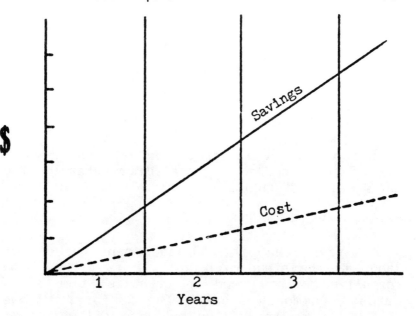

period of years. This would certainly increase the amount of the savings. However, it could be argued that most savings would not truly endure to the end of the contract. Probably something would occur during that time which would have not allowed the full potential of the savings to occur. By limiting it to 12 months into the future, an organization is staying in line with almost all others. Also, it makes claims for savings much more reasonable and conservative. Thus, management will find the numbers much more acceptable.

Cost

Cost will include everything that is related to the savings that have been claimed by the Circle. The greatest portion of the cost will be the amount of time spent by the Circle holding meetings. This is true regardless of whether the meetings were held during their normal working hours, or afterwards on an overtime basis. There

is also a much smaller amount to be considered to
cover the cost of the facilitator's time.   One
more cost that has to be considered for some of
the Circle projects is the cost of implementation.
While Circles generally are dealing with the
smaller, seemingly less significant problems,
they nevertheless still exert a tremendous amount
of ingenuity and conservation in selecting the
solution they will recommend to management.
All of these costs are totaled to determine the
savings-to-cost ratio.

Standard Hours

A favorite unit of measurement for direct
labor is the standard hour.   It is set by some
formalized method used to establish time standards.   Commonly used in the factory, it has
little use in the office setting at the present
time.   That is not to say it is unsuitable for
office application.   It simply means that relatively few organizations employ it.

This measure is not widely used for Quality
Circle activities.   Nevertheless, it remains as
one tool that can be employed.

The Learning Curve

There is a story about an aircraft executive
who accidently met an executive of a washing
machine company during a luncheon.   The conversation turned to manufacturing costs.   The appliance
executive commented that it took them at least a
year to determine the cost of a particular washing
machine model being manufactured.

The aircraft executive was surprised, and
explained that using the learning curve, he
could--in a matter of minutes--come within plus or
minus 10% of the actual cost.

A bet was made, with the lunch bill being the wager. The only information furnished to the aircraft executive was the cost of the first unit. For a few minutes, the aircraft executive worked with his pocket calculator. Then he announced, "Your 10,000th unit will cost you $116.75."

"Just drop the $.75," said the amazed appliance executive as he reached for the bill. "It actually cost us $116."

Theory Of The Learning Curve

This theory is really quite simple. A person learns as work is done. The more a certain operation is repeated the more efficient one becomes; therefore, the time required to produce each additional unit declines.

These facts have been long recognized. What was not known until recent years was that the rate of improvement remains regular enough to be predictable. Production tends to improve by a constant percentage each time production is doubled.

The learning curve applies to all products even though it originated in the airplane industry. Let's take an example of the typical learning curve for aircraft manufacturers. Their learning curve typically runs around 80%. Let's suppose that it takes 100,000 man-hours to build the first unit. If production follows strictly the 80% improvement curve, the second unit will take only 80,000 man-hours. Production has doubled; thus, the second airplane takes only 80% as much time to build.

At this point two airplanes have been built. It is necessary to look forward to the next time

production doubles. That will occur at the fourth
unit. The fourth unit should be built in 80% of
the time it took to build the second unit. That
would amount to 64,000 man-hours. This would be
continued as shown in the following table:

Unit	Man-Hours
1	100,000
2	80,000
4	64,000
8	51,200
16	40,960

and so on.

This may appear to be almost too mathematically precise to be true. Nevertheless, actual
experience and the study of production figures
demonstrate quite conclusively that trends of this
nature are found everywhere. Several organizations have reported that the learning curve has
dropped from, say, an 83% to a 78% curve during
the course of a contract. Although this does not
seem very dramatic, a change such as this over a
period of time can represent as much as a 50% drop
in the cost of completing a contract!

ATTITUDE IMPROVEMENTS

Quality Circles are supposed to affect
attitutes; but the question is how to measure
them. A remarkable number of people are thrown
into confusion about how they can possibly accomplish this. It's easy to say you have motivated
people through an involvement in worker-participation activities. It is much more difficult to
prove; However, there are ways to determine
employee attitudes. The following indicators are
examples of how this can be done in an indirect
fashion.

Absent Employees

A high rate of absenteeism generally reflects poor employee attitudes. Measures should be taken prior to the start of Circle activities and during them. Organizations have reported dramatic increases in the level of attendance after the implementation of Quality Circles.

Measurements taken prior to the start of Circle activities should be taken enough in advance so that the results are less likely to be distorted. This applies in the case of most measures that reflect attitudes. It is also applicable when taking attitude surveys. This will be discussed in the following section.

Tardy Employees

Those who fail to come to work on time may be reflecting a less than favorable atmosphere in the organization. This information is easily obtainable and should be charted also. One company using Quality Circles reported that the tardy rate was less than half of that of employees who were not in Quality Circles.

Grievances

The number of grievances in a given organization can be expected to fall off sharply as a result of the Circle activities. Being involved relieves much of the frustration that exists on many jobs. One organization reports that the number of grievances dropped to one-third of their previous level after Quality Circles were initiated. Another organization reported that a much healthier relationship developed between it and the union--one that was conducive to helping the organization into a better competitive position for the good of all.

Turnover

The average corporation in the United States has an incredibly high turnover rate of 25% per year! When one considers that the cost of each person who leaves an organization is at least $4,000 (this includes the cost of recruiting, training, and bringing the person up to full productive capacity), the overall cost is enormous. Yet, few organizations even consider this when evaluating their Quality Circle activities. Those that have, report substantial declines in levels of turnover.

ATTITUDE QUESTIONNAIRE

How an employee views such things as the supervisor, the organization, the manager, communications, the job, and the Circle can be important clues as to attitudes.

The following questionnaire is designed to measure employee attitudes.

EMPLOYEE ATTITUDE QUESTIONNAIRE

Please place a check mark (✓) in the column that most closely reflects how you feel.

	Definitely Disagree	Inclined to Disagree	Inclined to Agree	Definitely Agree
1. We can get into trouble by occasionally deviating from standard prescribed practices.				
2. Management is flexible enough that innovations are encouraged and will receive consideration.				
3. Our organization has a reputation for high standards.				
4. Our organization trusts individual judgment to the point that only rarely is one's work really checked.				
5. Employees take pride in being a member of this organization.				
6. Our organization subscribes to the philosophy of striving for constant improvement.				
7. Management does a good job of providing recognition for good work.				
8. Employees in our organization trust each other.				
9. We are a well-organized group around here.				

	Definitely Disagree	Inclined to Disagree	Inclined to Agree	Definitely Agree
10. In our organization employees take pride in turning out good work.				
11. Management does not expect you to check everything with them. If you clearly know what to do, you can move right ahead.				
12. Our promotion policies are designed to move the best people up. There are no favorites.				
13. Personnel in our organization are generally pleasant and friendly.				
14. Our quality and productivity rarely suffer because of poor planning and organization.				
15. In our organization, management sets challenging goals for us.				
16. In our organization, a person can occasionally "take the initiative" without getting into trouble.				
17. Management rewards us fairly according to the excellence of our job performance.				
18. Our organization is efficient and well managed.				

	Definitely Disagree	Inclined to Disagree	Inclined to Agree	Definitely Agree
19. Our organization is expanding because we are not afraid to take appropriate risks when the situation calls for it.				
20. The rewards and encouragement we get are normally greater than the threats and criticism.				
21. Management has a very close relationship with this organization's personnel.				
22. It is clear that management is anxious to improve performance in this organization.				
23. Policies and procedures are followed only when essential.				
24. There appears to be considerable loyalty toward the organization.				
25. In our organization there isn't much criticism.				

How to Administer

Locate a quiet room free from distractions. Explain to the employees that they have been randomly selected to fill out a brief questionnaire as a guide to management. Request employees to refrain from talking to each other and to be perfectly candid in their answers. Assure them

that it is not necessary to sign the questionnaires.

Allow 10 minutes to complete these questionnaires.

Timing

This questionnaire must be administered
sufficently ahead of time, or ahead of the an-
nouncement of Quality Circle implementation, so
that the results will not be affected by the eager
anticipation of getting involved in this "new"
activity.

Control Group

Increased validity of results is ensured
when a control group also takes the questionnaire.
Thus, at least two groups will be involved.
One group will later be presented with the opportunity to volunteer for Quality Circles, and the
other will not. Therefore, the possibility of
biased results is minimized.

Group Size

Sample size and accuracy go hand in hand,
assuming no bias. The large sample size assures
the greatest possible accuracy. If the sample
is too small, say 5 to 10, the results might
be regarded with skepticism. This is a time to
ask the advice of those in the organization who
work regularly with statistics. Examples include:
quality, industrial engineering, finance, and
personnel.

Score And Summarize

After the completed questionnaires have
been scored, they should be summarized and kept on
file for later comparison.

Follow-on Comparisons

This identical questionnaire can be administered to the same group, or other groups, at a later date to determine if attitude trends are developing. Frequency can vary; but the first follow-on questionnaire might be given as the pilot phase draws to a close. It can serve as another gauge to measure the success being experienced.

Who Should Administer

Experience can be helpful. Amateurs can make errors that will render the results invalid. Get help from the professionals. These individuals are usually found in personnel departments.

QUALITY CIRCLE ATTITUDE SURVEYS

Some surveys address attitudes toward Quality Circles in a very direct fashion. All of the questions reflect members' attitudes toward their activities in their Circles. An example of the kind of questions, and the responses, is included in the chapter entitled, "Results."

Many other questions have been used in surveys. The following are a few examples:

* How often do you attend Circle meetings?
* Have you spent time outside of normal work on Quality Circle activities?
* Has your Quality Circle involvement made your job more enjoyable, less enjoyable, or has it made no difference?
* Has Quality Circles affected your relationship with others in your regular work group?

* Has the Quality Circle activity affected your relationship with equals in other organizations?
* Has Quality Circles affected the productivity of your work group?
* How would you describe your feelings about making presentations to management?
* Do you think the cost of doing Quality Circles is justified by improvements in quality and costs?
* Should the Quality Circle activities be continued and expanded to other work groups?

OFFICE ACTIVITIES, CAN THEY BE MEASURED?

The following comparison between units of measurement from a production area and an office area help to illustrate the considerable similarity that exists. It should be further noted that office functions are quite measurable; and Circles operating in those areas should definitely conduct a measurement program.

ITEMS USED TO MEASURE QUALITY CIRCLE ACTIVITIES

Production	Office
Absenteeism	Same
Tardiness	Same
Savings per theme	Same
Turnover	Same
Safety performance	Same
Schedule	Same
Attitudes	Same
Grievances	Same
Yield rate	Same
Defects (errors)	Same

Repeated errors	Same
Rework costs	Same
Scrap costs	Same
Productivity	Same
Materials or supplies availability	Same
Omissions	Same
Repeated failures	Same
Volume of units produced	Same
Index of customer* satisfaction	Same
Customer complaints	Same
Customer rejections	Same
Rework costs	Same
Scrap costs	Same
Machine or computer downtime (malfunction)	Same
Labor cost per unit of product, page, report, etc.	Same

---

*"customer" may mean the consumer, retailer, wholesaler, or another department in the same company. In a governmental organization it could mean employees or even voters at large.

INSTRUCTOR GUIDELINES FOR TEACHING MEASUREMENT TECHNIQUES

The instructor providing information on how Circles should make measurements can use the following list of questions to guide the lesson and discussion. The whole subject of measurement of Circle activities is so important that it is worth taking the time to make sure that people get into a complete enough discussion so that they have a good understanding of how it works and whom they should contact for special expert advice.

INSTRUCTOR GUIDELINES

QUALITY CIRCLE MEASUREMENT TECHNIQUES

Questions to ask the class

* Name three general categories in which to measure
  Quality Circle progress.
* Why express Quality Circle measurement in terms
  of quality?
* What ways can quality be measured?

> Expected answers: Yield rates, defects,
>   scrap, spoilage, rework, scheduled
>   deliveries, customer complaints.

* Where do you get this information in your
  organization?
* Name individuals who can help provide information on quality.
* What are ways costs can be measured?

> Expected answers: Savings-to-cost ratios,
>   net savings (savings minus costs),
>   learning curves, standard hours.

* How will you know how many man-hours are being
  expended by you, your members, and others
  who occasionally assist them?
* How will you determine material costs?
* What organization(s) can provide assistance in
  helping you to determine labor and material
  costs?
* What group in your company is officially
  designated to evaluate cost savings?
* How can attitudes be measured?

> Expected answers: Absenteeism, tardiness,
>   grievances, turnover, surveys.

* Can you attach dollar amounts to these attitude
  measures?

Questions to ask the class   (continued)

* Who would be able to help you do it?
* Should you even try to measure attitudes in terms of dollars?
* Are "testimonials" a measure of the success of Quality Circles?
* If an attitude survey is conducted, would you prefer to do it? (Point out dangers when surveys are badly administered and result in contaminated data.)
* Give an example of a Circle's results that, while successful, might result in no measurable savings.

    Expected responses: Safety hazard reduction, grievance reduction, etc.

* How do you feel about posting, and occasionally adding to, a chart that summarizes completed Circle projects?

SUMMARY

Conducting proper measurements is so important that a Circle should call in an expert, if necessary, in order to make certain that it is being done correctly and according to the organization's policies and procedures. The facilitator does not need to know how to do the measurements. Every organization has someone on the payroll with the credentials to convince management that the measurement activity is being properly executed.

EVALUATING YOUR CIRCLE ACTIVITIES

The following questions can serve as a checklist to reveal how healthy Circle activities are in an organization, and what can be done to make them even better.

A periodic evaluation of Circle activities should be considered a must to ensure that good operational practices are being followed.

Evaluating the steering committee, the training, recognition practices, and management support might best be done by an outsider. That outsider could be a consultant, or an in-house specialist. The steering committee could use these questions to aid in evaluating the facilitator. The facilitator could use them to evaluate the leaders. The steering committee can then recommend required alterations.

EVALUATING THE STEERING COMMITTEE

_____ Have objectives been identified for Circle activities?

_____ What is the frequency of the steering committee meetings? (preferably at least monthly).

292

_____ Are funding arrangements for Circle activities clearly established? For instance, how are they charged and controlled?

_____ If a suggestion program exists, has a clear-cut policy been formulated regarding its relationship with Quality Circles?

_____ Were baseline measurements secured prior to starting Circle activities?

_____ Did the steering committee meet with the pilot program leader candidates prior to training?

_____ Does the steering committee regularly have a get-acquainted session with each group of new leader candidates?

_____ Does the steering committee allow for motions to be made? That is, is it one person, one vote?

_____ Does the steering committee operate as democratically as a Circle?

_____ Did the steering committee meet with the union president, or a committee from the union, to provide an informational briefing prior to the initiation of Circle activities?

_____ Do steering committee members, on occasion, attend Circle meetings or presentations?

_____ Has the steering committee clarified and communicated to Circles what is not contained in the Circle charter? (Examples include: personnel problems, grievances, wage and salary issues.)

_____ Has there been consistant increase in the number of Circles being formed?

_____ What kind of a dropout rate exists among Circles?

_____ Are several organizations represented on the steering committee? (Examples include: production, quality control, engineering, finance, personnel, education and training, suggestion program manager.)

_____ What organizations were omitted? Any particular reason?

_____ Has the steering committee at least one member who is a Circle leader? When this is the case, this individual usually rotates on a frequency of once a quarter or every six months.

_____ Does the steering committee have, or has it considered, having one member who is a Circle member? (When done, this individual usually rotates monthly or quarterly.)

_____ Are minutes of the steering committee maintained? Distributed?

_____ Has an implementation plan been developed to achieve Circle objectives?

_____ Has a Quality Circle policy and procedure been developed?

_____ What method has been used for identifying backup facilitator(s)?

_____ Were employees advised ahead of time about Quality Circles? (Typical ways this is accomplished may include: company newspaper, letters to homes, mass gathering in auditorium, numerous small group sessions, and one-on-one.)

_____ Have guidelines been established for Circle activities? Examples include: frequency of Circle meetings, duration of each Circle meeting, should meetings be held during normal working hours or conducted outside of regular working hours, or, should the leader have the choice to decide for himself or herself?

_____ Has there been any thought given to other steering committees being formed in your organization? An example is where other plant locations exist. Sometimes, a steering committee at corporate level sets overall guidelines and policies, with lower level steering committees operating within that framework.

_____ Does the steering committee make any kind of report of its activities to the Chief Executive Officer (CEO)?

_____ Was the original facilitator opening, as well as subsequent additions, advertised openly throughout the organization?

_____ Did the steering committee interview any of the facilitator candidates?

EVALUATING THE FACILITATOR

_____ Does the facilitator maintain a record of Circle activities?

_____ Has there been a consistant increase in the number of Circles being formed?

_____ What kind of a Circle dropout rate has been experienced?

_____ How many Circles have become inactive? (Inactive differs from dropout in that the former deals with Circles that have temporarily suspended activities for some reason.)

_____ Has each Circle made an absolute minimum of two management presentations during the past 12 months?

_____ Has each facilitator participated in teaching leader-training classes?

_____ Does your facilitator occasionally receive visits from facilitators with other organizations to exchange Quality Circle information?

_____ Does each facilitator have an understanding of, and the endorsement of, your quality control department?

_____ Is the facilitator salary range at least that of the highest rated supervisor?

_____ If there is but one facilitator in your organization, is there a trained backup?

_____ Does the facilitator consistantly play a background role, giving credit to the Circles?

_____ Is the facilitator a member of the Steering Committee?

_____ Does the facilitator have at least a weekly meeting with his manager?

_____ Does the facilitator have at least a monthly meeting with each manager who has Quality Circles in his/her organization?

_____ Does the facilitator have at least a quarterly meeting with each manager's manager who has Quality Circles?

_____ Does the facilitator prepare the weekly activity report? (Copies of the facilitator's weekly activity report go to several persons including: Circle leaders, managers with Circles, steering committee members, etc.)

EVALUATING THE CIRCLE LEADER

_____ Were Circle leaders volunteers?

_____ Did each Circle leader go through the leader training course prior to starting a Circle?

_____ Did each leader provide a general overview of Quality Circles to all employees in his/her work group?

_____ Did leaders take care not to preselect members for their first Circles? That is, did they make the selection on some kind of nondiscriminatory basis?

_____ Are minutes of Circle meetings maintained?

_____ Has each leader assigned a member to keep the minutes of each meeting?

_____ Has each leader appointed at least one assistant leader?

_____ Has each leader maintained a status of all Circle projects and assessed final dollar and/or other improvements?

_____ Does each leader maintain a variety of on-going records such as attendance, member training, status, etc.?

_____ Does each leader prepare an agenda for Circle meetings?

_____ When identifying a list of possible problems to work on, does the leader caution members to concentrate on those that are directly under control of Circle members?

_____ When selecting the problem the Circle will analyze, does the leader remind members to choose their own problems rather than those of others?

_____ Does each leader do a good job of involving everyone in the Circle?

_____ Does the leader occasionally ask members to assist in the training?

_____ Does the leader get maximum participation by members in a management presentation?

_____ Does the leader consistently help Circle members to develop a schedule for each project chosen?

_____ Has each leader helped the Circle to develop its code of conduct?

_____ Is the code of conduct for each Circle displayed in the meeting area?

_____ What is the dropout rate in a given Circle? Why?

_____ Are there suitable meeting rooms for Circle activities?

_____ Has any method been developed whereby Circle members can make a self-evaluation of their progress?

EVALUATING THE TRAINING

_____ Has a Quality Circle orientation briefing been provided to all managers?

_____ Are all supervisors regularly notified of up-coming leader training classes?

_____ Are Circle leaders required to attend Quality Circle leader training classes as a prerequisite to starting a Circle?

_____ Do all Circle members receive training in the use of the Quality Circle techniques?

_____ Which of the following Quality Circle techniques are taught to Circle members:

Case Study	_____
Problem Prevention	_____
Brainstorming	_____
Data Collection Techniques	_____
Data Collection Formats	_____
Charts & Graphs	_____
Decision Analysis (Pareto)	_____
Cause-&-Effect Problem Analysis	_____
Process C-&-E Problem Analysis	_____
Management Presentation Techniques	_____
Histograms	_____
Control Charts	_____
Stratification	_____

_____ Are lesson guides and training materials available to the facilitator to assist in teaching leader classes?

_____ Are lesson guides and training materials available to the leader to assist in teaching member classes?

_____ Are audio-visual materials available to the facilitator and leader to enhance and shorten the training process?

_____ Does each member have a training manual?

_____ Do all members take quizzes during training sessions?

_____ Are members encouraged to do worksheet problems?

_____ Are instruction aids such as projectors, black boards, flip charts, and tape recorders available for training purposes?

_____ Are Education and Training (E & T) personnel available to assist the facilitator in training leaders?

_____ Does E & T provide training completion certificates for those who have completed leader training?

_____ Does E & T provide training completion certificates to those who have completed member training?

_____ Does leader training include, in addition to the Quality Circle techniques, the following:

        Motivation?   _____
        Communication?   _____

Potential problems?   _____
Organizing the New Circle?   _____
Group dynamics?   _____
Management by objectives?   _____
Running meetings?   _____

EVALUATING THE
RECOGNITION POLICIES AND PRACTICES

_____ Has each Circle made at least one manage-ment presentation during the past six months to present status, achievements, and/or recommended solutions?

_____ Are Quality Circle activities reported on a regular basis in your organization news-paper?

_____ Are Circle activities regularly included in the weekly activity reports of managers who have Quality Circles in their organizations?

_____ Does the facilitator's weekly activity report regularly include recognition-type news items?

_____ Has there been at least one newspaper or magazine article about your Quality Circle activities published during the last 12 months?

_____ Has a facilitator, leader, or member been sent to at least one regional or national conference on Quality Circles during the past 12 months?

_____ Has at least one facilitator, leader, or member spoken at a regional or national conference on Quality Circles during the past 12 months?

_____ Has at least one of your facilitators, leaders, or members spoken at some community club function during the past three months?

_____ Has at least one of your facilitators, leaders, or members spoken at a school class during the past three months?

_____ Have Circles been recognized in the community newspaper, radio, or TV at least once during the past six months?

_____ Are Circle members provided with other recognition items such as plaques, trophies, etc.?

_____ Are bulletin boards ever used to publicize Circle activities?

Other recognition techniques include:

_____

_____

_____

_____

_____

_____

_____ Has the possibility of an in-house "conference" been discussed or has it occurred? (These usually last about one hour, are attended by all Circle members and executive management and include presentations by 3 or 4 Circles)

EVALUATING THE
SUPERVISION AND MANAGEMENT

_____ Has each manager with Quality Circles dropped in on a Circle meeting at least once during the past three months?

_____ Do executive management personnel regularly include Quality Circles in their annual objectives?

_____ Do middle managers regularly include Quality Circles in their annual objectives?

_____ Do department managers regularly include Quality Circles in their annual objectives?

_____ Has at least one manager included Quality Circles as part of his speech outside the company during the past three months?

_____ Has management allowed the facilitator to attend a conference during the past 12 months?

_____ Has management allowed either a leader or a member to attend a conference during the past 12 months?

_____ Have visitors from outside your facility been allowed to sit in on Circle meetings during the past three months? (This can be a learning experience for your people as well as the visitors.)

_____ Does management provide, or route, a copy of the Quality Circle Digest magazine published by the Quality Circle Institute in Red Bluff, California, and/or the IAQC Quality Circle Journal?

_____ Is a copy of either or both of the above magazines provided or routed to each manager who has Quality Circles in his department?

_____ Does management advise all supervisors of upcoming training classes?

_____ Has management provided for Quality Circle policies and procedures?

_____ Is Quality Circle participation on the supervisory and management levels voluntary?

PREPARATION FOR EXPANSION

The importance of having a solid base before moving forward is well established in every field of endeavor. The same applies to Quality Circles.

Most important, the people involved must be part of the plan and part of the commitment--in other words they must have ownership. In the case of Quality Circles, those people are: Circle members, leaders, facilitators, steering committee members, executive management, middle management, supervisory management, and staff management.

The key questions revolve around the "product" produced by the Circle: Creative solutions to the quality, cost, and attitude problems that affect the work the members do. How good is that "product"? Or, to put it another way, does it pay for itself?

But it is more than that. The organizational structure has to be in place. All employees, including management, have to be knowledgeable about its mode of operation and about the potential benefits. To many, the crucial question is, "What's in it for me?"

RESULTS

Reliable favorable accounting data are what convince management that the Circle activities should expand. Data covering improvements that have taken place in the following categories should be made available.

Quality

Quality is typically measured on one or all of: errors, defects, waste, spoilage, scrap, yield, customer complaints, or warranty costs.

Cost

Most improvements can be converted to dollar savings. In discussing cost improvements, most organizations refer to their savings-to-cost ratios. This varies between 2 to 1 and 10 to 1. For Circles meeting outside normal working hours at no pay, this may skyrocket to over 200 to 1!

Other cost measures include break-even points, learning curve improvements, and decreases in standard man-hour requirements.

Attitudes

Attitude improvements generally reflect beneficial changes in measures such as absenteeism, grievences, tardiness, turnover, and sick days.

Compare Progress in Different Sections of the Organization

Some areas of the organization will operate Quality Circles differently than others. Certain techniques will work better than others. Careful study of various methods employed will surface some that are so good they could be beneficially used throughout the organization.

EVALUATION CHECKLIST

The chapter entitled, "Evaluating Your Circle Activities" can help the steering committee assess the readiness for expansion. By all means, the checklist should be employed to determine the health of Quality Circle activities.

The evaluation checklist does more. It provokes an introspective assessment of one's weaknesses as well as strengths.

This inward assessment, periodically made, can serve to trigger the kind of appropriate, corrective action that speeds the establishment of a healthy Quality Circle activity.

SURVEYS OF ATTITUDES

General

Learning how people, at all levels, feel about Quality Circles, can be an important determinant as to the readiness of the organization to move into the expansion stage. How is this information gained?

Questionnaires have the advantage of pulling the maximum quantity of information in the minimum amount of time. Further, they assure that everyone will be asked the identical questions. An added advantage is that scoring and analysis are made easier because of this uniformity.

Open-end discussions add the kind of informality that may produce candid responses. It can be voiced in words that perhaps "tumble together," but nevertheless reflect the true views of the speakers. Even where it has been done on a tape, the degree of openness and honesty has been surprising. Naturally, analyzing this unstructured information can be quite time-consuming.

Who Conducts the Survey?

Often it is the facilitator, particularly when questioning the members, leaders, and the union. Steering committee members may get involved in talking to middle and executive management. Another alternative is to use an individual trained in these techniques. The garnering of data on attitudes will result in both positive and negative information. It is the negative feedback that may provide the greatest help in assessing the strength of Quality Circles.

Members

Elsewhere in this book, the reader will find information on questionnaires that can be used to determine the true feelings of members. An opportunity to ask questions on a face-to-face basis should be provided to let members expand on items they consider vital.

Leaders

The same questions that are directed to members can be, and usually are, asked of Circle leaders.

Middle Management

Specially designed questionnaires are possible, but less likely, at this level, because it involves fewer people. Whatever method is used to determine attitudes toward Quality Circles, listen for indications that:

*   They were not involved

*   They could not influence
            decisions

*   They did not know how Circles
            operated

*   They were unfamiliar with the
            analysis techniques

*   They were not being told what
            was going on

*   They were expected to solve
            problems the Circles had
            "dumped" on them

*   They were not held accountable
            for Circle success (there-
            fore, how important could
            it be?)

*   "The Circles are wasting time"

*   "Unnecessary powers being given
            to the Circles"

*   "Circles have tried to make us
            look bad"

*   "The facilitator goes around me"

    Unfortunately, there have been instances
where lack of management support occurs even when
the managers know that the Circle investment, as
measured in terms of quality, cost, schedules, and
attitudes has been paying off handsomely! When
this happens, it usually means that the manager
feels circumvented or left out. Lack of remedial
action can result in Circles being discontinued.
Perhaps it is analogous to the man who left a
good-paying job to take one at less, pay because

he didn't feel a part of things. Many decisions result in emotional responses rather than ones based on logic and facts.

Executive Management

Executive level management will likely be influenced more by result data than anything else. Certainly, they can't ignore feedback they receive from middle management and staff organizations. Their opinions are important; because the way they feel about Quality Circle activities is likely to be quickly mirrored by others in the organization.

Staff Support Organizations

Major negative concerns are likely to be:

*   "Circles are getting into our territory." (Industrial engineering, education, and training, etc.)

*   "Circles don't follow prescribed organizational channels"

*   "Circles get in over their heads, then expect us to bail them out"

*   "Circles don't give us credit for the help we give them"

*   "Circles cause us extra problems because they don't know the ripple effect their actions cause in other organizations"

Labor Union

When a labor union exists, it is advisable to communicate with the people in charge. A strong communication link with the union is as important as with any part of the organization hierarchy. Typically, the union is supportive. Perhaps it recognizes, more readily than most, the positive effect of a participative activity such as Quality Circles.

If negative concerns are voiced, they are likely to be in one or more of the following areas:

*   "Circles are allowed to discuss
    grievances, personnel matters,
    and other subjects covered by
    the bargaining contract"

*   "Circle concerns get management's
    attention much more readily than
    those of the union"

*   "We are the last to find out what
    is going on"

*   "Someday an employee is going to
    lose a job because of a Circle
    suggestion. When that happens
    it will be difficult for us to
    remain neutral"

WAYS TO STIMULATE ENTHUSIASM AND COMMITMENT

There is no one way to build a kind of enthusiam that will better equip Quality Circle activities to move into an expansion mode. Nevertheless, some techniques are as follows:

Ongoing Management Presentations

Almost anyone who has attended a management presentation is sold on the merits of this power-ful form of recognition. If there is any doubt, the members should be asked how they feel about it. In the member and leader attitude survey

reported in this book, there was unanimous agreement that it was a good idea. The author encourages management personnel who attend these
presentations to direct questions to the members
that will draw out their feelings. For example,
"Has Quality Circles been worth the effort?"
"How do you feel about your Quality Circle activities?" Even, "Wouldn't you have come up with the
same thing without having a Circle?" Managers who
don't need convincing might well initiate such
questions for the benefit of visiting managers who
need to be convinced.

Train All Supervisors As Circle Leaders

Some organizations put all their supervisors
through Circle leader training. It isn't a waste,
even if no follow-through on their part ensues.
They will benefit from it. It will affect the way
they manage. For some, it will convince them that
they want to start Circles in their areas.

Build A Core Of Part-Time Facilitators

There is a special strength to Quality
Circles in Japan. One reason is management's
involvement. Management involvement occurs in a
variety of ways, including participation as
part-time facilitators. Each part-time facilitator may handle two or three mature Circles.
Look for those who want to do it. Candidates
include managers, manager's managers, executives
(two company presidents are doing it!), supervisors, staff personnel, etc. Everyone knows the
value of involvement. It is just as essential at
the management level as with Circle members.

Encourage Observers At Circle Meetings

Seeing is believing--not for everyone, but
for many. Comments abound such as, "I was sur-

prised at the enthusiasum."   Or, "It is amazing
to see them using these techniques to solve
problems." Or, "What is it that turns them on?"
And, the enthusiasm they see is contagious!

Invite Observers To Circle Presentations

The excitement of a management presentation
isn't limited to just the Circle members.   The
leaders feel it.   The facilitator feels it.   So
does the manager.   Observers, some of whom are
doubters, will marvel at the commitment to perfec-
tion and efficiency being demonstrated by people
who may not previously have been part of the
team.   It quickly becomes obvious that before
Quality Circles, these people were definitely
underutilized.

Company Quality Circle Conference

A powerful stimulant results when an organization conference on Quality Circles is staged.
When Circle members attend, as do as many managers
and staff personnel as possible, organization
executives get an opportunity to see this "new"
concept in action.   It may last only an hour, but
will likely include three presentations from
better Circles. Perhaps certificates of appreciation are distributed by an executive. There is a
lot of handshaking, congeniality, and warmth.
Goodwill and enthusiasm run high.   It becomes
difficult to avoid being caught up in it.

General Publicity

General publicity, such as write-ups in
activity reports, photos on the bulletin boards,
newspaper releases, pins, plaques, visits from
outside organizations, etc., all serve as valuable
aids in building the enthusiasm necessary for
expansion.

Competition

Healthy competition between different plants, or various departments, can stimulate the flow of adrenalin. Even Circles can thrive on carefully administered suggestions that kindle the competitive spirit.

Results Data

The items discussed above are interesting; but until a major concern is addressed, many potential supporters will "hold back." That concern is, "Everyone is enthusiastic; but do Quality Circles pay their way?" Make results data available to all!

Training

All line management and support group personnel should be exposed to enough Quaity Circle training so they will know what it is, the philosophy, the objectives, how it operates, the types of training, ways to measure presentations by Circle leaders, members, or managers who are already involved.

The Management Workshop

Bernard Perry, formerly of the Naval Ordnance Station, Louisville (NOSL), Louisville, KY, is one of the pioneers and staunch advocates of "The Management Workshop." At NOSL, it is done in a series of eight 1-hour sessions. Attendance is mandatory. A light-hearted quiz is administered and discussed during the initial meeting. Attendees become involved. Supervisors and managers with Circles in their organizations take part as speakers. The final session takes the form of a debate between those in a pro-position and those who oppose it. At the conclusion of the debate, no one is asked to commit to whether there will be circles in his or her organization. They are asked to merely think about what they learned and to make their decisions, if and when it is determined that it is the right thing to do.

The management workshop has turned attitudes around, and has won new supporters for Quality Circles. With others, it provided the answers by which greater receptivity was fostered. It can be done in less than eight sessions; perhaps four would suffice in many organizations. It would depend on a variety of factors: management styles, organization philosophy, executive attitudes, educational backgrounds, experience levels, etc.

Consensus Management

The Japanese are credited with what is termed consensus management. Decisions are formed by any number of meetings and discussions until a more or less common policy emerges. The Western World would do well to emulate this practice whenever people will be substantially affected. While it takes longer, the payoff is more certain because consensus management creates a sense of ownership among everyone involved. Consensus management assures long-term benefits. Conversely, decisions coming from above, "unmolded" by the participants, will be assured of one thing only--fast initial action. Unfortunately, that may be followed by a "foot dragging" that soon results in failure of the project.

RESULTS CAN STIMULATE DESIRE FOR GROWTH

Persuasive rhetoric is useful; but verifiable facts are what executives prefer to use as the basis for decisions. Everyone involved with Quality Circles agrees to collect data, but many fail to do so. Those that do have programs that are effective have provided impetus; because they

are not only an attractive investment in people,
but also in building healthier organizations.

Types Of Results Data

> Quality improvement
> Cost reduction
> Attitude enhancement
> Safety improvement
> Energy conservation

These categories of results information are
important. Become familiar with them by reviewing
techniques on how to measure these types of
data.

Publicize the results data so that everyone:
executives, management, and employees learn about
it. Members, for example, can get just as excited
and enthusiastic as management over good news--
especially when they see their direct contributions to it.

Promotions

Results can take many forms. Circle leaders
become better managers because of experience
gained in managing Circle projects. Talents will
become visible. Potential candidates for promotion are certain to be observed. Many organizations have taken the further step of promoting
these men and women so that the organization
builds toward a stronger future. That delivers a
powerful message to everyone in the organization--
management and employees alike--that the Circles
are not only contributing, but that the effort is
being rewarded.

Comparisons

Results can motivate. Compare with industry
averages. Compare results from divisions within

the same organization. Compare departments.
Compare Circles. Caution: comparison of dollar
savings alone mislead; so it should be avoided.
A windfall savings of $100,000 might fall to one
Circle with little effort, while another might
contribute a masterpiece of superb management and
application of the problem analysis techniques and
save only $1,000.

Comparisons can provide the stimulus for
advancement. When on the low end of comparisons,
it can stimulate action by featuring goals to aim
for. When high, it causes the Circle to not let
its guard down lest its momentum slacken.

TAKING ACTION

There is a time for words and a time for
action.

Willingness to be Assertive

Changes may have to be made in a number of
areas.

The steering committee may be in need of revamp-
ing. Perhaps a member has become ineffective and
should be replaced. Maybe the policy and procedures are outdated and in need of re-evaluation.
The measurement plan may not be realistic. Worse,
it may be nonexistant. Implementation plans may
require updating. Too many organizations wrong-
fully assume that the implementation plan ends
when the first group of Circles goes into action.
Actually, the implementation plan is part of an
ongoing Circle activity.

Identifying "Energy Sources"

The energy sources are those who will provide
leadership for Quality Circles--not simply Circle
leaders--but in a number of capacities. Managers

who want Circle activities in their organizations, supervisors who strive to create Quality Circle activities, management and staff personnel who express a willingness to take on the roles of part-time facilitators, are some of these energy sources.

Change The Players

Coaches find that results sometimes follow a personnel reassignment or relocation. Organizations can stagnate if there is a continuing and persistant resistance to change. Often the fear of change results from a concern that, "If I had done a good job, changes would not be necessary." Such individuals must maintain that change is unnecessary. Rotating personnel will break down most resistance to change.

Learn From Mistakes

There is an old adage that says, "Anything worth doing is worth doing wrong." On the surface that seems contradictory and counterproductive. Yet, for example, if one looks at what the Wright Brothers did in 1903 on the plains of Kittyhawk, it would have to be concluded that their airplane design was dreadfully wrong. Nevertheless, it was still worth doing. Each subsequent model, while better, was still wrong. Even as one looks at the magnificent aircraft that criss-cross the oceans and continents, it could be safely said that there are aircraft marvels still waiting to unfold.

So, one can expect to make errors. Recognition of this fact of life can point the way to continual improvement in the Quality Circle activities. It is important to remember that the expansion that follows pilot activity is much larger than the pilot itself--thus, the effects, whatever they are, will be more widespread.

CONTENTS OF THE LEADER MANUAL AND MEMBER MANUAL
PORTION OF THIS BOOK

The balance of this book is excerpted from
leader and member training manuals published
by the Quality Circle Institute in Red Bluff,
California, and occasionally makes reference
to accompanying audio-visual training modules.

GENERAL INFORMATION

As a team leader, you are one of the most
important parts of a "movement" that is destined
to change   the work-life of millions of people.

You will guide a gathering of individuals who
have heard enough about this new concept to make
them want to meet with you to learn more about
it. The knowledge that you will help them to gain
will transform them into a highly skilled team
that can perform with an expertise and precision that is difficult to believe until you see it
in action.

The techniques that you will teach are
effective enough to enable your people to quickly
gather essential data, evaluate it, and put it to
use so skillfully -- so logically -- that management will not only listen to their recommendations, but will encourage them to make more.

You will see a marked improvement in communication. You will become aware that your people
tend to prevent problems whenever possible, and
overall morale will improve significantly. And,
probably the most satisfying "side-effect"
you will experience is that both you and the team

you lead will get a tremendous amount of enjoyment out of this activity.

The teams that accomplish the most are the ones whose members have the most fun working together!

TABULATED SUGGESTED AGENDA FOR CIRCLE MEETINGS

The tabulated suggested agenda is for use while the members are being trained and after the initial training is completed. The word "initial" is used because you are sure to want to pursue an on-going training program by presenting the various modules whenever you sense the need to refresh the members' minds on a particular phase of the team activity.

TABULATED SUGGESTED AGENDA

During Training	After Training	
X	X	Welcome members and guests
X	X	Introduce guests
X	X	Read and approve minutes
X		Review last lesson and re-do quiz, if needed
X		Discuss responses to worksheet exercise
X		Introduce the current lesson
X		Present the A-V module
X		Discuss the current lesson
X		Suggest completion of worksheet exercise
X	X	Work on a project
X	X	Give assignments, if appropriate
X	X	Post schedule and revise if needed
X	X	Suggest thinking about next project, or next phase of current one
X		Give quiz on current training module
X		Suggest members read about next lesson
X	X	Give date, time, and place of next meeting
X	X	Thank attendees for attention and co-operation
X	X	Make sure secretary prepares minutes
X	X	Confer with facilitator if required

GENERAL INSTRUCTIONAL SUGGESTIONS

The amount of time and attention you give
to this part of your manual will depend upon your
experience and knowledge; but, even if you are a
teacher with top quality credentials, it is
suggested that you read what follows, at least
once.

Everything appearing in this manual is
included for a solid practical reason -- it
has been proven to work. Teams that are implemented and operated according to these guidelines
are successful. They are cost-effective. And
the psychological effect on members results
in a dramatic boost in morale with all the
side-effects that go with it.

Training Aids

Prior to each meeting, be sure to arrange
to have available whatever you will need for the
efficient use of the time allotted. Here is a
list to serve as a reminder:

The appropriate A-V training module

Audio-Visual equipment

Flip-chart, pad, easel, marking pens

Overhead projector

Blackboard, chalk, eraser

Opaque projector

35mm projector

Relate Training to Actual Work Situations

There's no better way to make what you are
teaching the members "real" than to relate what is

covered in the training modules to their actual
work situations. You may be better able to see
tie-ins than they are, but try to get them to
discover them on their own. Encourage them to
give lots of attention to doing this. It is a
very effective way to learn a new concept - a new
way of thinking. Members can become potent
sources for assuring tie-ins.

Robert's Rules of Order

Many occasions will present themselves when
you will be called upon to be an expert parlia-
mentarian. You will have to make order out of
chaos - particularly when member enthusiasm shifts
into high gear. This will be especially evident
when the voting takes place after a brainstorming
session.

Members must always be encouraged to discuss
items being voted on if they feel the need. Apply
Robert's Rules of Order or any other applicable
system at the meetings. Robert's rules were
developed long ago, and they are designed to
maintain order and provide a fair and equitable
opportunity for all persons who participate
in meetings.

"Stop the A-V!"

If an A-V module is employed, the author
believes the A-V should be stopped in order
for you to reinforce understanding, emphasize
certain points, point out tie-ins with actual
on-the-job situations, and so on. This is important. It's easy for trainees to get their attention hung up on points that are unclear to them
and thus get very little out of what transpires
thereafter. As leader, you will be able, in many
instances, to sense this occurrence. Therefore,
you are strongly urged to stop the A-V at any
other points you feel necessary during the presentation. You are also urged to make it very clear

to the members that their questions and comments and requests to stop the A-V are welcome at all times during the presentation of the training module.   (This is one of the things we often remind you to do throughout this book. It's <u>that</u> important!)

It takes two way communication to maximize the effectiveness of the training sessions. Encourage it!

An Enjoyable Experience

The group you lead has an excellent chance to be effective and successful because of the potential that's built into the activity.   The concept is based on proven principles of the behavioral and managerial sciences.   But if the activity is an enjoyable experience, both for you and your members, there is no visible limit to the success that can be attained! Make it fun! Draw people out! Get everyone involved! Give attainable assignments!   Help the members and everyone they work with to <u>win</u>!   There's a whole lot of potential in your group; and the concepts of employee participation will bring it out!

QUESTIONS & ANSWERS

FOR MEMBERS

WHAT IS IT?

A group of people who voluntarily meet together on a regular basis to identify, analyze, and solve quality and other problems in their area.

WHERE DO MEMBERS COME FROM?

Ideally, members of a particular team should be from the same work area, or who do similar work, so that the problems they select will be familiar to all of them.

HOW MANY MEMBERS ARE IN A TEAM?

An ideal size is seven or eight members. The size can vary from a low of three members to a high of about fifteen. The size must never be so great that each and every member cannot have sufficient time to participate and contribute at each meeting.

325

WHAT ARE SOME OF THE WESTERN WORLD COMPANIES THAT HAVE INSTALLED THIS TYPE OF EMPLOYEE PARTIC- IPATION PROGRAM?

A partial list includes plants or divisions of the following organizations: J. C. Penney Co., U.S. Naval Ordnance, Uniroyal, Federal Aviation Administration, Ampex, Super Sagless, Armstrong Cork, Firestone, R. J. Reynolds Tobacco, Salt River Project, Bendix Corp., C.T.S., Yazaki - Australia, Hysla - Mexico, Singer-Kearfott, Amerock, Perfex, Victor Business Machines, Visual Graphics, Michigan Bell Telephone, Rolls Royce - England, Volvo - Sweden, Johnson & Johnson - Brazil, and many, many others.

WHAT ARE THE OBJECTIVES?

*   *Reduce errors and enhance quality*
*   *Inspire more effective teamwork*
*   *Promote job involvement*
*   *Increase employee motivation*
*   *Create a problem-solving capability*
*   *Build an attitude of "problem prevention"*
*   *Improve communications*
*   *Develop harmonious manager/worker relation- ships*
*   *Promote personal and leadership development*
*   *Develop a greater safety awareness*
*   *Promote cost reduction*

WHY THE EMPHASIS ON QUALITY?

A higher level of quality will make for happier customers and promote repeat business. Further, reduced levels of defects and scrap are directly translatable into higher productivity and profits -- profits that spell increased job security.

WHAT ORGANIZATIONS CAN USE IT?

Every organization offering goods or services needs to involve its people in a quality consciousness. Every business, every industry and every organization, regardless of its product or purpose can benefit greatly from the participation of all its people. They are now used in such diverse industries as merchandising, hospitals, banking, insurance, and many more.

IS THIS A NEW IDEA?

These teams (called Quality Circles) were conceived in Japan, in 1961, under the leadership of Dr. Kaoru Ishikawa, then an engineering professor at Japan's prestigious Tokyo University. Dr. Ishikawa, under the sponsorship of the Union of Japanese Scientists and Engineers (JUSE), tied together the theories of behavioral scientists such as Maslow, Herzberg, and McGregor, to the quality sciences introduced to Japan by Drs. Deming and Juran. The result was a "system" that was called Quality Control Circles. The first Circles were registered with JUSE during May, 1962.

HOW IS THE PROGRAM ORGANIZED?

The program is an integrated system made up of several parts:

* *The members themselves*
* *The leaders*
* *The facilitator (program coordinator)*
* *Steering committee*

HOW MANY TEAMS IN A GIVEN AREA?

In a clerical operation, for example, where 25 individuals do identical jobs, how are the 7 or 8 persons selected? No selection is made, nor is membership rotated. If all 25 want to be members, then three groups are formed. Remember, the team represents an investment in people and in the organization. Experience shows that the three teams in this instance would not duplicate each other's activities. Each will contribute in its own way and that contribution will benefit the others.

HOW LONG DO MEETINGS NORMALLY LAST AND HOW OFTEN ARE THEY HELD?

As a rule of thumb, meetings occur once a week and each meeting lasts for approximately one hour. However, some organizations have introduced variations. An example is a half-hour meeting once a week. Another variation is to hold a one or two hour meeting every two weeks.

HOW DOES THE PROCESS WORK?

The following diagram graphically depicts the steps involved:

Problem identification results from any of:

* *   *The members*
* *   *Management*
* *   *Staff or technical experts*

Typically, several problems are identified. Problem selection is a prerogative of the members. Problem analysis is performed by the members, with assistance, if needed, by the appropriate technical experts.

The members make their recommendation directly to the manager using a powerful communication technique described as "The Management Presentation." This technique is described in greater detail in a later section of this book.

WHAT TAKES PLACE DURING A MEETING?

Any of several activities may occur during a meeting such as:

* *Identifying a theme or problem to work on*
* *Getting training as required to better enable members to analyze problems*
* *Analyzing a problem*
* *Preparing recommendations for implementing a solution*
* *Participating in a presentation to management*

HOW SHOULD MEMBERS APPROACH PROBLEMS?

Members should approach problems with a positive attitude -- one that says, "We can do it!" There is a tendency to shrug off problems with, "Why bother, management will not listen anyway." The fact is that well in excess of 80% of recommendations are approved by management. Open discussion and brainstorming, with everyone participating in a positive and cooperative manner, will shed new light on any problem.

*HOW IMPORTANT IS IT FOR MEMBERS TO ESTABLISH
OBJECTIVES AND MILESTONES?*

*Very important.   Members are encouraged to estab-
lish an objective and develop a plan to achieve
it.   The plan is further broken into milestones so
that progress can be constantly measured against
the plan.   In fact, the training includes the use
of charting techniques so that progress can be
posted and serve as a constant reminder.*

*WHAT IF A PROJECT OVERLAPS INTO OTHER ORGANI-
ZATIONS?*

*This should be avoided.   Usually, there are plenty
of problems in one's own area.   However, if an
overlap does occur, an effort should be made to
work with the employees in the affected area.
Also, management of all organizations involved
should be kept advised.*

HOW DO MEMBERS USE THE SERVICES OF SPECIALISTS?

*Although members are largely "do-it-yourselfers,"
it is frequently necessary for them to contact
the organizations' experts in given fields,
such as quality, engineering, safety, maintenance,
etc.   This communication is strongly encouraged,
and the invitations to attend meetings and offer
advice and consultation should be made by the
facilitator through normal channels.   The specialists thus called upon to serve as consultants
while the members retain responsibility for
solving the problems.*

WHAT IS THE STEERING COMMITTEE?

*Fundamentally, the steering committee must set
goals and objectives for the team activities.   It
establishes operational guidelines and controls*

the rate of expansion. It should be presided over
by a chairperson and decisions reached by democratic process -- one person, one vote.

WHO SHOULD BE ON THE STEERING COMMITTEE?

Representatives from major departments within the
company should be members of the steering committee.   The facilitator should be a member
also.

WHAT IS A FACILITATOR?

The facilitator is the individual responsible for
coordinating and directing team activities within
a given organization.

WHO IS THE LEADER?

Experience demonstrates that member activities
will have a greater chance of success when the
supervisor is the initial leader. The concept
gains quicker acceptance when it fits into
the existing organizational structure.   The
supervisor is already designated to perform a
leadership role in that structure. If it did
not operate within the existing organizational
set-up, it might be viewed by some as a competing
organization.

CAN ANYONE OTHER THAN THE SUPERVISOR BE THE LEADER?

Of course. It will probably evolve in the following manner. The supervisor becomes the first
leader. Later, the leader identifies another
individual, usually a lead person to act as an
assistant leader.

IS THERE A RELATIONSHIP BETWEEN TEAM ACTIVITIES AND THE JOB?

The members are people who normally work together. The projects they select to work on always relate to the work they do.

WHAT ARE GENERAL PROBLEM AREAS SELECTED BY MEMBERS?

Paperwork, hardware, communications, service and processes are but a few of the general categories of problems worked on by members. Virtually anything which affects the quality of their work is a candidate.

DO MEMBERS EVER RUN OUT OF PROBLEMS?

No. They may occasionally think so, but a brainstorming session usually surfaces many problems that need immediate attention.

IS "PROBLEM PREVENTION" AN APPROPRIATE THEME?

It is most appropriate and should be enthusiastically encouraged. When a team has passed the point of "putting out fires" and starts looking ahead for ways to prevent them, it has achieved a major milestone. This is a form of quality consciousness that insures that quality will be built into the product and not "inspected" in.

ARE SAFETY THEMES ACCEPTABLE?

Absolutely. Most safety themes also have a relationship to quality. But, whether the tie-in is there or not, safety themes should be encouraged.

DON'T SUGGESTIONS GET COSTLY TO IMPLEMENT?

Rarely.   90% of the recommendations either cost nothing or can be financed from normal department budgets.   Remember, members are encouraged to select themes where they are the experts.   Thus, they will likely be the ones that subsequently effect the recommended changes, and they typically do so in a most cost conscious manner.

ATTITUDE RESULTS

Opinion surveys taken among leaders and members consistantly result in unanimous or near unanimous agreement that:

* Quality has been improved
* Morale has been enhanced
* They are cost effective
* Activities should be continued and extended to others.

WHAT IS THE MANAGEMENT PRESENTATION?

A management presentation is where the leader and members describe to their manager what project they have been working on and what recommendations they wish to make concerning it.   Participants use charts that they have prepared.   This event represents a most exciting form of participation, communication, and recognition to all.

WHY ARE MANAGEMENT PRESENTATIONS IMPORTANT?

Management presentations promote communication. Managers are personally informed of activities and accomplishments. The members gain recognition for their contributions. Morale is bolstered by *this periodic opportunity to deal directly with the manager and to be reassured of support for their activities.*

WHEN IS A MANAGEMENT PRESENTATION MADE?

A presentation should be made to:

* Show completed projects
* Make recommendations
* Provide status on long term projects

WHAT IS THE RECOMMENDED FREQUENCY OF THE MANAGEMENT PRESENTATION?

Approximately every three months.

WHAT TRAINING IS PROVIDED?

Leader training is provided by the facilitator during a concentrated three-day class. The leader then trains the members (with help as necessary from the facilitator) during a portion of each meeting. This member training takes place over a period of several weeks. Thereafter, additional training is provided only as required or as a refresher.

WHEN ARE MEMBERS TRAINED?

During their meetings, which are used both for training and for the study of projects.

WHAT ARE THE TECHNIQUES?

The most common techniques are:

* Brainstorming
* Data Gathering (Sampling)

* *Check Sheets*
* *Pareto Analysis*
* *Cause-&-Effect Problem Analysis*
* *Presentation Techniques*

FIRST CIRCLE MEETING

This meeting launches the Circle. An outline for the leader to follow is described here to illustrate its simplicity. The instructional outline is not repeated in this book for each of the remaining techniques.

Welcome the members and guests.

Introduce the facilitator and any guests, if present.

Review the question, "What is it?"

Review what your organization's objectives are for this activity: improved quality, safety, better communication, cost reduction, improvement of competitive position, job security, etc.

Review what is not within the charter of members, such as involvement with pay rates, grievances, personnel matters, etc. Point out that there are other channels for dealing with such matters.

Briefly describe the details of how this activity operates. Point out that members will receive training in problem analysis techniques, they will be involved in selecting the problems in their work area that will be taken up as team projects, they will work out the solutions to problems they select for attention, and that they will be directly involved in presenting recommendations to management.

Distribute the manuals to the members. Call attention to the questions and answers in their manual. Urge them to remember to ask any un-answered questions at the next meeting. Also, point out that there are work sheet problems and quizzes to aid the learning process and suggest that they use them.

Introduce the training course. List the subjects that will be covered: Case Study & Problem Prevention Techniques, Brainstorming, Data Collecting Techniques, Data Collecting Formats Plus Graphs, Decision Analysis Using Pareto, Basic Cause-&-Effect Problem Analysis, Process C-&-E Problem Analysis, and The Management Presentation.

Explain that the A-V modules for those subjects contain everything that appears in the member manuals, plus many more illustrations, so the book should be set aside while the A-Vs are being presented.

Also, let the members know that it is all right to interrupt the A-V presentation with pertinent comments and questions. You will be glad to stop the A-V equipment at any point they would like you to do so, so that any misunderstandings can be cleared up.

Present the A-V module on Case Study & Problem Prevention Techniques, stopping where suggested in the manual and elsewhere if helpful.

Get maximum involvement in a discussion of the material presented. Be sure to ask for examples of tie-ins between what was presented and what is encountered in actual on-the-job situations.

Urge the members to complete the worksheet exercise.

Ask the members to give some thought to a nickname for their group, if they would like to have one. (Almost all do.)

Ask them to make a list of items they would want to include in a Code of Conduct, which they will create at the next meeting.

Give the quiz on Case Study & Problem Prevention Techniques.

Suggest that the chapter on Brainstorming be read before the next meeting.

Announce the date, time, and place of the next meeting.

Thank the attendees for their attention and cooperation.

While details are still fresh in your mind, write the minutes of this meeting. If practical, have them typed in an organized format, which will serve as a model, prior to the next meeting. This is the only time you will take the minutes. At the beginning of the next meeting you will either get a volunteer or select someone to handle this detail.

Confer with your facilitator if required.

CASE STUDY & PROBLEM PREVENTION TECHNIQUES

This case study will illustrate how a problem is handled. Just as important, perhaps even more so, it will present techniques of how to prevent problems in the first place.

STOP THE A-V

Comment: The Case Study you are about to see will introduce new terminology and techniques to show how they interrelate. Subsequent training sessions will prepare you to be able to use them easily.

Most organizations have a mailing room on the premises.

Most mail requires only normal handling. Some pieces are classified and need special processing. Certified and registered letters also call for extra attention.

In this case study the organization's mailroom doubles as a shipping department for cartons and crates going to customers.

The supervisor has just completed a leader training course. Also trained in the same class were supervisors from manufacturing and office areas.

The supervisor has a meeting with personnel to give them information and answer their questions about their upcoming group involvement.

They are introduced to the facilitator who coordinates all groups in the organization. The facilitator will stay in close touch and attend many of their meetings.

One of the important tasks is to have a member maintain the minutes of the meetings.

The leader lists the various training techniques they will be taught during their first meetings.

The leader explains that the first training session emphasizes problem prevention techniques. The message is clear -- the best way to control problems is to avoid them.

Brainstorming techniques are employed in a number of situations. Everyone gets involved and contributes.

To solve problems, data must be collected. The leader explains that ways to do this on a sampling basis will be described in one of the classes. Sampling permits it to be done in a way that saves time and effort for members.

A variety of forms are available and can be used to ease and speed the collection of data. The design and use of graphs and charts will also be demonstrated.

DECISION ANALYSIS *Using* **PARETO**

Decision analysis techniques aid members when choices must be made.

Basic Cause & Effect

PROBLEM ANALYSIS

Members do not simply identify problems for others to solve. Cause-and-Effect problem analysis is a favorite technique for them to use.

Process Cause & Effect

Problem Analysis

An interesting and specialized variation can be used most effectively to pinpoint major causes of problems.

Members learn how to communicate their recommendations to management in a most powerful way -- the management presentation.

This introductory session continues until all questions have been answered.

They start meeting on a regular basis wherein the various training techniques are presented.

After they learn the principles of brain-storming they decide to put this new knowledge into practice by having a brainstorming session to identify the various problems they might work on.

The number one item becomes the project for the group to work on. They decide on a course of action to do the analysis. Data is needed.

CHECK SHEET

IＮＺ	1	2	3	4	₩ₒ.
₅₊ᵢₖ	₩₩	₩₩ ₗₗₗ	₩₩ ,	₩₩ ,,	27
ₚₜₐₑ	₩₩ ₗₕₕ ₩₩ ₗₗₗₗ	₩₩ ₩₩ ₩₩ ₗₗₗₗ	₩₩ ₩₩ ₗₗₗₗ	ₗₕₕ ₗₗₗₗ ₩₩	70
ₑᵢᵥₐᵢ	ₗₗₗ	₩₩ ,	ₗₗ	,	12
ᵣₛₐₒᵧ	ₗₗ		,	ₗₗₗ	6
ₙₐₗᵢ	₩₩ ,	₩₩,	₩₩ ,	₩₩ ,,	25
ₘᵢₗ	35	42	30	33	140

They design a check sheet and use it to easily collect the data they need.

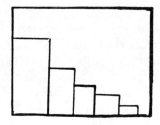

Decisions have to be made. The data collected on the check sheet is used to construct a Pareto chart that graphically depicts the degree and magnitude of the various alternatives.

The number one priority, as portrayed by the Pareto chart, becomes the target for a detailed Cause-&-Effect analysis. It is hoped that this will disclose the true cause of the problem. Let us assume the problem is "Incorrect postage on letters."

The Cause-&-Effect problem analysis is led by the leader but involves all of the members in suggesting every possible cause they can think of.

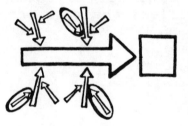

Next, each of these possible causes is examined and discussed to whatever depth desired prior to a vote. The causes gaining the most votes are circled.

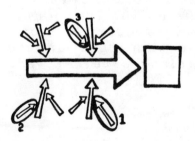

Finally, each of the circled causes is subjected to even further analysis and deliberation and voted on. The priority ranking: #1, #2, #3, etc. is written in as shown.

Verification. How do we verify if the number one most probable cause is the true one? Remember, the problem, was "Incorrect postage on letters." If the number one most likely cause is "Defective postage meter," members would suggest ways to verify it. Then, after selecting a method, they would test it before proceeding further.

Having verified the true cause, only one task remains -- that of determining the recommended solution. Total involvement is obtained by conducting a brainstorming session to surface a variety of possible solutions.

The all-important management presentation is where members recommend their proposed solution to the manager. The manager reviews the recommendation in light of the bigger picture and makes a decision whether to approve it. This is the first of a series of presentations that occur approximately every two to four months from now on.

Initially, members will spend time "putting out fires."

But, the phase that follows is the one that ultimately has the big benefits -- problem prevention.

The most advanced teams acquire an intense interest in preventing problems before they occur.

A "stitch in time saves nine" is a familiar phrase.

Problems are avoided by the simple expediency of taking simple precautions that require almost no expenditure of time.

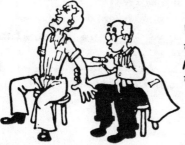

Vaccinations are familiar to most of us as a problem preventative technique.

Training in special skills can add assurance that the job will be done right the first time.

Detailed work instructions that have been carefully prepared will add assurance and confidence that the work will be correctly done in the first place.

Even greater assurance of compliance occurs when the work instructions are organized as a checklist. Thus, steps are not missed, are done in the proper order, and it becomes easier for someone else to pick up where another leaves off.

One member suggests increased use of "workmanship samples." These are completed units that are available for comparison purposes. One might be available to each employee or to a group of employees doing the same thing.

Another suggestion along the same line is the use of a photograph if the actual workmanship sample is not available.

Another points out that manufacturing employees are often provided with measuring instruments to check or gauge their own work. "Maybe we can somehow use the same concept here."

A member speaks up, "That would enable an employee to do something called a '1st Article Inspection.' It's done by the individual who has to make or process, say, 50 identical units. He does the first one, examines it carefully for flaws, and proceeds to make copies only when it is crystal clear that it is perfect."

"Sure, good idea," comments another member, "But that means making sure such instruments and gauges get regular calibration checks. Nothing stays calibrated for long."

There are other techniques to aid in the prevention of problems.

Absenteeism tends to cause an increased error rate. Reduced absentee-ism and problem preven-tion go hand-in-hand. Why? Because the absent employee is usually replaced with someone with less know-how and experience and with less capability of avoiding errors.

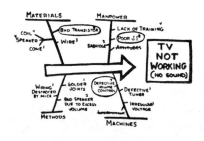

Cause-&-Effect problem analysis indirectly aids in holding down errors. How? The participation by members in identifying possible causes serves to alert members as to potential problem areas. Thus, a new problem prevention awareness is created.

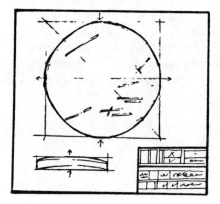

Use a drawing to mark the location of defects as they occur. This will provide new knowledge on what and where errors are happening and do so in a most graphic way.

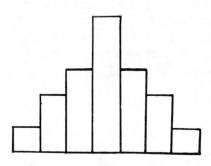

Information from samples becomes the basis for constructing histograms. These provide important clues that warn of problems.

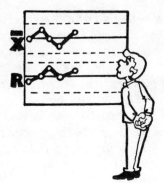

Data from samples can be used to easily construct $\overline{X} \cdot R$ control charts that plot trends that signal when a process is going out of control.

The Np control chart is similar in many respects. It signals the alarm when the process gets too close or exceeds the upper control limit line.

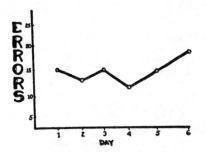

Then, of course, there is the plain and simple line graph -- that is, there are no upper or lower control limit lines. For many applications it is quite adequate to chart progress by this means.

The display of charts in the work area provides the all important feedback to members and other employees that can serve to reinforce their determination to prevent problems.

A most important tactic is to identify key points in the process that would trigger errors if they go out of control. Recognizing this, develop an <u>alternative</u> plan that can snap into action quickly in such an event to dramatically curtail the potential damage.

BRAINSTORMING

Brainstorming, explained in its most basic way, is using a group of people to stimulate the production of ideas.

It is almost always more effective than trying to generate ideas alone.

The effectiveness of brainstorming in unlocking the creative power of the group has long been recognized.

Prior to starting it is vital to identify what topic will be brainstormed. In this instance the members are being asked to determine what problems exist in their work area.

However, it is important to be as precise as possible in stating the topic to be brainstormed. Stating, "PROBLEMS WITHIN OUR WORK

352

AREA," is a decided improvement over simply stating it as "PROBLEMS." That is much too general.

This represents an even further improvement in stating the topic clearly and precisely.

Brainstorming works best when certain guidelines or rules are followed. The leader will review these prior to each session.

Each member, in rotation, is asked for ideas. This continues until all ideas have been exhausted.

Each member offers only <u>one</u> idea per turn, regardless of how many he or she has in mind.

Strive for quantity of ideas to maximize the effectiveness of the team process.

Not everyone has an idea during each rotation. When this occurs, just say, "Pass."

No idea should be treated as stupid. To
criticize or belittle someone is to surely
curtail the creativeness of team members.

For some it will be their
first attempt to speak
out during a brainstorm-
ing session. It may take
courage to start. Be
patient. Welcome and
encourage their ideas.
Their enthusiastic
support is essential.

Good-natured laughter and informality should
be encouraged to enhance the climate for
innovative activity. Obviously, on the other
hand, derisive laughter will have an unwelcome
and dampening effect.

Exaggeration should be
encouraged. It may add
humor and it certainly
adds a creative stimulus
to the process.

After the rules have been explained, the
brainstorming session commences.

The leader will often have to abbreviate a
lengthy idea into a few words. That's fine,
but the originator must agree.

During brainstorming, no evaluation of suggested ideas should occur. This applies equally to the leader. Not just a negative comment but even something like, "Hey, that's good!" No comments, please.

The process will be speeded if a member writes the ideas as they are given.

Finally, the brainstorming has been completed when all ideas have been exhausted. This massive number of ideas must be critically examined and narrowed down.

In the interest of time, a simple voting technique is used. It works because the members are the experts in their area. Members vote on each idea. The leader records each vote next to the idea. Members can vote for as many ideas as they feel have value. Only supporting votes are taken. No one is asked to vote against an idea.

Draw a circle around those ideas that received the most votes. The members decide how many of the top ideas will be so identified.

Now the members can focus in on a few important items instead of being somewhat confused by a large number of them. These important few will be voted on. Usually, each member gets only one vote at this time. Write the ranking number beside each idea that has been circled.

What about discussion? A member can halt the voting on any idea and argue for or against it. Others can join in if they wish. Only when the discussion has subsided will the vote take place.

There are a number of items to keep in mind as the group explores the subject of brainstorming.

An agenda distributed prior to the meeting will give members a chance to think about the upcoming brainstorming topic and perhaps have several ideas all set to go when the meeting starts.

A large sheet of paper
should be used when
brainstorming   Everyone
can read it and it be-
comes a permanent record
that can be used later
in a management presen-
tation.

Look to nature for
creative breakthroughs.

New ideas will be generated by thinking big.
Small aircraft spawned visions of huge air-
liners in the same way that small ships
preceded the mammoth ones that followed.

Combinations of existing
concepts or units may
lead to new and exciting
creations.   Such was the
case when the steam
engine and the paddle
were combined to power
early ships.

A shot of fantasy can aid in shedding the bonds that prevent us from doing creative thinking. An example is to imagine that the laws of gravity can be cancelled.

Or, if you are brain-storming for solutions, fantasize that money is absolutely no obstacle. Perhaps something like that happened when the great wall of China was conceived.

The pursuit of minification concepts during brainstorming may lead to new and sometimes superior products that often cost less.

Incubation often occurs after the initial brain-storming session. "Let's sleep on it," is a frequently voiced com-ment. Later, many innovative ideas may emerge.

DATA COLLECTING TECHNIQUES

DATA COLLECTING

TECHNIQUES

Information is absolutely essential both for the solution of problems; and, equally important, for the prevention of problems. In this section, the members learn how sampling techniques assist them in the collection of the data they need.

Why sampling? One very important reason is that it saves time.

When time is saved, money is saved, too.

Why is it necessary to collect data? There are two basic purposes:
(1)   Problem analysis
(2)   Problem prevention

To analyze a problem, the group must first collect information. Then it is in a position to successfully solve it.

A 100% examination is not always the most accurate. Fatigue can reduce a person's attention to detail.

Further, there are numerous examples where sampling has produced more accurate results. It is less costly. It requires less time and it may afford the chance to do a more thorough and careful examination of the sample.

The sample (n) can be expected to accurately represent the barrel of wine (N).

It's easy to see how sampling can save time and money in collecting information. How about the question, "How many boys in our community play soccer?" Sampling should be quite adequate.

Some products are destroyed in the process of examining and testing them.   Sampling mini- mizes this loss.

An expensive form of destruct testing is when specialized types of information must be collected.   Obviously, sampling is the only way to do it.

There are six steps to be followed in sam- pling.

Step 1.   Learn the facts.   For example, a pollster wants to forecast who is going to be elected mayor of the city.   Some things he must learn include: What groups, ethnic and otherwise, make up the city's population? Relative size of each? Average age? Employment statistics of each group?   Income levels? Past voting trends? Educational level, etc.?

Step 2.   Learn how large the lot size is.   This is also called the "popula- tion" and is abbreviated with the letter capital "N."   In the case of the pollster, "N" is the total number of people eligible to vote.

3. n

Step 3. *A sampling table will indicate how large the sample should be to achieve the desired degree of accuracy. Staff personnel skilled in these techniques can be helpful at this time. An excessive sample size would be a waste of money.*

The larger the sample size, the greater the probability of accuracy. In coin tosses, one should get 50% heads and 50% tails, but only 10 tosses could easily result in something like 7 heads and 3 tails. One thousand tosses would be very close to the true odds of 500 each.

Step 4. *Select the sample. In the example the pollster decides what voters would form a representative sample. The sample selected would contain voters from all socio-economic levels. In other words, to avoid biasing the results, it would be a "stratified" sample.*

Step 5. *Each person in the sample group is asked carefully chosen questions.*

Step 6.   A prediction is made based on the results of the sample.   The word "prediction" is used because one cannot be absolutely certain that the sample accurately reflects the condition of the entire lot.

It should be remembered that, although sampling can save time and effort in the process of collecting the data needed to solve problems, care must be exercised or the results of the sampling may be misleading.

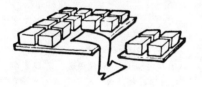

This is an example of bias.   The sample comes from one portion of the lot instead of being randomly selected.

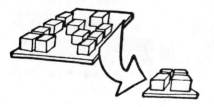

The likelihood of bias is dramatically reduced when the sample is drawn at random from all portions of the lot.

Stratification. Poll-sters must be sure they are taking stratified samples because of the very small sample sizes they depend on. Small samples save money but are potentially very dangerous. Great care must be exercised to select the correct proportion of individuals from every occupation group with additional responsiveness to age, income, education, etc.

Here is a brief look at ways the members use the information they have collected.

A convenient format to record the data collect-ed is in some form of check sheet. It speeds the collection process and makes the data more readily adapt-able to comparison and analysis.

Decision analysis tech-niques depend on first collecting information; then it is possible to construct charts.

Information must be collected to post charts such as line graphs.

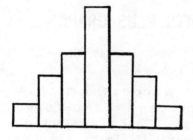

Histograms are often used to measure the uniformity of processes in both production and office areas.

On-going control of a process is maintained very well with a special type of line graph called an $\overline{X}\cdot R$ control chart.

Another kind of control chart is displayed in this illustration.

The presentation to management will tell the story most convincingly when it is based on a foundation of carefully collected data.

DATA COLLECTION FORMATS PLUS GRAPHS

The purpose of this section is two-fold. First, "Data Collection Formats." These are the forms members construct to save time in collecting the data they need. The second section is an introduction into the construction and use of various kinds of graphs and charts.

Members need data if they are to solve problems. The use of techniques that speed and simplify this process are welcome. A variety of data collection formats, designed by members, will help accomplish this goal.

366

WAYS TO COLLECT DATA

1. Check List
2. Drawings
3. Check Sheet

Three approaches that enable members to shorten the time it takes to collect the data needed to solve problems will be studied: (1) Checklists, (2) Drawings showing the locations of defects, (3) Check sheets.

A review of each way will be helpful. First, a common example of a checklist is the grocery list that everyone is familiar with.

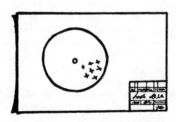

The second type is the drawing that is used to show the location of defects, such as on this record.

CHECK SHEET

ERROR	JUNE				TOTAL
	1	2	3	4	
ADDITION	₩	₩ ₩	₩	₩ ₩	27
MULTI-PLICATION	₩ ₩ ₩ ₩	₩ ₩ ₩ ₩	₩ ₩ ₩	₩ ₩ ₩	70
DIVISION	₩	₩	₩	₩	12
ROUTING	₩		₩	₩	6
TYPING	₩	₩	₩ ₩	₩ ₩	25
TOTAL	35	42	30	33	140

The third way is with the use of check sheets. They are equally applicable in the office or the factory.

Several examples of checklists indicate their usefulness.

As mentioned, the grocery list is a very familiar type of checklist.

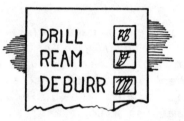

A work order assures that each step will be completed and in the correct sequence.

Before a newly designed airplane is flown, a lengthy checklist is used to assure that all systems are in proper working condition.

The family that uses a checklist will forget fewer items that are essential to a successful vacation trip.

Next, drawings can be used to record the exact location of defects.

One example is an engineering drawing of a music record disc. The location of scratches is indicated right on the drawing.

A company manufacturing face masks for hockey goalkeepers painted its mask to show the locations where stitches would have occurred if a well known player had not been protected. Sales went up sharply.

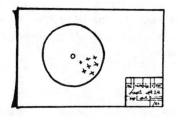

Back to defects. "X's" show the location of scratches on record discs. This is the result of one day's production.

Instead of "X's" one could draw the actual scratch shapes and locations on the drawing.

The communication process during the management presentation is heightened by the inclusion of drawings that show the locations of defects.

Check Sheets are another popular technique for collecting data. Several steps should be followed:

First, the time period must be determined when data should be collected. It may take only a few hours or it might require days or possibly months.

Second, a decision is made as to the variety of information that must be collected. It is usually a good idea to collect more than one thinks necessary. This <u>may</u> result in subtantial future savings in time if the added data is later deemed important.

Third, a form is designed that will facilitate the collection of the needed data.

Fourth, the data is recorded on the check sheet just designed.

Where does the data come from? In an office it might be found by examining records.

In the factory, the examination of several rejection tags might supply the necessary information for the check sheet.

So, a check sheet is as useful in the office as the factory. But, why collect data? The answer is, "To provide the information we needed to analyze problems." Sometimes this also means using the data to build graphs.

One example is a line graph.

Another might be a histogram.

*Still another could be a Pareto chart.   These
are just a few of many possible examples.*

*A specialized type of
check sheet allows the
collection of information
that can easily be used
to construct a histogram.
It should be used when
repeating the same
measurement on identical
units.   (This check
sheet has already taken
on the appearance of a histogram.)*

*This becomes even more apparent if one imag-
ines a dotted line running along the perimeter
of the tick marks.*

*Whenever possible,
the information collected
should be converted into
a graph.*

*It has been said that a picture is worth a
thousand words.   There is little argument that
pictures save time in the communication
process and help the audience to stay alert.
They are excellent for use in a management
presentation.*

Column or bar graphs are a favorite way to present data.

The Pareto chart graphically prioritizes information for decision analysis purposes.

The histogram can provide the result if the same measurement is taken on many identical units.

The pie chart clearly depicts the factory output of three competitors.

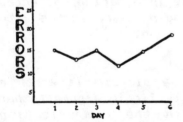

The line graph is frequently employed to visually represent data.

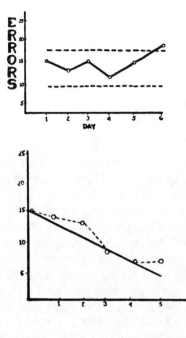

This is the same line graph with control limit lines added. Anytime the line breaks out beyond a control limit it can indicate a problem exists.

Establishing a target or plan can be done by drawing in a heavy solid line. The actual results are posted with the dotted line as they occur.

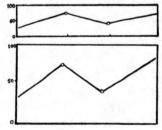

It is important to be careful not to mislead. Although these graphs do not appear to be similar, they actually display identical information.

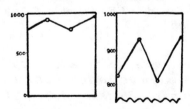

Here's another example of how graphs can mislead. Again, identical information is portrayed, but the impression on the viewer may be completely different.

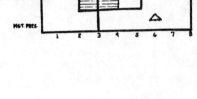

Every project should be accompanied by a milestone chart. This simplified chart is filled in as the work is done, and indicates that the work is ahead of schedule.

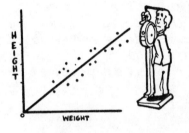

The scatter diagram displays the relationship between two kinds of data. Each plot point represents the height and weight of one man. When a number of people are thus posted the scatter diagram takes on this appearance. A pattern is formed. The shape of that pattern provides clues that assist in understanding the results.

Pictographs are simply graphs that employ pictures to add visual punch to a chart. This format should be avoided because, without explanation, it may lead the viewer to believe that the number of jobs increased fourfold when actually it only doubled.

The same information can be conveyed without danger of misinforming if this format is used. The use of a partial symbol is demonstrated during the third year.

Graphs can communicate the group's recommendation to management convincingly and with minimum expenditure of time.

DECISION ANALYSIS USING PARETO

Decisions must be made on a variety of subjects. One decision analysis tool used by teams is the Pareto chart.

Decisions are often difficult to make. The Pareto chart makes the process easier by quantifying the data so that comparisons can be made that are based on facts.

Pareto was a European scholar who lived during the 19th century.

He triggered alarm by graphically depicting the disproportionate distribution of wealth between the various social classes.

Those who talk about the 80-20 rule are referring to the concept of the "major few and the trivial many." For example, 80% of sales may be made by 20% of the salesmen.

Or, 80% of the office errors may be made by 20% of the employees.

80% of the scrap may be generated by 20% of the work force.

How To

CONSTRUCT

There are several steps in constructing a Pareto chart.

Step 1. The time period data to be collected must be determined. Although it may be only a few hours, it may require days or even months.

Step 2. What data is to be gathered must be decided. Careful consideration at this time will better assure a minimum of trouble later.

Step 3. A form must be designed for use in collecting the necessary data. This is the check sheet. Ideally, it should be general enough to allow the information to be arranged in a variety of ways in case the first one selected fails.

Step 4. *The data is recorded on the check sheet.*

CHECK SHEET

ERROR	JUNE				TOTAL
	1	2	3	4	
ADDITION	⊬⊬	⊬⊬ ⁄⁄⁄⁄	⊬⊬⁄	⊬⊬ ⁄⁄	27
MULTIPLICATION	⊬⊬ ⊬⊬ ⊬⊬ ⁄⁄⁄⁄	⊬⊬ ⊬⊬ ⊬⊬ ⁄⁄⁄	⊬⊬ ⊬⊬ ⁄⁄⁄⁄	⊬⊬ ⊬⊬ ⊬⊬	70
OMISSION	⁄⁄⁄	⊬⊬⁄	⁄⁄	⁄	12
ROUTING	⁄⁄		⁄	⁄⁄⁄	6
TYPING	⊬⊬⁄	⊬⊬	⊬⊬⁄	⊬⊬ ⁄⁄	25
TOTAL	35	42	30	33	140

This is the completed check sheet.

Step 5. *The data on the check sheet is used to construct the Pareto chart.*

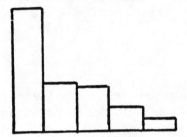

This is the result -- a completed Pareto chart with the columns arranged, as usual, in descending order.

Step 6. *This is where the group learns to construct the cumulative or "cum" line. The members know that the stack reaches a height equal to 140 units, or 100%.*

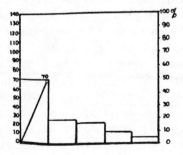

Starting at zero, the cum line is extended to the top right-hand corner of the first column. It is now at the 70 level.

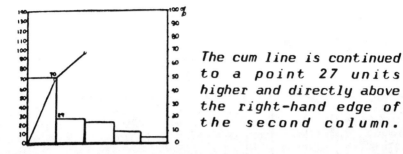

The cum line is continued to a point 27 units higher and directly above the right-hand edge of the second column.

The same is done for the next column of 25 units.

Then the line is extended for the column of 12 units.

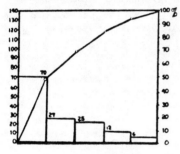

The cum line is complete when it reaches the 100% level per the percentage scale on the right side.

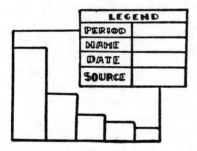

Step 7. A legend is added so that anyone can understand the meaning of the chart.

There are several points to remember.

The Pareto chart clearly
highlights the number one
problem; and it does so
with visual impact.

The cum line can also be of assistance.

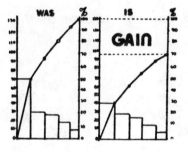

The foremost use of the
cum line is to visually
compare the before and
after situations.

*Thus far a Pareto chart based on errors has
been discussed. At times, money is the better
choice.*

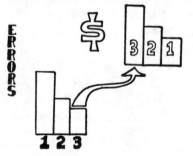

This dramatically illus-
trates how a minor column
might become the major
choice when the Pareto
chart is arranged by
money instead of errors.

CHECK SHEET

ERROR	JUNE				TOTAL	WEIGHING FACTOR	WEIGHED TOTAL
	1	2	3	4			
ADDITION	‖‖‖	‖‖‖ ‖‖‖	‖‖ ‖	‖‖‖ ‖‖	27		
PARTS PLACING	‖‖‖ ‖‖‖ ‖‖‖ ‖‖‖	‖‖‖ ‖‖‖ ‖‖‖ ‖‖	‖‖‖ ‖‖‖ ‖‖‖	‖‖‖ ‖‖‖	70		
	‖‖‖	‖‖‖ ‖	‖‖	‖	12		
	‖		‖	‖‖‖	6		
TYPING	‖‖‖ ‖	‖‖‖	‖‖‖ ‖	‖‖‖ ‖	25		
TOTAL	35	42	30	33	140		

Sometimes the analyst must exercise judgment based on his specialized knowledge of the subject. For example, he or she may look at a check sheet containing defect information and decide to assign priorities to each item. To do this, two columns are added to the right as shown.

What are some of the reasons weighting factors are used? No one wants an unhappy customer, for example. "Know what your customer places the greatest value on and respond accordingly."

Urgency is another reason one might decide to use weighting factors. Two examples might be legal considerations or governmental pressures.

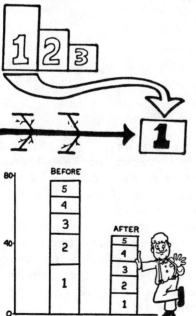

Here is a question. After the Pareto chart has identified the major problem, then what? That number one problem is then subjected to Cause-&-Effect Analysis to find the true cause.

This is another variation on how to present a before-and-after comparison. The columns of the two Pareto charts are simply stacked.

Pareto charts can be posted in the work area to keep employees informed.

Management presentations are more effective when visual aids, such as Pareto charts, are displayed.

There are endless applications for this versatile tool.

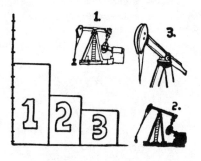

The number of safety days without an accident for each work group can be shown on a Pareto chart.

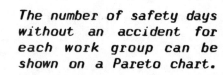

Oil well production can be illustrated on a Pareto chart.

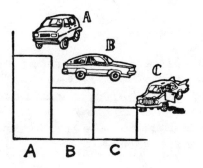

Some automobiles hold their value better than others as this chart suggests. Pareto charts can be a most effective way to make decisions on a variety of topics. It's a good idea to use this valuable time-proven technique whenever practical.

BASIC CAUSE-&-EFFECT PROBLEM ANALYSIS

The primary purpose of this technique is to help the group solve problems.

The problem is the effect and is written in the box to the right. The possible causes for the problem are written in the area to the left.

One look at the first completed Cause-&-Effect Problem Analysis will show why it is often called a "fish bone diagram."

Members select a problem to analyze from within their areas of work responsibility. Several steps are involved.

Step 1 is to state the problem. In this case the problem is a television set that doesn't operate properly. An effort should be made to define the problem as precisely as possible.

If, for instance, it is known that the sound is absent, this should be stated in the definition of the problem. This knowledge will assure more accurate pinpointing of possible causes. The net effect should be a savings in time to solve the problem.

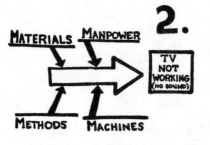

In Step 2 the major groupings for the possible causes that will be identified are determined. Any number of such groupings is permissible, although three or four are quite common. The 4 M's: materials, manpower, methods, and machines, are favorites.

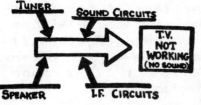

More experienced groups are likely to consider incorporating major groupings more specifically tailored to fit the problem.

3.

In Step 3 all members get involved by participating in a brainstorming session.

Brainstorming works best when certain rules are followed. The leader reviews these prior to each session.

A member should indicate the major grouping he or she wishes his or her idea included under. For example, he or she should say, "Under Manpower, 'Attitudes'."

Occasionally, a cause can be added as a branch off a cause already on the chart. It should be stated as, "Under Manpower, as a branch off of 'Attitudes' put 'excess absenteeism'."

The picture of the completed brainstorming session should show similar ideas grouped together in clumps. Thus, it will be simpler to analyze.

The brainstorming is over when everyone says, "Pass."

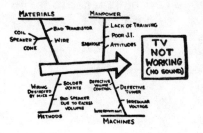

The Cause-&-Effect diagram may look like this at that time.

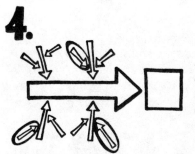

In Step 4 the ideas collected during brainstorming are critically examined to identify those that are best.

Identifying the best causes can be a time consuming process involving a critical analysis of the pros and cons of each.

Or the process can be speeded immeasurably by giving members the opportunity to vote for each cause they believe to be important. It may not seem scientific but experience has demonstrated that it works quite well.

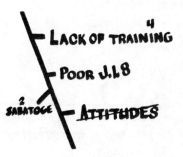

The leader informs members they can vote for as many of the ideas as they wish. The leader begins by pointing to one of the causes and asking, for example, "How many wish to vote for 'Lack of Training'?" The vote, in this case, 4 is recorded

on the diagram. This procedure is followed
until all causes have been voted on. When
no votes are received, a line is simply drawn
through that cause.

Next, those with the highest number of votes
are circled. Usually this means at least two
and up to five or six; but there is no set
number.

In this instance the
three causes receiving
the maximum number of
votes were circled.

When examining each
cause, members should
look for something that
has changed. Few
things serve as better
clues.

They should look for deviations from the
norm. If one's weight increases unexpectedly,
it might tie into an accompanying variation in
diet or exercise patterns.

Police look for clues of recurring "patterns"
that will help them in identifying criminals.
"Patterns" are useful tools in any field of
problem analysis.

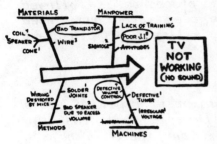

This is the Cause-&-Effect diagram with the major causes circled. Now members can focus in on just a few causes -- much less confusing!

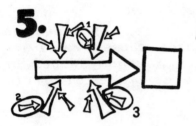

In Step 5 the most probable causes will be ranked in order of importance.

To do this the group looks only at those causes that have been circled. A _discussion_ of each takes place.

After the discussion is completed, members are asked to vote.

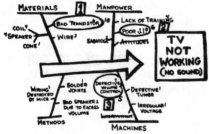

Finally, the priority ranking is added beside each of the major causes.

6.

In Step 6 the one most likely cause is tested in an attempt to verify it. This step may be easy in the case of most TV repairs, or, occasionally difficult and time-consuming. But, it must always be done.

The top cause is labeled #1. <u>That</u> is the one the group will want to attempt to verify.

A good way to do this is a brainstorming session. Members are asked for their suggestions on how to verify it. They usually suggest a number of common sense ways to do this. They prioritize these suggestions and then actually test the top idea or ideas.

After the true cause has been verified, there is an important follow-up to the Cause-&-Effect Problem Analysis: The Recommended Solution.

RECOMMENDED

SOLUTIONS

Cause-&-Effect Problem Analysis aids in discovering and verifying the true cause of the problem Then, the group can prepare a recommended solution.

Member involvement is encouraged in identifying various ways to correct the problem -- another excellent opportunity to utilize the brainstorming techniques. Again, members can be counted on to suggest a variety of ways to solve the problem.

Cause-&-Effect Problem Analysis is usually employed to solve problems. However, a couple of other applications should be considered.

Occasionally, there is a pleasant surprise when something unexpectedly takes a turn for the better. Unless the reason for the occurrence is discovered, that something may resume its former characteristics just as suddenly. Cause-&-Effect Analysis can be used to find the cause of the "good" problem.

Some leaders have found the Cause-&-Effect diagram to be an excellent teaching device. The effect might be, for example, "The Job Description." The brainstorming session would be where members suggest all those things that cause it to be right.

ACTION ITEMS

Item	Action	Who	Date	
			Target	Actual

The way to get results is to identify problems or objectives, specify the action needed, state who will follow through and set a target date for completion.

There are some items to remember when using this versatile tool.

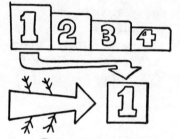

The problem selected often comes as a result of Pareto analysis.

The diagram is not finished until a legend that gives information such as a date, the group that did it, and the name of the leader is recorded on it.

PROCESS CAUSE-&-EFFECT PROBLEM ANALYSIS

**Process
Cause & Effect**

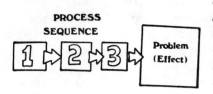

Problem Analysis

Process Cause-&-Effect Problem Analysis provides a way to use this valuable technique in a most effective manner.

Process Cause-&-Effect Problem Analysis is similar in some respects to Basic Cause-&-Effect Problem Analysis. There are, however, some important differences.

The process involves several steps.

1.

⇨ **Problem (Effect)**

In Step 1 the problem is identified as precisely as possible. (No difference here from Basic Cause-&-Effect Problem Analysis.)

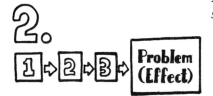

In Step 2 the process sequence is determined.

Usually, the process sequence begins with the first step and those that follow are taken one-at-a-time.

But, sometimes it is easier to work backwards.

An example to work through is a problem that just might be easy to relate to -- being late for work!

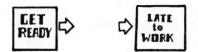

The first block in the sequence is easy. It is labeled "GET READY"; and it includes what is done from the time of awakening until one is dressed.

The second block is labeled "EAT"; and it covers what takes place at breakfast.

The final block in the sequence is labeled "DRIVE," to describe the task of driving to work.

An example in an office might be the excessive delays in the flow of certain paperwork. The sequence or flow of work can be identified easily. First, a draft is prepared. Next, it is typed. Finally, it is mailed.

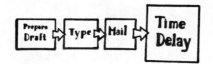

The sequence is depicted graphically in this Process Cause-&-Effect illustration.

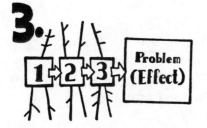

Step 3 is the brainstorming session where all members of the team get involved in suggesting possible causes.

After the rules have been explained, the members can commence the brainstorming process.

The process moves at a much faster pace when the leader is assisted by a member who writes down the ideas as they are called out.

Back to the first example. Attention should be concentrated only on the block titled, "GET READY." Brainstorming is used to identify possible causes for being late to work.

When the first block in the sequence is completed, the group moves to "Eat" and does the same.

Then they move to the
final block in the
sequence. The brain-
storming is completed
when each person says,
"Pass."

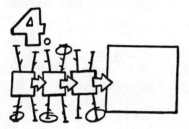

Step 4 is where the ideas
collected during brain-
storming are critically
examined to select those
that are best.

Each cause must be evaluated to determine
its degree of merit. This may involve considerable time and detailed analysis.

However, time is a luxury usually in short
supply. Voting is comparatively rapid and the
results are usually impressive.

Next, those with the highest number of votes
are circled. Usually this means at least two
or three, but could include more.

This is the diagram
showing the major causes
circled.

5.

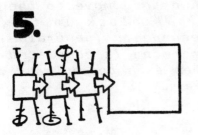

In Step 5 the causes highlighted in Step 4 are ranked in order of importance. To accomplish this, only those causes that have been circled are examined.

Each cause that is circled will be voted on.

Members are asked to vote <u>only</u> on these major causes. Discussion of <u>each</u> circled cause takes place <u>prior</u> to the voting.

The number of votes is jotted down next to each circled cause.

Then each is ranked in accordance with the number of votes received.

6.

In Step 6 the number one most likely cause is tested in an attempt to verify it. Perhaps the alarm must be set to go off earlier!

The number one cause is the one to be verified.

A good way to do this is a brainstorming session to get the ideas of all members.   They will prioritize this list to determine the best ways to verify the number one most likely cause.   Then they will test it.

There is an important follow-up to the verification process: The Recommended Solution.

Brainstorming is used to get member involvement in identifying various solution alternatives.

The pros and cons of the top alternatives are debated by the members to achieve a consensus.

The selected solution becomes part of the management presentation.

There are several things to remember.

During the brainstorming phase, concentration is on one block at a time rather than scattering the groups thoughts by jumping back-and-forth.

Here is a review of how one might save time and effort during brainstorming. It may be quite obvious that one block is the source of the true cause.

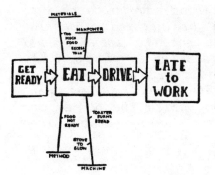

It is assumed that the group wants to focus in on the block titled, "EAT." Therefore, brainstorming is centered

Steps 4 and 5 are taken while continuing to focus in on the same block.

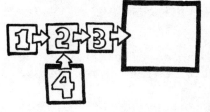

The blocks are usually in sequence but occasionally one of the blocks is offset if that reflects how the process actually occurs.

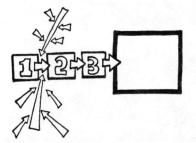

It is possible that the members will decide to brainstorm what may have occurred during transportation between blocks. This is done in the manner indicated. If this step had been anticipated earlier, it could have been added as a separate block!

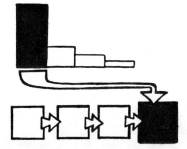

And, of course, although it may be very basic, the problem selected for analysis often came about after using Pareto analysis to select it.

THE MANAGEMENT PRESENTATION

The management presentation is an important and rewarding feature of these activities. This section is designed to prepare the group to carry off this technique in the most effective way possible.

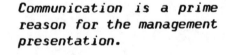

Communication is a prime reason for the management presentation.

Why not simply submit a written recommendation? Prime reasons include: It may be misunderstood, it lacks the impact of face-to-face two-way communication, and it fails to adequately recognize efforts of members.

400

The members recommend _solutions_ to the problems they have identified and analyzed.

Sometimes it is used to provide status on a long, drawn-out problem that is still being worked on. Not only will this keep management informed but it often generates renewed enthusiasm.

The meeting area should be free from distractions.

A checklist is used to assure that everything is ready. Typical items include: Extension cord, projector, screen, blackboard, chalk, etc.

The room should be set up ahead of time. Equipment should be in place and the charts ready to use.

A name card should be placed in front of each person, including members.

Starting at the scheduled time makes a good impression.

It is essential to have an agenda that lists the sequence of items and the speakers. Each attendee should receive a copy.

Each member is introduced at the beginning of the presentation.

As many members as possible should be involved as speakers.

Each should again be introduced immediately prior to speaking.

Sometimes one can get the feeling of losing the audience. Visual aids can liven up a talk.

Charts that illustrate the techniques that have been mastered, such as Pareto and Cause-&-Effect, should be used. They make a good impression; and they get the messages across quickly. Charts that were prepared during the analysis should not be "cleaned up." It is simpler to use them as is and adds a note of realism.

Flip charts allow the room to remain brightly illuminated while material is presented.

There is an additional advantage to flip charts. As each sheet is used, it can be hung on the wall for later referral by the speaker or others.

It is important that <u>everyone</u> in the room can read the charts. Few things can "turn off" an audience like chart wording that's too small to read.

Pictures are <u>almost always</u> more effective than words alone. The generous use of graphs can save an audience both frustration and time in understanding a message.

General words such as "pet" evoke different reactions from people. Care must be used to be as specific as possible so as to prevent mis-understanding.

The agenda must be used to set the direction for the course of the presentation and it must be adhered to. Distractions must be avoided if possible.

To get the group's message across, it is important to talk the audience's language! Achievements should be expressed, when practical, in terms of schedule, quality, cost, and safety.

The KISS principle: Keep It Sweet and Simple. One highly successful executive practiced his presentations on younger members of his family to assure his speech was understandable and that he could capture and hold their attention.

If possible, bring an example of the actual hardware or paper and at the appropriate time let the audience handle and examine it. Few things work more effectively to clearly get a message across.

If handouts are distributed too early, the audience may decide that the material is more interesting than the speaker.

Those who have helped the group should be thanked. It makes both them and the members look good; and it establishes the trust to assure a continued "win-win" cooperation.

To what level of management should the presentation be made? To the manager to whom the leader reports.

Enthusiasm should show. It's contagious! However, it is often easier said than done. Many tend to tense up and inhibit their actions when speaking to an audience. The solution? Practice. If one over exaggerates in practice, it becomes easy to let his or her natural enthusiasm show in public.

A big smile relaxes both the speaker and the audience and better allows enthusiasm to come through.

Gestures can add impact and clarity to the communication process. Practice will help perfect skill at doing this.

Cue cards containing key words are a superb way to assure portions of the talk will not be forgotten.

If preferred, members may write out their "speeches," word for word. But if it is read, the speaker should frequently look up at the audience.

A dry run prior to the presentation eases tensions and paves the way for a smoother and more effective presentation.

Some members find it more comfortable to work in pairs during a presentation -- a good way to build confidence!

What's the next project for the group? Usually, it has already begun. It is quite important that, before adjourning, someone should provide a brief status report including a forecast of when it will be completed. The manager will be impressed; and it serves as a commitment that will stimulate member activity.

How frequently should a management presentation be made? As often as necessary, but the group should strive for every three months or so. Sometimes more than one project is covered during a single presentation.

Everyone benefits from this remarkable communication process -- members, management, and the entire organization.

The presentation must not be used as a means of circumventing the normal chain of command so as to force a favorable response.   That is not a "win-win" technique and will surely result in future problems.

The manager should never be shocked by being put on the spot with unexpected requests for solutions, funding, or manpower increases. No surprises, please!

The management presentation is a splendid opportunity for members to communicate their ideas and achievements to management.   It is a rewarding experience for all.

MINUTES
QUALITY CIRCLE MEETING

_____   _____   _____
Circle Name   Organization   Leader's Name

Attendees:

_____   _____   _____
_____   _____   _____
_____   _____   _____

Minutes:

Action Items:

_____   _____
Recorder's Name   Date

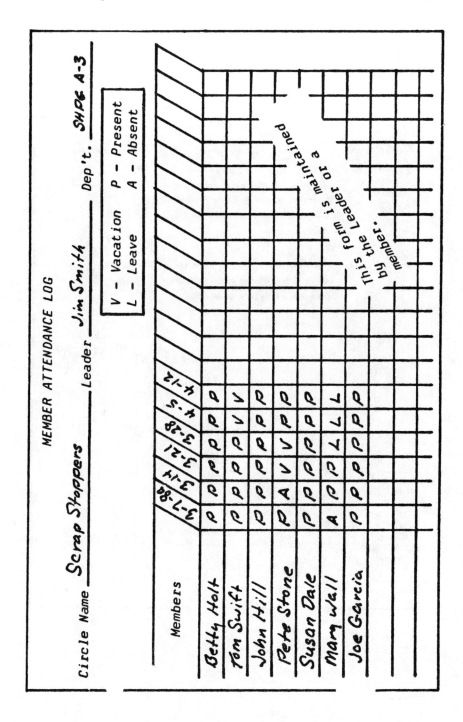

INDIVIDUAL GROUP ACCOMPLISHMENTS

Name ___"Impactors"___

Date Started	Leader	Project Description	Date Completed	Savings or Result
3-17-79	Jones	Broken cases - cause unknown. Investigation showed cause due to "jarring" due to machine handling. Bumper cushions installed at cost of $140.	4-9-79	$3,240
4-2-79	Jones	Malfunction of circuit breaker units. Cause due to excessive heat from use of Type K solder guns.	4-30-79	8,660

This form is maintained by the facilitator or leader. It is an on-going record of one groups', achievements. It does more than inform others of accomplishments -- it informs the leader and members how well they are doing. As each new item is added, see that (among others) the facilitator receives a copy.

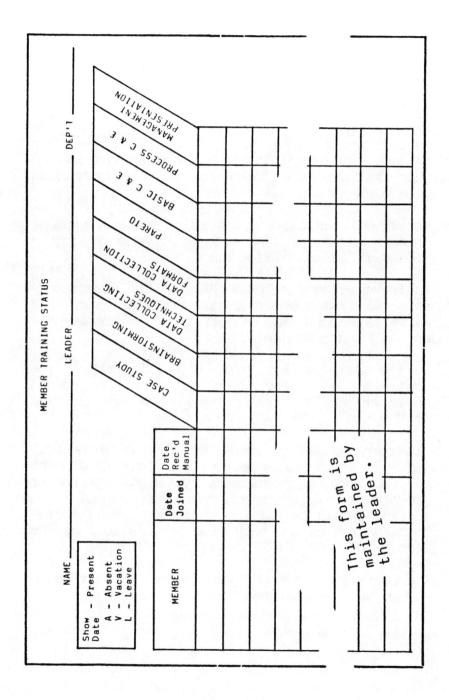

PROJECT SUMMARY

The Project Summary Report is prepared by the leader with guidance from the facilitator.

Essentially, it records the team project and the various actions taken to solve it. Indicate which persons and organizations were contacted and on what dates. Describe what analysis techniques were employed.

Answer the questions regarding the management presentation, the manager's acceptance or rejection, and implementation data.

In the section labeled RESULTS, list any measurable gains such as error rate decrease, scrap and waste fall-offs, decrease in customer complaints, and dollar improvements.

In the same section, make note of attitude improvements as reflected by such items as reduced absenteeism, turnover, and other morale-type indicators.

The audit summary should be done by a neutral party -- perhaps someone in an official cost evaluation group, maybe done by the same person or group that evaluates employee suggestions. The auditor should be able to depend on cost information entered on the back side of this form by the leader, members, facilitator, and others.

The facilitator, and probably others, will receive a copy of the completed form.

PROJECT SUMMARY   Side 1

_____   _____   _____
     Circle Name   Organization   Leader

Title of Project _____

_____

Date Started _____   Date Completed _____

Summary of Actions Taken (Include individuals, organizations, dates, etc.)

DATE OF MGMT. PRESENTATION _____ ACCEPTED?_____ IMPLEMENTED? _____
If not accepted, why not?

_____

RESULTS:
Measurable (Work related):

Attitude Improvements:

_____

AUDIT SUMMARY   (Work sheet of savings & expenses on back side)

               Total Estimated Savings $ _____
               Total Costs   _____
               Savings   _____

_____   _____   _____ _____
     Auditor   Organization   Telephone   Date

PROJECT SUMMARY
Work Sheet

Side 2

VARIOUS ESTIMATED COSTS as determined by Leader, members, facilitator, etc.

Total
Costs

ESTIMATED SAVINGS as calculated by the leader, members, facilitator, etc.

Total
Savings

COMMENTS